# PALESTINIAN SECULAR TERRORISM

Profiles of Fatah, Popular Front for the Liberation of Palestine,
Popular Front for the Liberation of Palestine-General Command,
and Democratic Front for the Liberation of Palestine

## YONAH ALEXANDER

 *Transnational Publishers*

Published and distributed by Transnational Publishers, Inc.
Ardsley Park
Science and Technology Center
410 Saw Mill River Road
Ardsley, NY 10502

Phone: 914-693-5100
Fax: 914-693-4430
E-mail: info@transnationalpubs.com
Web: www.transnationalpubs.com

**Library of Congress Cataloging-in-Publication Data**

Alexander, Yonah.
　　Palestinian secular terrorism : profiles of Fatah, Popular Front for
the Liberation of Palestine, Popular Front for the Liberation of
Palestine-General Command and the Democratic Front for the
Liberation of Palestine / by Yonah Alexander.
　　　　c. cm.
　　Includes bibliographical references.
　　ISBN 1-57105-307-7
　　1. Arab-Israeli conflict.　2. Fatò (Organization).
3. Jabhah al-Shaayah li-Taorar Filasoan-al-Qiyadah al-mmah.
I. Title.

DS119.7.A6425 2003
956.04—dc　　　　　　　　　　　　　　　　　　　　　2003048409

Manufactured in the United States of America

# CONTENTS

# PREFACE

Contemporary Arab nationalism, which began with the Islamic intellectual awakening and cultural revival in the second half of the nineteenth century, gained momentum with the end of the Ottoman Empire fifty years later, and reached its peak in the post-World War II period. Arab nationalism is dominated by two ideas: independence and unity. The concept of independence is manifested in the continuing struggle of individual Arab countries to achieve and maintain sovereignty; the notion of unity is reflected in the "Pan-Arab" dream of uniting all Arabic-speaking peoples, Moslems and Christians alike, and also in the "Pan-Islamic" idea of bringing under one flag all Moslems, Arabs, and non-Arabs.

In short, Arab nationalism is a paradox. On one hand it represents deep-rooted feelings of separatism and parochialism stemming from territorial, dynastic, ideological, and personal rivalries; on the other, an equally compelling sense of solidarity and harmony nourished by consciousness of a common historical legacy, cultural heritage, and unfulfilled aspirations.

Regardless of the conflicting, divisive, and cohesive elements of these ideas and forces, the predominant, most immediate aim of Arab nationalism is the removal of the last vestiges of colonialism from Arab lands. The Arabs are firmly convinced that without total elimination of imperialism and foreign influence, there can be no de-balkanization or unification of the fragmented Arab world, and that without a unified Arab nation, widespread economic development and social progress are impossible. Thus, perpetuation of a highly active xenophobia, combined with threats and use of force, is an inseparable component of Arab nationalism as long as the main objective—unity—remains unattainable.

It is against this background that the Arab-Israeli conflict must be considered, for the battle over the control of Palestine is, to many Arabs, a continuation of the struggle against foreign intervention and domination in the Middle East. As such, this conflict must be viewed on two levels: first, as the problem of an Arab Palestine occupied by a Jewish entity; and second, as a question of national geopolitical antagonism that exists between Israel and most Arab states. Throughout the last 55 years the emphasis has shifted from one level to the other depending on the needs of the Arab ideologists at a particular stage in the evolution of the conflict. Whether it is a clash between Palestinian nationalism and Zionism, or an antagonism between Arab and Jewish states, the focal point has always revolved around the physical and emotional concept of "Palestine," and the implications arising therefrom. It is not surprising, therefore, that despite the signing of the peace treaties between Israel and Egypt in 1979 and bewteen Israel and Jordan in 1994, as well as the initiation of the 1993 Oslo Peace Process between Israel and the Palestinian leadership, the conflict in Spring 2003 seems to defy any foreseeable potential solution.

More specifically, although afflicted with centuries of colonialism and with numerous attempts by its foreign rulers to separate it from the Arab cause, Palestine has always been considered by the Arab people an extension of Arab soil. Similarly, its inhabitants have consistently been regarded an integral part of the Arab nation. The Arabs assert that, since the rise of Islam, Palestine has formed an organic geographical unit of Arabdom, linking the Fertile Crescent, the Arab peninsula, and the Nile Valley, while connecting the continents of Asia and Africa with the only land bridge between them. Moreover, the recognition of the sanctity of Jerusalem as a religious center has made Palestine the heart of the Islamic world, physically as well as spiritually.

The Arabs also maintain that the indigenous Palestinian people, both Moslem and Christian Arabs, are mainly descendants of the Canaanite native population long established in the land before being invaded by Hebrew tribes about 1500 B.C. Not only did they survive Israelite rule, but they also retained control over a large part of this territory throughout that period. When the Arabs arrived in the seventh century, the Palestinians readily intermingled, as with the Crusaders some four hundred years later, and as Arabized people have continued to reside there regardless of waves of invasions and successive Turkish, British, and Zionist domination.

Although this rationale for the authenticity of the Arab character of Palestine has been long acknowledged, it is rather surprising that prior to World War I no distinct Palestinian politico-ideological parties developed simultaneously with other Arab national movements elsewhere. In fact, Palestine was regarded as "Southern Syria" and the Palestinians sought to merge this sector of the Middle East together with "Greater Syria" on the basis of common political, judicial, social, and economic foundations.

Nevertheless, concern for the fate of Palestine as part of the Arab world began to be articulated as soon as the Arab press published reports on the emergence of Zionism as a national ideology in the 1880s. Anxiety over the future of the area reached a fever pitch after successive blows to Arab national consciousness: the Balfour Declaration of 1917; the reneging of the British on promises of post-war support of Arab independence in return for Arab help against the Turks during World War I; and the subsequent British encouragement of Zionist efforts to make Palestine the first "Jewish National Home" in two thousand years.

The Palestinian Arabs revolted sporadically in the 1920s and 1930s, resorting to terrorism against the Jewish community in British Mandated Palestine. These efforts to change the political map by force were ultimately crushed by the "foreign intruders." But it was with the establishment of Israel in "Arab Palestine" (or "usurped Syria") in 1948, regarded by the Arabs as the "greatest disaster" to befall them, that the existence of a Jewish entity in the Middle East became irretrievably linked to them with foreign domination.

They were firmly convinced that the dismemberment of the Arab territory would not have occurred if Zionism had not been initiated to solve the "European Jewish problem," and as such was intrinsically linked to European imperialism. They saw the Zionist pattern of colonialism, particularly in South Africa and Southern Rhodesia (currently Zimbabwe), where white settlers formed political entities in non-European lands

Thus, while acknowledging that de-colonization—which had begun after World War I and culminated in the events that swept the British and the French out of the Middle East some three decades later—was completed, Palestinians, nevertheless, regard Israel as the last alien pocket in the usurped Arab homeland, representing an anomaly and a radical distortion of the trend of contemporary world history.

This strange phenomenon led Palestinians to the unshakable conviction that there exists an international plot, specifically a Western conspiracy, directed against the Arab world. They see a continuing diplomatic, economic, and military relationship between the West and Zionism, including, inter alia, Western support of the United Nations Partition Plan of 1947; the tri-partite Israeli-French-British collusion in the Suez episode of 1956; the "direct involvement" of the West during the Six-Day war; the aid provided by the United States to Israel since its emergence; and the continuing Western support of Israeli "aggressive" policies and actions against Palestinians.

Palestinians also regard Zionism as an imperialist ideology apart from its connection with and support by the forces of reaction and the various forms of neo-colonialism. They view Jewish nationalism, by its very nature, as motivated by a "superiority" philosophy because it seeks to fulfill "biblical prophecies" for "God's Chosen People" in a "Promised Land" that rightfully belongs to others. It is inevitable, therefore, that this "missionary complex" should be based on racism, aggressiveness, and unlawfulness—elements that characterize other types of colonial ideologies.

Palestinians are convinced that racial and religious prejudices are inherent in the Zionist ideology and exploited by the state of Israel. The encouragement of a dual loyalty and allegiance among Jews in countries outside the Jewish state are cited by Palestinians as a case in point. Another striking example, according to their view, is that Israel precludes integration of Jews by non-Jewish societies, promotes Jewish racial purity and exclusiveness, and practices racial supremacy not only with respect to the indigenous Arab population but also vis-à-vis Jewish immigrants from Arab countries. The Arabs also asserted that was this Zionist logic of self-segregation that brought about the "final solution" of the "Palestine Problem" resulting not only in the suppression of an Arab minority in an artificial Jewish state but, more tragically, in the displacement of an entire people from their ancestral territory.

The Palestinians also see Zionism as an aggressive ideology that deliberately, methodically, and invariably resorts to imperialistic methods such as psychological intimidation and terror, physical eviction and expulsion, systematic looting and confiscation, brutal persecutions and massacres, planned provocations, terrorist campaigns and military attacks. They believe, for instance, that Israel, as a classic example of the colonial state, cannot be satisfied only with the de-Arabization of Palestine but must also expand at the expense of its neighbors in order to facilitate the settlement and absorption of unlimited Jewish immigrants and to establish a homeland within the historical boundaries of "Eretz Yisrael" (Land of Israel) thus realizing the ancient dream of an empire from the Nile to the Euphrates.

The progressive aggrandizement of the Jewish state from several agricultural colonies in Palestine at the beginning of the last century to the occupation of substantial parts of Egypt, Jordan, and Syria in the June 1967 war (including the West Bank and Gaza) must be seen as a continuing process whose limits cannot be predicted. In fact, some Arabs are seriously convinced that Israel is not a state but a "movement" in the course of implementing its "missionary" designs, namely, the complete domination of the world.

Finally, Palestinians view Zionism as lacking morality and legitimacy. They regard Israel as an illegal entity created and sustained on the basis of fait accompli brought about by the aggressive use of force in violation of the principles of self-determination, human rights and justice; in disregard of the territorial integrity and political independence of other countries; and in defiance of international law.

In sum, Israel represents to the Palestinians both Western imperialism and Zionist colonialism. It is viewed as a foreign, malignant body in the heart of the Arab world, a presence that is ideologically alien, morally and legally indefensible, diplomatically an affront, politically an injustice, and militarily a constant threat to their security in an independent Palestinian state and their hopes for unity and economic and social advancement.

The psychological trauma of being humiliated, victimized and threatened inevitably foments among most Palestinians residing in the occupied territories an intense antipathy toward and an extreme intolerance of Zionism and the state of Israel. Although the Arab Palestinians constituted the main force resisting the pre-1948 Jewish community, their active role was greatly diminished by the intervention of the Arab states after the establishment of Israel. Moreover, despite their existence as a distinct group with a common national origin, shared experience, and a unified purpose, they were unable to voice their grievances and demands effectively until after the Six-Day War because the Arab states were unwilling to solicit, let alone follow, their views.

Yet the Palestinian "Fidayun," those who sacrificed themselves for the cause, were not totally ignored. In fact, some of the more radical Arab states, such as Iraq and Syria, for ideological as well as tactical reasons within intra-Arab rivalries, have molded their own Palestinian groups to be the vanguard of national liberation. It is not surprising, therefore, that other Arab states, each having their particular policy needs, have joined in supporting the activities of various emerging resistance units.

As a consequence of these developments, the "Palestinian Revolution," regarded by the Arabs as an integral part of the international liberation movement, is not a monolithic body in terms of its ideological disposition. Although the defeat of Egypt, Jordan and Syria in the Six-Day War has made the loosely organized guerrilla groups realize that the success of their revolution will depend, in the final analysis, on their own efforts, they have been unable, thus far, to form a common ideological base for the confrontation with the Jewish state. On the contrary, with the involvement of a younger, predominantly leftist and Islamist Palestinian leadership, ideological and theological differences between the resistance movements have deepened, contributing to further misunderstanding and conflict. For instance, Fatah (the Palestine Liberation Organization's major movement), has no political ideology except the recovery of Palestine through an armed struggle, while the Democratic Front for the Liberation of Palestine is a Trotskyist group committed to total revolution aimed at Zionism, imperialism and "Arab reaction." Furthermore, "holy terrorism" in the name of higher Islamic imperatives is the theological motivation of movements such as Hamas and Islamic Jihad. These differences have resulted in bitter internal rivalries between the various terrorist groups, and have weakened the growth and effectiveness of the movement in general.

Moreover, the insistence of Palestinian national liberation movements that the Arab states on the borders of Israel provide them with sanctuary and logistical support has "Vietnamized" the area, leading to a series of bloody civil wars such as the September 1970 and the summer 1971 "massacres" in Jordan, and the Lebanese episodes in 1973 and 1982. No wonder that the Arab countries had rejected the Palestinian notion of "state within a state" and have been unwilling to compromise their sovereignty even for the sake of Palestine. Thus, any agreement between the Arab states and the Palestinians, as well as among the Arab countries themselves, reflects a particular balance of forces and specific political circumstances that surround and affect the situation.

While these antagonistic relationships have had obvious psychological repercussions on the Arab world, the setbacks suffered have not altered two basic facts: first that it was Zionism that has led the Arab states to regard Palestine as an Arab cause and that has awakened in the Palestinian Arabs aspirations for independence; and second, that Israel exists—in many Arabs' eyes—as an imperialist base threatening their very survival, making its removal imperative.

To be sure, the Arabs recognized as far back as their first defeat in 1948 that before Israel's elimination was fully achieved, they would have to fight many battles in a hard and protracted struggle. But they found comfort in the fact that it took them some 75 years to liberate the occupied part of the Arab world from the Crusaders. Some Arabs have predicted an even longer war with Zionism.

The Arab plan for Israel's annihilation has, therefore, included a number of steps designed to gradually tighten the noose around the neck of the Jewish state: diplomatic offensives to isolate it politically; boycotts and blockades to strangle it economically; propaganda campaigns to demoralize it at home and discredit it abroad; and terrorist and military attacks to weaken it physically.

Indeed, in 1964 the Arab League (consisting of twenty-two Arab states) established the Palestine Liberation Organization (PLO) to serve as the vanguard force in a low-intensity warfare activities directed against the Jewish state. Although this movement was engaged in terrorist activities for the next two decades, by 1988 Yasser Arafat, the PLO's Chairman, renounced terrorism, recognized Israel, and declared his willingness to engage in negotiations with the Jewish state. Although the Oslo Peace Process in 1993 and subsequent agreements that were signed ushered in a new page in the turbulent history of Palestinian-Israeli relations, the second Intifada (uprising), which began in September 2000 and continues unabated in spring 2003 cast a doubt as to the peaceful resolution of the conflict between the antagonists.

The purpose of this volume is to present the record of the terrorist connection of the PLO's Fatah and several of its secular affiliate groups, particularly the Popular Front for the Liberation of Palestine (PFLP), Popular Front for the Liberation of Palestine—General Command (PFLP—GC), and the Democratic Front for the Liberation of Palestine (DFLP). This publication is designed to provide an easily accessible reference for academics, policymakers, the press, and other interested individuals. The study exposes much of the mystique of these groups and thereby places these organizations in perspective as some of the many challenges facing the international community in its war against terrorism—whether it is waged in the Middle East or elsewhere.

To be sure, the current internationalization and brutalization of modern terrorism makes clear that we have entered an age of super and cyberterrorism, with serious implications to national, regional, and global security concerns. Perhaps the most significant dangers are those relating to the safety, welfare, and rights of ordinary people; the stability of the state system; the health of economic development; the expansion of democracy; and perhaps even the survival of civilization itself.

It is not surprising, therefore, that the academic community—in recognition of its intellectual obligation as well as its moral and practical responsibility to participate in the international effort to arrest the virus of terrorism—has over the years developed multidisciplinary research initiatives focusing on a broad range of issues related to this challenge. For instance, in the aftermath of the February 26, 1993 bombing of the World Trade Center in New York City, the Terrorism Studies Program at George Washington University organized a research project on the selected Middle East perpetrators. This study grew out of the realization that "if contemporary society is to make terrorism, initiated in the name of supposedly 'higher' ideological and political purposes, a less inviting tactical and strategic tool and a more costly weapon to its precipitators and their nation-state supporters, then it is critical to expand our knowledge of the motivations and capabilities of these groups."[1]

It is against this background that the Inter-University Center for Terrorism Studies (a consortia of academic institutions in over thirty countries), in collaboration with the International Center for Terrorism Studies at the Potomac Institute for Policy Studies, is continuing its various research projects to increase our understanding of some of the most notorious contemporary terrorist movements around the world. Three studies have already been published in this series.[2] It is hoped that *Palestinian Secular Terrorism* will advance public understanding of the nature of the challenges terrorism poses in the upcoming months and years. This study is particularly relevant at the time when the United States and its coalition allies defeated Iraq on the battlefield and have initiated a roadmap towards Palestinian Statehood through peaceful means.

The research for this study, particularly since the Intifada beginning in September 2000, was coordinated by Jason Korsower, a Research Associate of the Inter-University Center for Terrorism Studies. Also, important contributions were made by Joy Kolin and Alon Lanir (Johns Hopkins University) as well as the research team at the International Center for Terrorism Studies comprised of Kerrie J. Martin, Tyler Richardson, Jonathan C. Koltz, Matt Burruano, Debby Cohen, Lauren Gershenson, Brett Jarvis, and Brendan Dillon.

In addition to these researchers, other individuals in the United States and abroad have contributed to this project. We are particularly indebted to the encouragement of Michael S. Swetnam (CEO and Chairman of the Board, Potomac Institute for Policy Studies), and the continuing academic advice of Professor Herbert M. Levine of the Inter-University Center for Terrorism Studies and Professor Edgar H. Brenner, Co-Director of the Inter-University Center for Legal Studies (International Law Institute in Washington, DC).

Finally, this volume draws on unclassified information generated over the past four decades from dozens of international seminars and conferences, numerous interviews, media reports, court cases, and field-work in the Middle East, Europe, Asia, and Latin America.

Yonah Alexander
April 25, 2003

[1]    Yonah Alexander, *Middle East Terrorism: Selected Group Profiles*. (Washington, DC: JINSA, 1994) pp. Vi–vii

[2]    Yonah Alexander and Michael S. Swetnam, *Usama bin Laden's al-Qaida; Profile of a Terrorist Network* (Ardsley, NY: Transnational Publishers, 2001); Yonah Alexander, Michael S. Swetnam and Herbert M. Levine, *ETA: Profile of a Terrorist Group* (Ardsley, NY: Transnational Publishers, 2001); and Yonah Alexander, *Palestinian Religious Terrorism: Hamas and Islamic Jihad* (Ardsley, NY: Transnational Publishers, 2002).

# CHAPTER 1

# FATAH

Fatah is an acronym for *Harakat al-Tahrir al-Wataniyyeh al-Falastiniyyeh,* or The Movement for the National Liberation of Palestine, spelled in reverse. In English, the word means "conquest."

## BRIEF HISTORY

Fatah was formed in 1958 by Yasser Arafat (a.k.a. Abu Ammar), Khalid al-Wazir (a.k.a. Abu Jihad), Salah Khaleb (a.k.a. Abu Iyad) and Faruq al Qaduwi (a.k.a. Abu Lutf) during their student days at the University of Cairo, out of a desire to create a Palestinian-run organization dedicated to armed struggle against Israel. Initially, Fatah stood in relative opposition to the Palestine Liberation Organization (PLO), which was founded in 1964 and controlled by the Arab League and Egyptian President Gamal Abdul Nasser. Arafat and his colleagues were disappointed with the fact that this movement, which sought to destroy the State of Israel, was not conceptualized among the Palestinian Arab populace. In the same year, Arafat's group of associates struck against Israel's National Water Carrier, an incident that established Fatah as a violent revolutionary organization. After the Six Day War against Israel in 1967, the group reconciled and merged with the PLO to become its largest member, and soon after Arafat became the PLO's leader (1969).

Fatah is a secular nationalist Palestinian movement created to liberate Palestine from Israeli occupation through armed struggle and subsequently establish a Palestinian state in its place. Fatah's initial ideological approach to armed resistance was supported by two main influences.First, the victory of the *Front de Liberation National* (the National Liberation Front of FLN) over French colonialism in Algeria served as an example to Fatah members of a successful armed struggle.[1] Second, the writings of anti-colonialist revolutionary writer, Franz Fanon, influenced Fatah members to initiate armed struggle.[2] These influences helped to solidify Fatah's stance that armed struggle was necessary in order to unite the Palestinian people into a popular movement and alter public opinion in recognizing Palestinians as a people, even in the face of Israel's military superiority (particularly after the Six Day War).[3] Later, in an attempt to broaden support among

Arabs, the organization integrated its goals with the concept of Pan-Arabism; the establishment of a Palestinian state, in addition to redeeming the Palestinians from oppression, would serve as a critical step in ridding the Arab world as a whole of Western imperialism.[4]

Initially the group enjoyed support from Egyptian President Nasser, who viewed Fatah as another tool in which to chip away at Israel. However, Nasser's support for the group waned after the President adhered to a 1957 cease-fire agreement with Israel and subsequently placed restrictions on Fatah's activities. As a result, Arafat and Fatah leaders relocated to Kuwait and Qatar, where support and funding from local Palestinians were plentiful and where its operational capabilities were less inhibited.[5] Despite this move, the organization still continued to operate in the West Bank and Gaza, and carried out its first commando action from these territories in 1965 under the auspices of its military arm, *al-Asifa* (the Storm).

Following the 1967 war, Fatah leaders moved to Jordan, where a large number of Palestinians resided after the establishment of Israel and subsequent Arab-Israeli war in 1948. In 1968, Fatah merged with the PLO. Additionally that same year, Fatah militants clashed with Israeli forces at the Battle of Karameh, which ideologically was a significant event for the group. In spite of the many Palestinian casualties and the destruction of its command, Fatah considered this battle a victory and a symbol of honor (*karameh* is the Arabic word for honor). The re-inventing and re-telling of this battle became popular throughout the Arab world, which in turn enhanced Fatah's stature among Arabs. Soon after, Arafat took over the leadership of the PLO.

In September 1970, PLO/Fatah momentum faced a serious challenge. That month Popular Front for Liberation of Palestine (PFLP) terrorists successfully hijacked and destroyed three commercial airplanes in Jordan. In response to these actions, under already mounting tensions with Palestinian armed groups, Jordanian King Hussein deployed his troops into battle against Fatah and other Palestinian organizations residing within his territory. The event, known as "Black September" was a defeat for these terrorist organizations and forced the PLO to flee to Lebanon (via Syria) where its headquarters would remain for more than a decade.

The collective expulsion of PLO forces by Jordan did little to improve Fatah's relations among rival factions other than to generate a shared contempt for the Jordanian authorities. Many Palestinian groups still openly challenged Fatah's lead of the PLO. Particularly troubling to Fatah leaders was the growing status of the PFLP in the PLO, arising in part from its success in conducting international terrorist operations to promulgate the Palesinian cause. This growing concern over rival factions coupled with the desire for revenge against the Jordanian Monarchy and further world attention to the Palestinian cause led to the establishment of the Black

September group, designed to clandestinely carry out international terrorist operations in order to increase Fatah's stature in the PLO.[6] The group catapulted itself onto the international scene by assassinating Jordan's Prime Minister, Wasfi Tal, in November of 1971, and the murdering of eleven Israeli athletes at the Munich Olympic Games in September of 1972. Arafat, who wished to be seen as a moderate among Palestinian leaders, formally denied any connection with the group. However, strong evidence implicating him has been subsequently revealed.[7]

In Lebanon, Fatah established headquarters in Beirut and stationed approximately 15,000–20,000 troops in southern Lebanon, from the northern Israeli border to the Zaharani River. The presence of Fatah members in southern Lebanon was so widespread that the region became known as "Fatahland." Once situated firmly in Lebanon, Fatah changed its tactics, and by the late 1970's focused more on military attacks against Israel's northern border and less on international terrorism. In 1975, civil war broke out in Lebanon, and Fatah forces joined the fight. At the same time, Fatah activists routinely conducted mortar and shooting attacks on northern Israeli towns and villages. In one notorious attack, terrorists crept across the Israeli-Lebanese border into Kibbutz Misgav 'Am and seized control of a packed nursery house, holding all inside captive and eventually killing three before Israeli forces regained control.[8] In response to increasing attacks by Fatah forces and other Palestinian secular groups, the Israeli Defense Force (IDF) launched operations "Litani" in 1978 and "Peace in the Galilee" in 1982, both into Lebanon.

IDF advancement into Beirut in 1982 forced the PLO leadership to flee to Tunis, with other members escaping to Algeria, Yemen, and Iraq. Fatah headquarters remained in Tunis until 1994. This expulsion affected the organization both physically as well as ideologically. Fatah's operating power was weakened as it now planned and managed regional attacks from a greater distance and exerted less control over Palestinians in the West Bank and Gaza. Ideologically, the group once again shed its skin, this time adopting a new strategy of gradual political dialogue and recognition of Israel after its latest attempts to defeat Israel in a war ended in defeat.[9] Furthermore, the organization now turned to the United States to play a substantial role in the Middle East after exclusive aid from other countries (mostly Arab countries) ended in disappointment.

The Intifada (Arabic for uprising) of December 1987 in the West Bank and Gaza Strip holds great importance to the Fatah movement. The uprising drew international attention to the Palestinian claim for self-determination and promoted the start of multi-lateral negotiations in Madrid in 1991, which ultimately led to the 1993 Oslo Peace Accords. Although the PLO was still banished from these territories, Arafat's loyalists in the West Bank and Gaza, the Fatah Hawks, were key players during the uprising and helped to maintain the group's Palestinian popularity and commanding power in these territories.

The Oslo Peace Agreement brought the exiled PLO/Fatah leadership to the West Bank and Gaza to form the Palestinian Authority (PA) on condition that Arafat and his leadership "cooperate in the fight against terrorism and the prevention of terrorist attacks."[10] The subsequent Oslo II Interim Agreement of September 1995 specified the creation of a 12,000 strong police force to assist the PA in combating terror. On the basis of these commitments, Israel withdrew from most of the West Bank and Gaza.

Despite promises by PA Chairman Arafat to renounce terror and assist in the prevention of attacks, Fatah has never willingly rescinded any of its calls for armed conflict with Israel. The Fatah constitution still calls for the destruction of Israel long after the chairman signed an agreement promising to rescind any resolutions in the Palestinian National Convention that advocates the annihilation of Israel.[11]

The al-Aqsa Initfada that began in September 2000 dismantled any precarious security cooperation that existed during the Oslo years between Israel and the PA. Fatah leaders strengthened support for the uprising by popularizing and legitimizing terror attacks with in Israel among the Palestinian populace. For example, Hussein Sheikh, a Fatah leader in the West Bank, stated shortly after these attacks began that, "if Israel attacks Palestinian militant leaders inside the Palestinian Authority, it is legitimate to attack Israeli civilians in Israel."[12] Attacks by Fatah members increased and spread into Israel's pre 1967 borders with the upsurge in violent rhetoric.

The discovery of the *Karine-A* ship marked a new chapter in Israel and PA relations. In early January 2002, IDF forces captured a ship in the Red Sea loaded with both light and heavy arms originating from Iran for delivery to the West Bank and Gaza. Soon after Israeli authorities discovered that Senior PA officials including PA Chief Financial Officer, Fuad Shubaki, were involved in the smuggling operation. The capture of the ship provided clear evidence that not only was the PA violating agreements made under Oslo, it was actively promoting the opposite; preparing for armed conflict by smuggling in arms. The Oslo agreements, signed by the Arafat, permitted PA police to carry light arms in order to maintain order and combat terror, and to keep accurate records of these weapons. Possession and use of heavy arms were strictly prohibited, as was smuggling in arms of any kind. Further evidence suggests that the PA has been involved in additional arms smuggling operations with origins in Iraq and from supporters in Jordan and Egypt by way of tunnels that run under Israel's borders.

As a result of Israel's complete lack of faith in the PA's desire to reign in terrorists and in response to increasing number of suicide bombings in Israel, particularly the Passover bombing in March of 2002, the Israeli government initiated operation "Defensive Shield" in the West Bank to arrest terrorists, confiscate weapons and destroy terrorist enclaves. The operation weakened Arafat's control over the PA and has led to his calling for new elections in 2003. Meanwhile, Fatah continues to carry out attacks against Israeli military and civilian targets.

## IDEOLOGY AND OBJECTIVES

New Fatah recruits must take the following oath of allegiance:

"I swear by God the Allmighty,

I swear by my honor and my conviction,

I swear that I will be truly devoted to Palestine,

That I will work actively for the liberation of Palestine,

That I will do everything that lies within my capabilities,

That I will not give away Fatah's secrets,

That this is a voluntary oath, and God is my witness."[13]

The following articles constitute key elements in the Fatah Constitution:

## THE MOVEMENT'S ESSENTIAL PRINCIPLES

The Fatah constitution specifies the following articles:

**Article (1)** Palestine is part of the Arab World, and the Palestinian people are part of the Arab Nation, and their struggle is part of its struggle.

**Article (2)** The Palestinian people have an independent identity. They are the sole authority that decides their own destiny, and they have complete sovereignty on all their lands.

**Article (3)** The Palestinian Revolution plays a leading role in liberating Palestine.

**Article (4)** The Palestinian struggle is part and parcel of the world-wide struggle against Zionism, colonialism and international imperialism.

**Article (5)** Liberating Palestine is a national obligation which necessities the materialistic and human support of the Arab Nation.

**Article (6)** UN projects, accords and resolutions, or those of any individual which undermine the Palestinian people's right in their homeland are illegal and rejected.

**Article (7)** The Zionist Movement is racial, colonial and aggressive in ideology, goals, organisation and method.

**Article (8)** The Israeli existence in Palestine is a Zionist invasion with a colonial expansive base, and it is a natural ally to colonialism and international imperialism.

**Article (9)** Liberating Palestine and protecting its holy places is an Arab, religious and human obligation.

**Article (10)** Palestinian National Liberation Movement, "**FATEH**," is an independent national revolutionary movement representing the revolutionary vanguard of the Palestinian people.

**Article (11)** The crowds which participate in the revolution and liberation are the proprietors of the Palestinian land.

## GOALS

**Article (12)** Complete liberation of Palestine, and eradication of Zionist economic, political, military and cultural existence.

**Article (13)** Establishing an independent democratic state with complete sovereignty on all Palestinian lands, and Jerusalem is its capital city, and protecting the citizens' legal and equal rights without any racial or religious discrimination.

**Article (14)** Setting up a progressive society that warrants people's rights and their public freedom.

**Article (15)** Active participation in achieving the Arab Nation's goals in liberation and building an independent, progressive and united Arab society.

**Article (16)** Backing up all oppressed people in their struggle for liberation and self-determination in order to build a just, international peace.

## ORGANIZATIONAL STRUCTURE

Fatah's historical political institutions include the General Conference (the supreme decision-making body), the Revolutionary Council (dealing with political and operational affairs when the General Conference is not in session), and the Central Committee (composed of Fatah's top leadership, in charge of everyday policies).[14]

The Fatah movement was composed of three brigades: Yarmuq, Karami and Qastel in the Palestinian Liberation Army (PLA) and numerous terrorists groups such as Force 17, al-Asifa (Storm), and the Hawari/Special Operations group. The al-Asifa group was responsible for the first Fatah attack, in 1965, and was Fatah's primary militant group. Fatah also had three security branches. The first, United Security, focused on organizational and security problems. The second, Security and Information dealt with internal security, preventive action, and provided information to the other security branches. The third, Central Operation, coordinated activities with other military groups.[15] Following the Oslo peace agreement, signed in 1993, the Fatah movement formally became the Palestinian Authority (PA).

A number of new security organizations and armed factions emerged with the establishment of the Palestinian Authority. The most substantial security apparatus is the Preventive Security Forces (PSF). Force 17 changed its operational definition to become Yasser Arafat's private presidential guard. Lastly, two new, armed factions were established: the Tanzim in 1995, and the al-Aqsa Martyrs Brigades, in 2000 during the second Intifada. The following is an overview of these new bodies as well as older entities still active in the post-Oslo process.

## TANZIM

Tanzim (Arabic for "organization") is the armed faction of Fatah. It was founded in 1995 by Yasser Arafat and Fatah leaders as an ideological replacement to the Fatah Hawks, the armed faction active during the first Intifada of 1987–1992 that subsequently dissolved as a result of the Oslo peace agreements. The organization adheres to a no compromise position on the peace process, especially on the issues of Jerusalem and right of return, and violently pursues the implementation of these goals.

The group is based in Ramallah but has local branches throughout the West Bank that actively recruit new members. Many local branches recruit heavily from Palestinian high schools and universities, and as a result Palestinian students and graduates comprise a significant number of Tanzim members. Other faction members consist of personnel from the Palestinian security offices who were active in the first Initifada and Fatah members who were imprisoned in Israel. Reportedly, every Fatah member who was imprisoned in Israel belongs to the Tanzim.[16]

Tanzim mostly operates against Israeli military and civilian targets in the West Bank and Gaza, organizing massive violent demonstrations and executing deadly attacks. For instance, members have organized violent demonstrations, such as the "Tunnel riots" of September 1996 and the "Nakba riots" of May 2000, and have carried out other attacks, such as the targeted killing by a Tanzim sniper of 10 month old, Shalhevet Pass, in March 2001.[17] The group has also been at the forefront of the al-Aqsa Intifada. Tanzim members (along with PA security officers) have been active since before 2000 in preparing large numbers of young Palestinians for the violent escalation by running summer camps that teach basic military training and pro-Fatah political ideology. The organization claims to have trained thousands of Palestinian youths in these camps. After the start of the al-Aqsa Initfada, armed members routinely mixed with demonstrating children (who were many times brought to these demonstrations in school buses by Tanzim members) and opened fire on Israeli troops from within the crowd, in an effort to provoke IDF soldiers to return fire in the direction of young demonstrators.[18] The reasoning behind this strategy is that the more civilian Palestinian deaths (preferably children) from Israeli return fire the group can cause, the easier it becomes to win local and international sympathy towards its ends.

Tanzim plays two important roles in the Fatah organization. First, the faction serves as Fatah's paramilitary force that counter-balances the increasing power of armed Palestinian Islamist groups. The need for such a force grew after violent confrontations erupted in 1994 between PA security forces and Hamas in Gaza and have continued to occur throughout the latter part of 2002.[19] Tanzim can be used as Fatah's crushing tool should fighting escalate or should these Islamic groups attempt to dethrone Arafat and Fatah.

Nevertheless, despite possible future clashes between Fatah and Palestinian Islamic groups, these organizations are united in their struggle against Israel. In this battle, Tanzim plays a crucial role in unifying the terrorist campaign by organizing mixed terrorist cells with Hamas and Palestinian Islamic Jihad activists that have been involved in bombings and road ambushes against civilian targets.[20] For example, the Return Brigades, a fusion of Fatah-Tanzim and Islamic terrorist groups have claimed responsibility for several attacks on Israeli soldiers and civilians, including the murder of an Israeli civilian in the Atarot industrial zone of Jerusalem.[21] The Saladin Brigades, a cover name for a group of Fatah-Tanzim and Hamas operatives, were responsible for an attack on an Israeli Merkavah tank that killed three soldiers on February 14, 2002.[22]

Tanzim's second role is to increase PA and Fatah popularity on the Palestinian street and to play down its image as a corrupt and self-interested organization of "outsiders." The faction works to counteract local opposition and popular criticism by being actively involved on a communal rather than national level, and by recruiting new members from local Palestinian communities and promoting them to leadership positions within the organization. The fact that many Tanzim members are also graduates of the first Initfada further increases its popularity among Palestinians. It is even at times a framework for the grassroots to express their disapproval of the PA leadership.[23] Consequently, Tanzim's presence allows Fatah and the PA to more effectively pool for radical Palestinian support that might otherwise exclusively support other terrorist organizations such as Hamas, PIJ, or PFLP.

Another reason Tanzim enjoys such popular support is through its West Bank leader, Marwan Barghouti. He is seen by many as a defender of Palestinian rights and one willing to speak out against the corruption of the Palestinian leadership. In a poll taken in late 2002, Barghouti's popularity was second only to Arafat, and CNN reported that he is "the driving force behind the Intifada."[24] However, Barghouti's future as a Palestinian leader and rival to Arafat remains uncertain. He was arrested by Israeli Security Forces on April 14, 2002 during operation "Defensive Shield" and as of early 2003 is on trial in Israel for murder.

There is mounting evidence that Arafat plays a significant role in Tanzim terror attacks. Documents collected from IDF raids on Fatah and PA offices during Israel's operation "Defensive Shield" suggests that Tanzim (and al-Aqsa Martyrs Brigades) were involved in a larger movement led by Arafat to employ terrorism as part of a strategy of attaining Palestinian goals.[25] Documents seized by Israeli authorities (during this operation as well as after the expulsion of the PA from the Orient House in Jerusalem in August 2001) show PA financed terrorist activities and indicate that high PA officials were directly supporting the activities of Tanzim and other terrorist groups. Furthermore, Arafat's involvement in choosing senior faction leaders and maintaining ongoing relations with faction commanders suggests that he had specific knowledge of these activites. However, despite mounting evidence, Israeli intelligence still has not been able to clearly establish how much control Arafat has over Tanzim members. Most sources agree that this uncertainty has allowed Arafat to play a double hand; by maintaining this vague connection, Arafat is able to use the Tanzim to conduct terrorist attacks while at the same time claim that he is working for peace.

## AL-AQSA MARTYRS BRIGADES

The al-Aqsa Martyrs Brigades is another armed faction of Fatah and takes its name from the al-Aqsa mosque, located on a site holy to both Jews and Muslims. The faction was recognized in late September 2000 during the outbreak of the second Intifada. The majority of its members are young radical Tanzim activists who grew up in West Bank refugee camps, with a concentration of members coming from Ramallah and Nablus. The West Bank town of Jenin is considered to be an al-Aqsa stronghold, which is part of the reason for IDF advancement into the town during operation "Defensive Shield."

The Brigades quickly established themselves as one of the most ruthless terrorist organizations operating in Israel and Palestinian held territories. Along with Tanzim, the Brigades have committed more than 300 attacks resulting in Israeli civilian deaths.[26] It was responsible for a sixth of the 689 Israelis that have been killed in attacks from September 29, 2000 through December 15 2002, or approximately 115 deaths.[27] Similar percentages could be applied to the numbers injured (4,887 by mid-December) by the Brigades during the last two years. Additionally, the al-Aqsa was the first Palestinian terrorist organization to use female suicide bombers, of which there have been three as of Spring 2002. The organization has been listed on the United States State Department's Foreign Terrorist Organization (FTO) since March 27, 2002.

While Fatah and the PA officially continue to deny involvement with the organization, evidence would indicate otherwise. The Israeli government maintains that most of the Brigades' leaders receive salaries from the PA and are listed as security forces. For example, in one of the documents found in Jenin, Marwan Barghouti requested to employ and register 30 al-Aqsa activists to the PA security apparatus.[28] In addition, other top PA officials including Fa'ak Kana'an (head of Fatah in Tulkarem), Hikham Balawi (Secretary of the PA's National Security Supreme Committee), and Fuad Shubaki (the PA's main financial official) gave out instructions for the payment to Brigades' members.[29]

Perhaps the strongest evidence for linking Fatah and the PA to the al-Aqsa Martyrs Brigades comes from individual testimonies of group members. Maslama Thabet, who leads the Brigades in Tulkarem, was quoted as stating, "Our group is an integral part of Fatah. We are Fatah itself, but we don't operate under the name of Fatah. We are the armed wing of the organization. We receive our instructions from Fatah. Our commander is Yasser Arafat himself."[30] Additionally, the Brigades were confirmed to be "loyal to President Arafat" by his foreign media spokesman, Mohammed Odwan.[31]

## FORCE 17

Force 17, also known as *al-Amn al-Ri'asah*, was founded by Ali Hassan Salameh in the mid 1970s, during the PLO's active presence in Lebanon. The origin of its name, though shrouded in mystery, is believed to have come from either Salameh's Beirut telephone extension or from its supposed headquarters at 17 Faqahani Street in Beruit.[32] Initially, the Force was established solely to provide security to Fatah leaders, and did not play a significant role in carrying out terror attacks. However, most of its leadership (including Salameh) did have a history of terror involvement and, specifically, many were targeted by Israel for their involvement in the 1972 "Munich Massacre" of Israeli athletes during the Olympic games.

By the early 1980s, Force operations had branched out from its previous security role to include gathering intelligence and acting as a combat unit during Israel's operations in Lebanon.[33] After PLO forces were expelled from Lebanon by Israeli forces, Force 17 expanded its area of operation to Europe, where members built a terrorist infrastructure with a network of safehouses from which to conduct attacks against Israeli and enemy targets and to proliferate arms. For instance, in 1985, the organization claimed responsibility for an attack that killed three Israelis in Cyprus. Most notably, the group was responsible for the assassination of Nagy El-Ali, a British citizen and a Palestinian cartoonist known for his caricatures against the Palestinian leadership. The rigorous investigation into his murder by British authorities led to the arrest of numerous Force members as well as the seizure of a large amount of arms.[34] Other activities were conducted under a different group name that was comprised of Force 17 members, and the "Hawari apparatus," a group designed by Arafat and the PLO to act as a clandestine subsidiary organization that, unlike Force 17, could conduct operations without any apparent connection to its parent organization.

Though active in Fatah operations outside of the West Bank and Gaza, Force 17 played no role in the first Palestinian Intifada. As a result, the group is still seen as representing "outsiders" by many Palestinians and Force leaders who are not as popular or well known as other faction leaders.

The Cairo Agreements in 1994 marked the 'official' end of the organization. Henceforth, it was dismantled and incorporated into the General Security Service (GSS), or the newly formed umbrella organization for all PA security forces. The vast majority of former Force officers who returned from Tunisia in 1994 became part of the Presidential Security unit, or *Al-Amn Al-Ri'asah*, which was to be placed under the GSS. The organization was designed to work to preserve the existence of the PA, and to protect its leaders.

Arafat, in breach of the Oslo agreements, kept the new unit apart from the GSS and solely under his command. Additionally, two subsidiary units were created under the Presidential Security unit's command that were not agreed to in the accords, the Force 17 Intelligence Unit and the Presidential Guard. Force 17 Intelligence Unit was given the task of gathering information about the activities of opposition movements and additional domestic threats.[35] The Presidential Guard consisted of several dozen elite members known for their unquestioned loyalty to Arafat who were given the task of providing security and preventing assassination attempts on the PA president.[36]

In its new role, Force 17 operations expanded to include counterterrorism as well as apprehending suspects accused of collaborating with Israel. For example, in 1998 the Force kidnapped and murdered Mahmoud Ali Jumhour for collaborating with Israel by selling West Bank land to Israelis.[37] Since the start of the al-Aqsa Intifada, Israeli authorities have accused Force members of carrying out shooting attacks, roadside bombs and mortar attacks against Israeli civilian and military targets.

## PREVENTIVE SECURITY FORCES (PSF)

[A.K.A.—Palestinian Security Services (PSS), Palestinian Preventative Security Services (PPSS)]

In May 1994, the PA and Israel signed the Cairo Agreement on the status of Gaza Strip and Jericho Area, creating the Palestinian Directorate of Police Force, or General Security Service (GSS), a conglomeration of ten separate offices that are under the command of PA Chairman Arafat. The Directorate includes four departments that are not part of any signed agreements, as well as two organizations, the Special Security Force and the Presidential Security (commonly known as Force 17), that fall outside the rubric of the Directorate. Two of these organizations have been implicated in terrorism against Israeli targets: The Presidential Security, which was previously addressed under the section on Force 17, and Al-Amn al-Wiqa'i, the Preventive Security Forces (PSF). The PSF is considered the largest of the PA's intelligence forces, consisting of approximately 5000 security men. Its main tasks are to prevent terrorist or other opposition groups from carrying out attacks against the PA, as well as to provide information on Israeli activities.[38] The group regularly arrests Palestinian civilians, who are detained and interrogated in PSF run prison installations. Interrogations have been known to be extremely violent, in some instances causing death, and have led to abundant accusations of human rights violations.[39] As a result, the PSF has become one of the most brutal organizations operating in the territories.

Though most Palestinians fear the organization, PSF leaders enjoy broad popularity. Mohammad Dahlan led the PSF in the Gaza Strip and Jibril Rajoub heads the group in the West Bank. Both leaders were former Fatah leaders that were active in the first Initifada and have prior prison records in Israel. Due to their revolutionary backround, both leaders are popular among local Palestinians. Dahlan and Rajoub also have formed close contacts within the PA leadership. These contacts coupled with substantial public support gave the two leaders significant political power.

During the years following the Oslo Accords, both Dahlan and Rajoub worked closely with Israeli Security Forces in overseeing security and counter-terrorist operations. However, after the start of the al-Aqsa Initfada, cooperation halted between the two parties. In the 2001 and 2002, PSF forces were involved in attacks against Israeli targets in the Gaza Strip. Reportedly, Dahlan was responsible for directing these attacks.[40]

## SELECTED FATAH LEADERSHIP AND MEMBERSHIP

### Abd al-Rahman Abd al-Rauf Arafat al-Qudwa al-Husseini (aka Yasser Arafat, "Abu Ammar," "al-Khetyar")

Born in Cairo, Egypt on August 27, 1929 to a wealthy family originally from Gaza,[41] Arafat's father was a member of the Muslim Brotherhood, an Islamic fundamentalist movement that sought to drive the British out of Egypt through the use of violence. In 1952, he enrolled in King Fuad University under the name Yasser Arafat, where he studied civil engineering, was president of the Palestinian Student Union, and afterwards served as a second lieutenant in the Egyptian Army. While attending university, he met Salah Khalaf and Khalil al-Wazir, two future Fatah leaders. Arafat and his colleagues became increasingly politically active on Palestinian issues, leading to several arrests by Egyptian authorities. After these arrests, Arafat and his associates moved to Kuwait and officially formed Fatah in 1958.

In 1968, Fatah joined the PLO and Arafat was elected chairman in 1969. Over the course of his role as chairman, Arafat has had to move the PLO headquarters three times: from Jordan, in 1970 after the 'Black September' massacre; from Lebanon, in 1982; and from Tunisia, in 1994, with the signing of the Oslo Accords with Israel, legitimizing Arafat's regime.

In 1996, Arafat was elected as chairman of the Palestinian Authority, the official representation of the Palestinian Arab people residing in the West Bank and Gaza Strip. During IDF's operation "Defensive Shield" in April 2002, Arafat was placed under unofficial house arrest in Ramallah. He movement became unrestricted after 35 days.

### Khalil Ibrahim al-Wazir (aka "Abu Jihad")

Along with Yasser Arafat, Abu Jihad helped to found Fatah and became the organization's military commander. He also commanded the "Western Front" which was responsible for numerous terror attacks in the 1980s. Abu Jihad was assassinated by Israeli agents in Tunis in April 1988.

### Hussein Abayat

Abayat has been involved in anti-Israel activities since 1982, when he was arrested for smuggling arms. After five years of incarceration, he returned to his home in the Bethlehem area and eventually became a Tanzim leader. In the first few months of the 2000 Al-Aqsa Intifada, the IDF charged Abayat with the deaths of three soldiers and for his involvement in shooting attacks against Rachel's Tomb and the Jerusalem neighborhood of Gilo, which borders the PA-controlled village of Beit Jala.[42]

On November 9, 2000, IDF helicopters and reconnaissance units killed him and injured his deputy Khalcd Salahat in a car attack near the town of Beit Sabour. Abayat was the first Palestinian leader to be targeted by IDF operations.

## Hussein Al-Sheikh

Arafat has used Ramallah-based Al-Sheikh as a means to control the factions and leaders of the PA who pose a threat to the current leadership. For example, as the result of staged elections for the Tanzim leadership in the West Bank, Al-Sheikh shares the titles of head of the Supreme Committee of the Fatah Movement and leader of the Tanzim in the West Bank with his rival, Marwan Barghouti. Soon after the elections, Arafat ordered Al-Sheikh to replace West Bank Palestinian Preventive Securities Services (PPSS) chief Col. Jibril Rajoub.

After the targeted killing of Hussein Abayat on November 20, 2000, Al-Sheikh told reporters that "we see ourselves free to operate with all means against Israel" and "there can be no limitations during war."[43] He has also stated: "The change in Fatah methods [towards Israel] began with the second month in order to reduce the number of Palestinian victims and to inflict human losses on the Israeli side since they had resorted to assassinations and quality operations. It's a war."[44] In addition, he said, "Carrying out an action within the Palestinian territories allows Palestinians from this point forward to carry out military actions anywhere."[45]

## Smahadna and Abu Rich families

The two Bedouin families located in the city of Rafah in the southern Gaza Strip controlled the Fatah Hawks, a group which was active during the first Intifada of 1987 and was supposed to have been disbanded. The Smahadna clan is also a supporter of the Popular Resistance Committees, a conglomeration of national and Islamic terrorist organizations, which operate out of Rafah and the northern part of Gaza. The Committees have claimed responsibility for shooting attacks against Israeli military targets as well as Palestinians who disagree with their ideologies.

## Salah Tamari

Tamari currently chairs the Palestinian Legislative Council's Committee on Land and Settlements. Residing in Bethlehem, he is known to be a former PLO field commander in southern Lebanon. Although critical of Arafat and the PA, Tamari remains a loyalist.

## Dr. Thabet Ahmad Thabet

On December 31, 2000, IDF units assassinated Dr. Thabet, formerly the Secretary-General of Fatah in Tulkarm, Director-General of Inspection of the Palestinian Ministry of Health, and a member of the Supreme Fatah Committee in the West Bank. His family and Israeli left-wing leaders claim he was an active supporter of peace, but Israeli officials maintain that he was behind several attacks against Israelis.

## SELECTED TANZIM LEADERSHIP AND MEMBERSHIP

### Marwan Barghouti[46]

Barghouti is currently the leader of the Fatah Tanzim on the West Bank. He maintains a constant presence in the media, despite the fact that he does not represent all Tanzim fighters, or all Palestinians in the West Bank. Although he has authority in his home of Ramallah, he does not have much influence in other cities (such as Nablus or Hebron). PA Chairman Yasser Arafat has repeatedly tried to undermine Barghouti's leadership. For example, Arafat staged an election for the leadership of the Tanzim in the West Bank, in which his loyalist Hussein Al-Sheikh allegedly "won." Although he attempts to portray his involvement as purely political, Barghouti has been implicated both directly and indirectly for a number of shooting attacks against Israeli targets since September 2000. Barghouti's signature has appeared on documents in 2002 captured by Israeli forces that illustrate his involvement in numerous terrorist attacks. Israel maintains that he is involved in at least nine attacks against Israelis. On April 15, 2002 he was captured by the Israeli military. In August 14, 2002, Barghouti was indicted in a Tel Aviv District Court on charges of murder, attempted murder and involvement in terrorist organizations. He is the first Palestinian to be tried in an Israeli court since the Oslo accords.

### Sharif Muhammed Yousouf Naji

Naji is the senior Tanzim operative from the Amri refugee camp belonging to the terror cell that prepared and participated in several suicide attacks in Tel-Aviv, Jerusalem and the Maccabim check point. Naji was involved in organizing attacks, including housing and transporting suicide bombers on their way to attacks. He also played a role in the acquisition and preparation of explosive devices, including explosive belts for suicide bombers. Naji was captured by Israeli forces in the fall of 2002.

### Zafer A'a—Juad A—Rahman Rimawi

Rimawi is the senior Tanzim operative and intelligence officer from Beit Rima. He has been responsible for both planning and carrying out terrorist attacks and supplying weapons and providing safe houses; he also acted as a liaison between Tanzim and Force 17 senior officers. He was captured by Israeli forces in the fall of 2002.

## Ahmed Hils

Hils is the Fatah Tanzim leader in Gaza Strip.

## Moutasem Sabee[47]

Sabee is the Fatah Tanzim leader and Fatah Shabiba in Jenin.

## Jehad al-Amarin

Al-Amarin is a local leader of the al-Aqsa Martyrs Bridages in Gaza and is also known by Israeli intelligence as a colonel in one of the Palestinian security apparatus. He was killed when his car exploded in Gaza in July 2002.

## FORCE 17 LEADERSHIP AND MEMBERSHIP

## Ali Hassan Salameh

Salameh is the former first commander of Force 17. He was implicated in the 1972 Munich Olympics massacre, and was assassinated by Mossad (Israeli Secret Service) agents in 1979 in Beirut.

## Mohammed Natur (aka Abu Tayyib)

Abu Tayyib is the former second commander of Force 17. He currently works for the Palestinian Special Security.

## Yusuf Ali Ahmed Abdullah (aka Dr. Yusuf)

Dr. Yusuf is the commander of the Force 17/ Presidential Guard.

## Abu Fadih

Fadih is the deputy commander of Force 17. Abu-Fadih served as deputy to Mahmoud Dumah Abu Awad. He was killed by Israeli forces in March 2002.

## Mas'oud Hussein Mahmoud Ayad

Ayad is the Lieutenant Colonel of Force17. Apparently he is aligned with Hizballah. Ayad led a group of Force17 members in a mortar attack on Netzarim in Gaza in February 2000. Israeli forces assassinated Ayad a few days after the attack.[48]

## Faisal Abu Sharkh

Abu Sharkh is the Force 17 commander (fall 2002).

## Mahmoud Dumah (aka Abu Awad, Abu Awdh)

Abu Awad is the head of Force 17 in Ramallah. He was implicated in the murders of Israeli settlers Binyamin and Talia Kahane on December 31, 2000 and the attack at Wadi Haramiya on November 13, 2000.

## Usama Al-Najjar

Al-Najjar is the current commander of Force17 (fall 2002) in the Ramallah region.

## Bashar Hatib

Hatib is a member of Force 17. He was involved in the October 30, 2000 murder of Esh-Kodesh Gilmore.

## Muhand Abu Haliwa

Abu Haliwa is a Force 17 member who was involved in the October 30, 2000 murder of Esh-Kodesh Gilmore.

## Khaled Suish

Suish is a member of Force 17. He was involved in the October 30, 2000 murder of Esh-Kodesh Gilmore.

## PREVENTIVE SECURITY FORCES (PSF) LEADERSHIP AND MEMBERSHIP

### Mohammed Dahlan

Dahlan was head of the PSF in Gaza until June 2002. He was subsequently appointed as Arafat's National Security Advisor. Dahlan has played a key role in negotiations with Israel. Both Dahlan and Jibril Rajoub were recruited from the ranks of Arafat's Fatah faction to carry out a security mandate largely aimed at reining in militant groups. Dahlan, 41, was a student leader in the first Intifada of the 1980s and was deported by the Israeli government. He continued to orchestrate the protesters from exile in Tunis where he won Arafat's confidence. Analysts see Dahlan as a possible successor to Arafat and in April 2003 he was appointed to the newly formed Palestanian cabinet.[49]

### Jibril Rajoub

Rajoub was the head of the PSF in the West Bank until June 2002. He was fired by Arafat, but refused to resign. Only after Arafat applied pressure, did Rajoub stepped down. Both Rajoub and his Gaza counterpart, Mohammed Dahlan, were exiled to Tunisia in 1988, in connection with leading the first Intifada in 1987. Since his return to the West Bank in

1994, Rajoub has been involved in a number of power plays with Arafat loyalists and opponents, as he is considered more attuned to the "streets" than those Fatah members who were exiled to Tunisia in 1982. In the mid-1990's, he attempted to interrupt Marwan Barghouti's plans to turn Fatah into a more political party, and less militant. Arafat has tried to undermine his popularity in the West Bank by establishing the Palestinian General Intelligence, led in the West Bank by Tawfiq Tirawi. In October 2000, Arafat attempted to overthrow Rajoub with Hussein Al-Sheikh, head of the Supreme Committee of the Fatah Movement and leader of the Tanzim in the West Bank, but failed. By 2003 Rajoub is no longer a major player in security affairs.

### Colonel Amin al-Hindi

Israel has implicated al-Hindi as one of the main perpetrators of the massacre of Israeli athletes at the 1972 Munich Olympics; for which "Black September" took responsibility for the attack. Apparently, the group was an offshoot of Fatah, and Arafat may have even been behind the operation.[50] Al-Hindi, who is himself not a Palestinian, was with Arafat during the PLO's exile in Tunisia, and recently held the title of Chief of Palestinian Authority General Intelligence Service.

### Tawfiq Tirawi

Tirawi is the Palestinian Authority Intelligence Chief in the West Bank. He was implicated by Israel for being behind the kidnapping of Arab Israeli journalist Yousef Samir.

### Jamil al-Bakri

Al-Bakri heads the PSF in the Hebron area. Members of PSF have been implicated in several shooting attacks against Israelis in the West Bank and the Gaza Strip.[51]

### Fatah Tanzim members from the Church of the Nativity that were deported to Europe in May 2002:[52]

### Ibrahim Musa Salem Abyat "Abu Galif"

Abu Galif is a prominent Tanzim operative from Bethlehem who heads a military cell. After the death of Ataf Abiat, in October 2001, he became the Tanzim Bethlehem commander. He was responsible for numerous terrorist attacks.

### Jihad Yousouf Halil Ja'ara

Ja'ara is a Hamas and Tanzim operative and member of the PSF from Bethlehem. He has been continuously involved in terrorist attacks targeting IDF forces and Israeli civilians.

### Abdullah Daoud Mohammed Abdullah Khader

Khader serves as the Head of the PA's General Intelligence in Bethlehem. Daoud assisted senior Fatah Tanzim operatives and provided courses and training to Tanzin members and weapons. He took part in the February 25, 2002 shooting at the Tekoa junction.

### Ismail Musa Muhammad Hamdan

Hamdan is a Tanzim operative and a member of Ibrahim Abu Gali`f's cell in Bethlehem. He was involved in numerous terrorist attacks near Gilo, a Jerusalem neighborhood.

### Muhammad Sai'd Attallah Salem

Salem is senior Tanzim operative from Dehaishe refugee camp. He was involved in planning and dispatching suicide attacks in the neighborhood of Beit Israel on March 2, 2000 and the supermarket in Kiryat Yovel in Jerusalem, on March 29, 2002.

### Mohammed Fouzi Mohammed Muhaneh

Muhaneh is a member of the Special Forces of the General Intelligence apparatus. He recruited a terrorist cell in El Aroub, prepared explosive charges, and planned attacks against Israeli civilians in the West Bank and Jerusalem.

### Khaled Mohammed Abd el Hamid Abu Najimeh

Najimeh is a member of the General Security Special Forces and of a Tanzim cell responsible for a number of terrorist attacks, among them the woman suicide bomber attack in a Jerusalem supermarket on March 29, 2002.

### Ahmed Mohammed Ahmed al Hemamreh

Al Hemamreh is a Tanzim operative. He is wanted by Israeli authorities for transporting a suicide bomber and an accomplice to Jerusalem for a mission.

### Khalil Mohammed Abdullah Nawareh

Nawareh is a Tanzim member and aide to Ibrahim Abayat. He has taken part in a number of terrorist attacks.

### Annan Mohhammed Hamis Tanjeh

Tanjeh is known as a Tanzim operative and member of the al-Aqsa Martyrs Brigades. He took part in a number of shooting attacks in Bethlehem and Gilo.

### Kamel Hassan Hamid

Hamid is responsible for the financing of the Tanzim operations in Bethlehem, including the purchase of weaponry and explosives. Hamid is believed to be in direct contact with Marwan Bargouti and responsible for disbursing funds to his operations.

## ISRAEL'S MOST WANTED FATAH MEMBERS

### Ra'ed Karmi

He was a key member of the Fatah /Tanzim in Tulkarm and responsible for numerous shooting attacks in the area. Karmi was killed by the IDF on January 15, 2002.

### Atef Abaiat/Abu Jaliaf

He was a member of the Bethlehem Fatah/Tanzim group and responsible for the planning and execution of dozens of bombings and shootings in the Bethlehem area. He was killed by Israeli forces on October 18, 2001.

### Riad Alamur

He is a member of the Bethlehem Fatah/Tanzim cell and responsible for dozens of shooting attacks against Israelis.

### Yihya Daamsah

He is a member of the Dehaishe refugee camp Fatah/Tanzim group and responsible for dozens of bombing in the Bethlehem area.

### Marwan Zalum

He is a member of the Hebron Fatah/Tanzim and responsible for numerous shooting and bomb attacks in the Hebron area.

### Khatem Jamal

He is a member of Fatah/Tanzim in Hebron and responsible for a number of shootings in the Hebron area.

## FINANCIAL SOURCES OF SUPPORT

The PLO received approximately $125 million dollars per year from the Gulf Arab states until 1990 when Yasser Arafat supported Iraqi President Saddam Hussein's invasion of Kuwait. At this time, the amount significantly decreased.[53] In order to increase its annual budget, the PLO began selling property it owned around the world in the early 1990's; the sales amounted to nearly $125 million dollars.

As head of both Fatah and the PA, Yasser Arafat has direct control over the dispersal of funds to the various sections of his regime. Prior to the establishment of the PA in 1993, Fatah maintained secret bank accounts in Saudi Arabia and other Gulf states. Fatah also was involved in a number of criminal activities such as narcotics trafficking. Reportedly, the money went directly to the Fatah leaders.

The PA currently receives grants from the European Union (EU), the United States, and several other sources. European aid from 1994 to 1997 amounted to approximately 1.68 billion ECU, of which 700 million ECU was for economic aid (which included training for police forces and the 1996 elections in the PA). Following the 1998 Wye River Memorandum, an additional 3.2 billion ECU was to be provided over a five-year period (to 2003).[54] Since the end of 2000, Arab states transferred $45 million a month to the PA, and from April 2002, this sum has increased to $55 million a month. The EU transfers approximately 10 million ECU a month—the equivalent of 10% of the PA's budget.[55]

Evidence suggests that a large sum of financial support for Tanzim and the al-Aqsa Martyrs Brigades comes from international aid.[56] Documents seized by the Israeli government in operation "Defensive Shield" show that the PA legitimized militant activists by making them National Security employees. By doing so, international aid from the EU and Saudi Arabia designated to assist in the operation of the PA can be diverted to Tanzim and al-Aqsa activists.[57] Some of the documents reveal invoices for $80,000 to establish an arms workshop in the office of a senior PA officer, Fuad Shubaki. Documents captured in Marwan Barghouti's office show that the PA financed terrorist activities. Money was funneled through PA salary accounts and then transferred to Tanzim branches in the West Bank. In this manner, the PA also financed Fatah youth movement branches (Shabiba), and student groups in Bir Zeit University. The allocations range between $750 and $4,300.[58] The PA countered that the documents found by the IDF are not authentic, that Israel has a history of fabricating documents to incriminate Arab countries and that the documents do not prove that the PA is linked to terrorism. The PA claims that Israel has shown no evidence that the individuals mentioned in the documents were actually involved in terrorist attacks.[59]

Israeli reports state that Saudi Arabia transferred approximately $135 million to Palestinian terrorists and their families since September 2000. The families of suicide bombers receive up to $33,000—an amount generally equal to six years of work.[60] During the Arab League summit in March 2002, the participating Arab countries pledged to the PA $330 million over a period of six months and an additional $150 million to support the Intifada.[61]

Iraq also funded some of the PA's activities, and funneled $12 million to the PA as aid. Furthermore Saddam Hussein promoted suicide bombings in Israel by providing money to the families of suicide bombers. In February 2002, Saddam Hussein increased the amount of money given to suicide bomber's families from $10,000 to $25,000, and has vowed to indefinitely continue his support of Palestinian terrorism.[62]

## AFFILIATED GROUPS

Al-Aqsa Martyrs' Brigade
Battalions of the Al-Aqsa Victims
Fatah Hawks[63]
Fatah Shabiba (Youth Movement)[64]
Fatah Tanzim
Fatah Uprising
Four Martyrs[65]
High Co-ordinating Committee of National and Islamic Factions
Martyrs of the Intifada
Omar al-Mukhtar Forces[66]
Palestine Liberation Organization[67]
Saladin Brigades[68]
Thabet Brigade[69]
High Coordinating Committee of National and Islamic Factions
Hizballah
Islamic Resistance Movement (Hamas)
Palestinian Islamic Jihad
Popular Army Front
Popular Palestinian Resistance Forces
Popular Resistance Committees (*Lijan al-Moqawama al-Sha'biyyeh*)

Although one of Fatah's functions is to quell and eliminate any Islamic-backed opposition to Arafat's leadership and the PA, Fatah has in the past sided with such opposition during times of conflict with Israel. For example, between the 2000 and 2002 round of violence, Fatah militiamen have trained and cooperated with Hizballah based in Lebanon.

Fatah leaders have been positioned in the main Palestinian refugee camps located around Beirut and the Israeli border ever since their arrival to the region in 1970. Their goal has been to recruit more members into the organization. In the camps, the nationalist Fatah members have collaborated with Hizballah forces, and have established new ties with Iran (who is the primary financial supporter of Hizballah).[70]

The Israeli unilateral withdrawal from southern Lebanon and the dissolution of the Southern Lebanese Army (SLA) in 2000 were seen as immense victories for Hizballah among Palestinians in the Territories. Fatah leaders called not only for a "Lebanonization" of the struggle against Israel, but also for a popular resistance, suggesting an alliance between

Fatah and Hizballah.[71] Also, despite fears of an Islamic opposition to the PLO/PA, Arafat has sought to recruit Hamas members to join the PA.[72]

Following the establishment of the PA in 1994, Palestinian and Hamas leaders came to an agreement regarding the relations between the two groups. Hamas was committed not to attack the PA itself, while still initiating terrorist attacks against Israeli targets. Muhammad Dahlan, the then head of Palestinian security in the Gaza Strip met with Hamas leaders during the bombings. Israel urged the PA to arrest those responsible for the bombings, but the PA did not do so.[73]

With the onset of the al-Aqsa Intifada in September 2000, Fatah attempted to establish new connections with their ideological opponents—Hamas and Islamic Jihad. Members of Fatah and Fatah Tanzim have grown increasingly weary on two fronts—the ongoing fighting with Israel and the political dealings with Palestinian Authority Chairman and Fatah Chairman Yasser Arafat. Many Tanzim members wanted to see the situation escalate by increasing the amount of anti-Israeli attacks. Because Arafat's role prevented him from making any outright calls for escalation, Fatah and Fatah Tanzim members have taken control by affiliating with Palestinian Islamic organizations. As a result, is new groups surfaced during the months of violence, claiming responsibility for terrorist attacks as well as incitement among the Palestinian people. Such groups included Hizballah-Palestine, *Lijan al-Moqawama al-Sha'biyyeh*, or Popular Resistance Committees, and High Coordinating Committee of National and Islamic Factions. These new alliances demonstrate how otherwise rival organizations and factions can reach a level of cooperation with regard to their common goal: "The liberation of all historic Palestine by liquidating the Zionist entity at the military, political, economic and cultural levels."[74]

Another link made between Fatah/PLO and Islamist factors is the allusion to the Hudaybiya Agreement, a non-aggression treaty signed by the Prophet Mohammed and the Quraysh tribe in 628 CE. After acquiring a sufficient amount of arms, Mohammed and his men three years later conquered and destroyed the enemy tribe.[75] Yasser Arafat has continually referred to the Oslo Accords of 1993 as a Hudaybiya Treaty, a treaty of détente until a sufficient amount of armaments and personnel are accumulated. At that point, the Palestinians will annul the agreement.[76]

The Committees, or PRCs, have become a major player in the uprising against Israel by using members of Fatah as well as those from Hamas and Islamic Jihad to facilitate attacks on a more constant and severe basis. Fatah-affiliated organizations have the capacity to carry out attacks that they would otherwise be unable to perform. An example is the April 28, 2001 mortar attack on a settler youth clubhouse in the Gaza Strip. An offshoot of Fatah claimed responsibility. Until that time, only Hamas and Islamic Jihad used mortars in attacks against Israelis. Another example is the car bombing in Jerusalem on February 8, 2001. The Popular Palestinian

Resistance Forces claimed responsibility for the bombing. The PRC is based in the southern Gaza Strip city of Rafah in addition to the northern sections.

Fatah and other terrorist groups also cooperated during the Gilo shootings in December 2001. According to Israeli security sources, while the PA was obeying orders from Arafat to refrain from shooting at residential homes in Gilo, Fatah-Tanzim members from Bethlehem paid Hamas and the Palestinian Islamic Jihad (PIJ) members approximately $50 to $500 to continue the shooting attacks.[77]

The PRC not only targets Israeli civilians, but also targets those who oppose their own interests or those suspected of collaborating with Israeli forces. For example, the PRC claimed responsibility for a gun battle outside the home of the PA military intelligence chief, Moussa Arafat, stating that he was arresting Palestinian militants.[78]

At a press conference held at the Palestinian Media Center in Ramallah in August 2001, Tanzim leader Marwan Barghouti called for all Palestinian factions to join together, in order to "fortify the internal front and continue with the Intifada until the end of the Israeli occupation."[79] He also stated: "Whoever participates in the struggle for liberation and resistance against the occupation and makes sacrifices has the right to be part of the political decision-making process."

Documents discovered during Israel's operation "Defensive Shield" have revealed that the PA's general intelligence headquarters in Jenin, and Hamas and PIJ groups are collaborating to carry out terrorist attacks. The PA shared information it received from American and Israeli sources regarding wanted terrorists, and provided weapons to Hamas and PIJ members. The Israeli security forces also have identified "cocktail cells," which include Tanzim, Hamas, and PIJ members. Numerous suicide attacks since the beginning of the second Intifada have been carried out by a number of combined terrorist groups.[80]

## AREAS OF OPERATION

### WEST BANK, GAZA STRIP, AND ISRAEL

In the West Bank, regional leaders, warlords, and strongmen control the different Palestinian towns and villages. While Hussein Al-Sheikh was appointed by PA Chairman Yasser Arafat to oversee Fatah in the West Bank, the Fatah leader in a given town may pledge his allegiance only to Arafat as his commander. These regional leaders exert a great deal of power, but only in their jurisdictions. Leaders such as Marwan Barghouti, who was situated in Ramallah, attempted to represent all of Fatah in the West Bank, but was not able to exert any influence in Nablus or Hebron.

In the Gaza Strip, just as in the West Bank, regional leaders control the area, rather than the head of Fatah Tanzim in Gaza, Ahmed Hils. In the southern Gaza town of Rafah, a group calling itself the Fatah Hawks controlled the area. Two tribal families, Smahadna and Abu Rich, were in charge of the group.

The Fatah Hawks were active in the first Intifada and were disbanded with the signing of the 1993 Declaration of Principles. Tanzim fighters are also active in Gaza. They band together in small militias and are dispersed among the different warlords in the region.

Jenin has been targeted as an area of Tanzim and al-Aqsa Martyrs Brigades activity and has been dubbed the "suiciders' capital." In the recent Intifada, 28 of the suicide attacks originated in Jenin. These groups were severely crippled as a result of the IDF offensive into the Jenin refugee camp termed operation "Defensive Wall." Large quantities of arms and explosives laboratories were discovered, as well as many terrorist activists killed or captured.[81]

Jenin is also an example of trans-organizational cooperation, resulting in joint terrorist attacks. The joint PIJ-Fatah suicide attack on November 2, 2001 at the Afula bus terminal involved such cooperation.[82]

Nablus and Bethlehem are additional Palestinian terrorism infrastructure centers. In April 2002, over 40 Tanzim terrorists fled from the IDF to the Church of the Nativity in Bethlehem, where they found refuge.[83]

## HEADQUARTERS

There is no one central headquarters of Fatah. Although PA Chairman Yasser Arafat remains president of the organization, regional leaders are in control.

Each Palestinian-administered enclave (created in 1993 with the signing of the Declaration of Principles), has its respective Fatah leader, as well as its own company of Tanzim gunmen.

According to intelligence gathered in operation "Defensive Shield," Nablus has served as a coordinating center for a number of terrorist groups, namely Fatah, Hamas, and the Popular Front for the Liberation of Palestine (PFLP). Israeli raids captured significant amounts of arms, including "18 explosives laboratories, 10 explosive belts, and hundreds of kilos of explosives; 7 Qassam rockets and their production labs."[84] In addition, wanted terrorists were located abetted in the homes of the mayor of Nablus and the Palestinian Police. The main Fatah cell in Nablus planned the logistics for other cells in Tulkarm, Qalqiya, and Ramallah. These groups operated under the al-Aqsa Martyrs Brigades banner, and led by Marwan Barghouti, head of the Fatah Supreme Council.[85]

The enclaves include:

GAZA STRIP: Gaza City, Khan Yunis, Rafah.

WEST BANK: Bethlehem, Hebron, Jenin, Jericho, Qalqilya, Nablus, Ramallah, Tulkarm.

## MEMBERSHIP

*Fatah:* Membership numbers are unknown.

*Tanzim:* Estimates as high as ten thousand.

*The al-Aqsa Martyrs Brigades:* Estimates at several hundred

*Force 17:* Thirty-five hundred members: Two thousand men in the Gaza Strip. Fifteen hundred men in the West Bank, mostly deployed in Ramallah.

*Preventive Security Forces:* Approximately five thousand agents in the West Bank and Gaza Strip.

Additionally, many Palestinians involved in terror activities have double or triple affiliations with different terrorist organizations. For instance, members of Tanzim may be involved in operations under the al-Aqsa Martyrs Brigades. Similarly, many employees working in factions under the PA General Security Services that are not involved in terrorist activities may in fact carry out terror attacks under a different name, such as al-Aqsa.

## STRATEGIES AND TACTICS

Fatah members have claimed responsibility for attacks which thus far have been confined to the West Bank and Gaza. Civilian and military targets were struck by roadside bombs, mortar attacks, grenades, and gunfire. Since October 2001, Tanzim and al-Aqsa Martyrs Brigades members have also targeted Israeli civilians in Israeli proper and increasingly utilized suicide bombers to carry out terrorist attacks.

The Fatah Constitution enumerates, in part, the following articles:

**Article (17)** Armed public revolution is the inevitable method to liberating Palestine.

**Article (18)** Entire dependence on the Palestinian people which is the pedestal forefront and on the Arab Nation as a partner in the fight, and realising [sic] actual interaction between the Arab Nation and the Palestinian people by involving the Arab people in the fight through a united Arab front.

**Article (19)** Armed struggle is a strategy and not a tactic, and the Palestinian Arab People's armed revolution is a decisive factor in the liberation fight and in uprooting the Zionist existence, and this struggle will not cease unless the Zionist state is demolished and Palestine is completely liberated.

**Article (20)** Achieving mutual understanding with all the national forces participating in the armed struggle to attain the national unity.

**Article (21)** Revealing the revolutionary nature of the Palestinian identity at the international level, and this does not contradict the everlasting unity between the Arab Nation and the Palestinian people.

**Article (22)** Opposing any political solution offered as an alternative to demolishing the Zionist occupation in Palestine, as well as any project intended to liquidate the Palestinian case or impose any international mandate on its people.

**Article (23)** Maintaining relations with Arab countries with the objective of developing the positive aspects in their attitudes with the proviso that the armed struggle is not negatively affected.

**Article (24)** Maintaining relations with all liberal forces supporting our just struggle in order to resist together Zionism and imperialism.

**Article (25)** Convincing concerned countries in the world to prevent Jewish immigration to Palestine as a method of solving the problem.

**Article (26)** Avoiding attempts to exploit the Palestinian case in any Arab or international problems and considering the case above all contentions.

**Article (27)** "**FATEH**" does not interfere with local Arab affairs and hence, does not tolerate such interference or obstructing its struggle by any party.

## EXAMPLES OF MODUS OPERANDI, 2000–2003

PREVENTIVE SECURITY FORCES AND FATAH HAWKS

November 18, 2000
A senior Preventive Security Forces member shot and killed two IDF sergeants stationed near Kfar Darom in the Gaza Strip. The Fatah Hawks claimed responsibility for the shooting.

FORCE 17
December 31, 2000
Force 17 members ambushed a civilian vehicle carrying an Israeli family near the West Bank town of Ofra traveling towards Jerusalem. The driver, Binyamin Kahane, and his wife Talia were killed in the shooting. The couple's five young daughters were injured in the attack. Although Kahane was the son of the late Meir Kahane (founder of the militant Jewish Defense League and Kahane Chai groups), the attack was assumed to have been committed at random.

March 26, 2001
A Force 17 sniper, who later told reporters he was working alone, fatally shot ten-month old Shallevet Pass in the head as she was being strolled over to her grandparents in the Avraham Avinu quarter of Hebron, in the

West Bank. Her father was shot in both of his legs. The sniper shot from the Palestinian Abu Sneineh neighborhood, which sits above the Avraham Avinu section.

## TANZIM

March 2, 2002
Tanzim claimed responsibility for the shooting of Jerusalem police detective Chief-Supt. Moshe Dayan. His body was discovered near the Mar Saba Monastery in the Judean Desert.

November 9, 2001
Tanzim members shot and killed an Israeli woman in her car near the village of Yabed, near the West Bank town of Jenin.

## AL-AQSA MARTYRS BRIGADES

January 18, 2002
Al-Aqsa gunmen carrying automatic weapons opened fire on a crowd at a bat mitvah reception in Hadera, in Central Israel, killing six people and wounding 30 others.

November 11, 2002
Al-Aqsa gunmen infiltrated Kibbutz Metzer and killed five Israelis, including a mother and her small sons. Kibbutz Metzer is a politically dovish community with good ties to local Israeli Arab communities, located just inside the pre 1967 Green Line border in the Galiliee

January 5, 2003
Two al-Aqsa suicide bombers tore apart the old central bus station frequented by foreign laborers in south Tel-Aviv, killing 22 people and wounding approximately 100 others.

## OMAR AL-MUKHTAR

November 8, 2000
Three Omar al-Mukhtar Forces members, a Fatah faction, fired automatic weapons at the car of 24 year old Noa Dahan while passing through the Rafah border crossing. The attack killed Dahan injured her nephew, who was traveling in her car.

## FOUR MARTYRS

April 28, 2001
The Four Martyrs, an unknown group claiming to be aligned with Fatah, launched a mortar attack on a clubhouse in Netzer Hazani, in the Gaza Strip. Five teenagers were wounded in the attack.

## THABET BRIGADES AND AL-AQSA MARTYRS BRIGADES

June 19, 2001
Gunmen attacked a three-car convoy near the entrance of Einav, east of the West Bank town of Tulkarem. One Israeli passenger was killed in the attack. The gunmen fled after one passenger returned fire. The Thabet Brigade and the al-Aqsa Martyrs Brigades claimed responsibility for the attack.

## SALADIN BRIGADES

December 28, 2000
Saladin Brigades claimed responsibility for detonating two remote controlled pipe bombs placed in the back of a Dan bus traveling from Tel-Aviv to Petach Tikva, in central Israel. The blast injured 13 passengers, but officials say many might have been killed if not for a malfunction of one of the explosive devices.

## ENDNOTES

1    On Nov. 1, 1954, a nationalist group of indigenous Algerians calling themselves the FLN launched a guerrilla war against French rule in Algeria. Advocating a policy of violent revolution and total independence, the group plummeted the country into an 8 year civil war that ultimately led to Algerian independence from France in 1963.

2    Frantz Fanon was an anti-colonialist revolutionary writer living in French ruled Algiers in the middle of the 20th century. In 1956, he resigned his post as head of the Psychiatry department of Blida-Joinville Hospital in Algeria to work for the Algerian cause. His two significant works, *Black Skin, White Masks* and *The Wretched of the Earth*, illustrate his philosophical view that a total revolution of "absolute violence" is required to create a free new world. This philosophy permeated through Fatah camps, and many reports confirm that the group handed out pamphlets of Fanon ideology to its members. For a brief summary on Fanon's life and works see www.emory.edu/ENGLISH/Bahri/Fanon.html.

3    Specifically, from 1965–67 Fatah strategy was rooted in an "entanglement theory" which involved border attacks on Israel in order to provoke Israel into adopting an offensive position that would eventually trigger regional war. See E Karmon, "Fatah and the Popular Front for the Liberation of Palestine: International Terrorist Strategies (1968–1990)" http://www.ict.org.il/articles/articledet.cfm?ariticle=145.

4    For more on Pan-Arabism see Helena Cobban, *The Palestinian Liberation Organization: People, Power, and Politics.* (New York: Cambridge University Press, 1984), pp.21–35.

5    See Yonah Alexander and Joshua Sinai, "*Terrorism: the PLO Connection*"(New York: Crane Russak, 1989), p.6.

6    Ibid. See also Aryeh Y. Yodfat and Yuval Arnon-Ohanna, *PLO Stategy and Tactics* (New York: St. Martin's Press), p.146.

7    Ibid.

8    This attack is noted in Security Council document s/13892 April 14, 1980, Letter from Yehuda Z Blum, Permanent Representative of Israel to the U.N. addressed to the President of the Security Council.

9    Opposition to this policy, particularly form Abu Nidal's Fatah Revolutionary Council, intensified cries to renew terrorism. In response, Fatah activists carried out several attacks such as the 1985 bombing in Larnaca and Barcelona. See E. Karmon's "Fatah

and the Popular Front for the Liberation of Palestine: International Terrorism Strategies (1968–1990)," p.13.

[10]    The Israeli-Palestinian Interim Agreement, September 28, 1995.

[11]    See articles 2,9,12 and 13 in the movement's essential principles in the chapter on Ideology and Objectives.

[12]    Sheikh was quoted in the *Jerusalem Post.*

[13]    Andrew Gowers and Tony Walker, *Behind the Myth: Yasser Arafat and the Palestinian Revolution.* (New York: Olive Branch Press, 1991).

[14]    Y. Alexander. & J. Sinai, Terrorism: The PLO Connection. (New York: Crane Russak, 1989), p.37.

[15]    ibid, pp.37–38.

[16]    Roni Shaked, "The Tanzim: Fatah's Fighters on the Ground." *Yediot Achronot,* October 3, 2000.

[17]    The "Tunnel riots" began when riots began after the Israeli government opened the tunnels under the Old city of Jerusalem. During the Nakba riots, Tanzim members were shooting at IDF outposts and border crossings. http://www.ict.org.il/inter_ter/orgdet.cfm?orgid=82.

[18]    http://www.ict.org.il.

[19]    In October 2002, Hamas members disguised as Palestinian policemen ambushed and killed PA riot police chief Rajah Abu Lehiya in Khan Younis in southern Gaza. Hamas officially tried to distance itself from the killing claiming the attack was a "family revenge" issue. However, heavy clashes followed between police and Hamas gunmen after police forces tried to arrest the suspects. The event sparked outrage throughout the Fatah organization. Fighting and gun battles between the groups in the Gaza Strip have continued to occur into November and December 2002 almost on a daily basis, leading the director-general of the Palestinian Ministry of Information, Hasan al-Kashef, to state that "the use of firearms in personal disputes and factional clashes has become widespread and can no longer be ignored." As late as December 15, 2002, PA Minister of Supplies Abu Ali Shahin charged "Hamas is concocting problems with Fatah in the Gaza Strip to weaken and marginalize the PA so it would replace the authority."

See "Inter-Palestinian clashes rock Gaza," *BBC News,* October 7, 2002; Toameh,Khaled Abu. "Civil War a real threat, says PA official" *Jerusalem Post,* December 9, 2002.; Toameh, Khaled Abu. "PA minister says Hamas trying to replace PA," *Jerusalem Post,* December 15, 2002.

[20]    Ibid.

[21]    Mathew Levitt, *Targeting Terror.* (Washington: The Washington Institute for Near East Policy, 2002).

[22]    Ibid.

[23]    www.ict.org.il/inter_ter/orgdet.cfm?orgid=82.

[24]    Kelly Wallace. "Arafat facing challenge from Barghouti." CNN. http://www.cnn.com/2002/WORLD/meast/12/09/arafat.barghouti/index.html

[25]    Ibid.

[26]    Yael Shahar, "The al-Aqsa Martyrs Brigades: a political tool with an edge" March 24, 2002. www.ict.org.il

[27]    www.imra.org.il

[28]    http://www.idf.il/english/announcements/2002/april/Fatah_Activists/7.stm

[29]    The Israeli government claims that the PA also utilizes extra budgetary funds such as oil and tobacco imports to finance additional terrorist attacks. Dani Naveh, "Involvement of Arafat, PA Senior Officials, and Apparatuses in Terrorism Against Israel . . ." www.mfa.gov.il/mfa/go.asp?MFAHOlomO p.4.

[30]    Matthew Kalman, "Terrorist says orders come from Arafat" *USA Today,* March 14, 2002.

[31]    Ibid.

32  www.ict.org.il

33  www.ict.org.il/inter_ter/orgdet.cfm?orgid=86, accessed 5/20/2002.

34  Ibid.

35  Gal Luft, *The Palestinian Security Forces: Capabilities and Effects on the Arab-Israeli Military Balance*. The Ariel Center for Policy Research (ACPR), October 2001, p.14.

36  Ibid.

37  Reuven Paz, "Force 17 The Renewal of Old Competition Motivates Violence" www.ict.org.il

38  See Gal Luft, *The Palestinian Security Forces: Capabilities and Effects on the Arab Israeli Military Balance*, p.15.

39  Ibid. For more information of PSF human rights violations see the Amnesty International Report 1997: Palestinian Authority (internet edition) and B'Tselem report, "Neither Law nor Justice," Report on the Palestinian Security Services," Jerusalem, August 1995.

40  Ibid.

41  Jillian Becker, *The PLO*. (London: Weidenfeld & Nicolson, 1984).

42  *Ha'aretz*, November 10, 2000. See also http://www.phrmg.org/english/Assassinations/Case1.htm

43  Kevin Whitelaw, "Rockets kill a Palestinian militia leader." *US News & World Report*, November 20, 2000.

44  "Palestinians change tactics in Intifada." *Reuters*, December 21, 2000.

45  Ross Dunn, "Palestinians warn that abductions by Israel are escalating conflict." *Sydney Morning Herald*, April 3, 2001.

46  For more information on Barghouti, see his personal website: www.mbarghouthi.org

47  Margot Dudkevitch and Lahoud Lamia, "Navy, air force hit targets in Gaza." *Jerusalem Post*, May 14, 2001.

49  http://www.us-israel.org/jsource/biography/Dahlan.html

50  Patrick Goodenough, "Munich Olympics Massacre said to be PLO Operation." *Conservative News Service*, May 5, 1999.

51  "Inside the PLO Forces." *Middle East Digest*, April 1997.

52  For additional information on the 13 Palestinian terrorists from the Church of the Nativity that were deported, please see http://www.mfa.gov.il/mfa/go.asp?MFAH01ou0

53  Mary C Cook, "Arafat-Rabin Agreement Comes at Depths of PLO Financial Crisis." *Washington Report on Middle East Affairs Special Report*, November/December 1993.

54  http://mondediplo.com/focus/mideast/europeanunion-en

55  http://www.mfa.gov.il/mfa/go.asp?MFAH01om0

56  The annual budget for the Tanzim has been cited at 2.4 million US dollars. Shaked, Roni, "The Tanzim: Fatah's Fighters on the Ground." *Yediot Achronot*, October 3, 2000. Translated by the Israeli Government Press Office.

57  www.mfa.gov.il/mfa/go.asp?MFA0lom0

58  http://www.idf.il/Fatah/english/main_index.stm

59  PLO Release, fact sheet, May 22, 2002.

60  http://www.aipac.org/result.cfm?id=1309

61  http://www.aipac.org/result.cfm?id=1306

62  Mohammed Daraghmeh, "Iraq Boosts Suicide Payment." *The Associated Press*, April 3, 2002.

63  Active in the first Intifada and now stationed in Southern Gaza and controlled by two families. See Section Leadership.

64  Shabiba is the youth wing of Fatah, which is funded by the Palestinian Authority. As of March 2000, the group won elections in the student councils at Al-Azhar University at Gaza and Bethlehem University, while Hamas won in similar elections in five other universities in the West Bank and Gaza Strip. IANA Radionet March 2, 2000. www.ianaradionet.com

[65] Claimed responsibility for the mortar attack on March 28, 2001 in the Gaza Strip. See section on Terrorist Attacks.

[66] Claimed responsibility for the attack on November 8, 2000 at the Rafah border crossing at the Gaza Strip. See section on Terrorist Attacks.

[67] As of 1968, when Fatah joined the PLO umbrella organization, the group has remained the largest faction.

[68] Claimed responsibility for the attack on December 28, 2000 in Tel Aviv. Saladin was an Arab general who thwarted the attempts of the Crusaders in the Holy Land. In the streets of the Territories, many Palestinians praise PA Chairman Yasser Arafat as a modern-day Saladin.

[69] Claimed responsibility for the two attacks on June 16, 2001 in the West Bank. See section on Claimed Attacks.

[70] Reuven Paz, "Hizballah and Fatah: A New Alliance against Israel." *ICT*, October 22, 2000.

[71] Ibid.

[72] Among the Hamas members recruited by the PNA are Iqrima Sabri, Mufti of Jerusalem, known for his statements denying any Jewish claim to the Temple Mount and Western Wall, and PA Communications Minister Imad Faluji, who stated that the recent Intifada was planned after Camp David II. Meyray Wurmser, "Terrorism and a Palestinian State." *MEMRI*, www.memri.org/staff/staff04.html

[73] Steve Emerson, "Hamas, the PLO and Terrorist Attacks Against Israel," Testimony of Steven Emerson, March 12, 1996, House of International Relations Committee, pp.12–13.

[74] "Rejection and Imposition." Official Fatah website editorial. http://www.fateh.net/e_editor/01/150701.htm The editorial issues several compliments for the "National and Islamic Forces," a coalition of secular and religious terrorists who have been the masterminds behind many of the incidents.

[75] "Although this treaty was violated within three years from the time its was concluded, most [Islamic] jurists concur that the maximum period of peace with an enemy should not exceed 10 years since it was originally agreed that the Hudaybiya Treaty should last 10 years." "Hudaybiya." *Encyclopedia of Islam*, 1967, p.546.

[76] Ibid. Arafat first compared Oslo with Hudaybiya in Johannesburg on May 10, 1994, when he said: "I'm not considering it [Oslo] more than the agreement which has been signed in 628 CE between the Prophet Muhammad and the tribe of Koreish."

[77] http://www.jpost.com/Editions/2001/12/07/News/News.39531.html

[78] Nidal Al-Mughrabi, "Police guard Palestinian official's home after clash." *Reuters News Agency*, July 24, 2001.

[79] "Barghouti calls for national unity government." *Jerusalem Times*, Vol. VII, No.392: August 10, 2001 (Internet edition).

[80] http://www.ict.org.il/spotlight/det.cfm?id=550

[81] Dani Naveh, p.43.

[82] Ibid., p.46, 48.

[83] Ibid., p.49, 55.

[84] Ibid., p.50.

[85] Ibid., p.52.

# CHAPTER 2

# POPULAR FRONT FOR THE LIBERATION OF PALESTINE

## ALSO KNOWN AS

PFLP

al-Jabha ash-Sha'abiya li-Tahrir Falestin, al-Jabha ash-Sha'abiya

Red Eagles

## BRIEF HISTORY

The Palestinian Popular Front for the Liberation of Palestine (PFLP) is a Marxist-oriented group that was established by Dr. George Habash in the aftermath of the Six-Day War in 1967. Dr. Habash, a Christian Arab, created the PFLP by merging three formerly autonomous groups: Heroes of the Return, the National Front for the Liberation of Palestine, and the Independent Palestine Liberation Front. In 1968, the group joined the PLO to become its second largest member (after Yasser Arafat's Fatah movement) in size and influence among Palestinian Arabs.

The PFLP's philosophy rests on three pillars: Palestinian uniqueness *(wataniyya)*, Arab unity *(qawmiyya)*, and Marxism-Leninism. In other words, the PFLP believe that the Palestinians are a distinct Arab people who require their own nation, and are essential to the unification of the Arab nations under a new Marxist-Leninist order. Within this framework, the organization first strives to solidify the national struggle of the Palestinian people for autonomy by uniting them under a Marxist secular government. Ideological support for this approach comes from Castro's revolutionary guerrilla teachings, which served as a guideline for PFLP activists.[1] Secondly, the Palestinian nation is to be achieved only by liberating all of Palestine from Zionist oppression. This liberation policy includes a no-compromise position with regard to negotiations with Israel, and an active terrorist campaign using any and all means necessary in order to bring about Israel's destruction. After the elimination of Israel is achieved, group efforts would next concentrate on uniting the Arab world under Marxist ideology by undermining pro-Western Middle East regimes. Thus, the establishment of a Palestinian state in place of Israel is seen as a catalyst and first step for altering the whole Middle East.

By the time the PFLP established its headquarters in Jordan, it had already become one of the most violent Palestinian terrorist groups. Initially, members conducted raids on targets inside Israel. However, because these border crossings failed to generate sufficient attention from abroad, the organization quickly changed tactics and turned to international terrorism in order to create global crises that would focus attention on the Palestinian cause.

In 1970, as a result of ideological inflexibilities, internal disputes, and personality conflicts, the PFLP split into three factions: the PFLP, the Democratic Front for the Liberation of Palestine (DFLP), and the Popular Front for the Liberation of Palestine—General Command (PFLP-GC). Habash remained in control of the original PFLP after the split, and established ties with other foreign leftist groups, such as the Baader-Meinhoff group, the Irish Republican Army (IRA), and the Japanese Red Army, in an attempt to increase worldwide leverage.[2] These links facilitated the PFLP's operations in Europe, and elsewhere including the Lod Airport Attack in '72, the Air France hijacking to Entebbe in '76, and helped to catapult the group into international notoriety.

Particularly notorious among PFLP operations was the hijacking and destruction of four international commercial airplanes, three in Jordan and one in Cairo, in September 1970. This attack (along with an attempted assassination on Jordanian King Hussein by Palestinian terrorists and increasing tensions) led to the events of "Black September" in Jordan, in which King Hussein forcefully expelled the Palestinian organizations from his territory. Afterwards, the PFLP transferred its headquarters to Lebanon and Syria, where it continued to plan high profile international terror attacks. After the death of the Front's operational planner, Wadi Haddad, in 1978, the group halted its high profile attacks, but continued its attacks against Israeli and moderate Arab targets.

Although a member of the PLO, the PFLP has, throughout much of its history, been in opposition to the policies of Arafat's Fatah. In the mid 1970s, the PFLP and PFLP-GC formed the Front of Palestinian Forces Rejecting Surrenderist Solutions—the Rejection Front after the PLO backed an idea of establishing a Palestinian state in March 1977. In 1985, the group established the Palestinian National Salvation Front (PNSF) in Damascus to counter an agreement signed by Arafat and King Hussein earlier that year calling for peace talks with Israel, and additionally demanded that Arafat resign as head of the PLO.

During the first Intifada in December 1987, PFLP activists called the "Red Eagles" carried out attacks against Israeli targets in the West Bank. Opposition to any peace plans with Israel led PFLP leaders to form coalitions with other PLO opposition groups (e.g. the DFLP and the "Damascus

Ten"), calling for a continuation of violence as well as a challenge against PLO Chairman Yasser Arafat's leadership in conducting peace talks. In 1993, the group formally separated from the PLO after the signing of the Declaration of Principles.

With the decline of the former Soviet Union and the end of the Cold War, the PFLP along with other leftist oriented groups were pushed to the periphery, leaving room for the ascent of Palestinian Islamic groups such as the Hamas and Islamic Jihad. In 1999, the PFLP reconciled with Arafat's Fatah movement after a six-year breach in the relations following the signing of the 1993 Oslo Peace Agreements between the PLO and Israel, though the group still opposed the agreement and insisted on no negotiations with Israel.

The decline of the Soviet Union, loss of public influence, and the reconciliation with the PLO caused the PFLP to alter some of its ideological points. For instance, as of the early 2000s, the group curbed its insistence on a Marxist state and a worldwide Marxist revolution, and instead chose to work from a more democratic platform. Today, the group calls for the establishment of a democratic socialist society.[3] It endorses "the establishment of a democratic state on the land of historic Palestine," and calls for a Marxist outlook "in its understanding and analysis of social reality."[4] Most important, however, is the PFLP's continued goal of destroying the Israeli state, and that its destruction is an essential part to tackling western influence in the Middle East. That the group still calls for the destruction of Israel is diplomatically expressed by referring to "historic Palestine," which signifies all lands from the Mediterranean Sea to the Jordan River. Furthermore, the PFLP would accept the establishment of a Palestinian state (with Jerusalem as its capital and right of return of refugees) along side an Israeli state, but only temporarily as a stepping-stone to completely replacing Israel as a distinct state.

In 2000, PFLP leader George Habash retired and was succeeded by the more radical leader, Abu Ali Mustafa. The new leader was previously permitted to reside in the West Bank, under Arafat controlled area, on condition that the PA would not allow him to conduct terrorist operations. Once Mustafa took control of the PFLP, he moved the group headquarters from Syria to the West Bank city of Ramallah and attacks against Israel shortly followed. During the summer of 2001 Israeli authorities captured and interrogated a six-man PFLP cell. The Israeli authorities learned subsequently that the group was plotting to bomb Israeli schools, other densely populated civilian structures in Jerusalem, and even the U.S. consulate in East Jerusalem.[5] Faced with little choice in preventing these attacks, Israeli forces rocketed Mustafa's office in August 2001, killing him and other members. Ahmed Sadat became the group's new leader and under his lead the PFLP assassinated Rechavam Zéevi, Israel's Tourism Minister, in a Jerusalem hotel in October of the same year in retaliation for the killing of Mustafa. Since then, its leadership has joined with umbrella groups, such as the National and Islamic Factions and the Popular Resistance Committees that call for an escalation of attacks against Israel.

## IDEOLOGY AND OBJECTIVES

"*The Military Thinking of the Front*," one of the PFLP's basic documents states:

"A basic condition for a true, radical revolution in our times is a revolutionary party, whose function is to orchestrate a national liberation war and lead it to victory. The structural basis of the revolutionary party is Marxism seeing Marxism as a guide to action, rather than a stagnant ideology. The Popular Front therefore adopts Marxism-Leninism as the basic strategic line for building a revolutionary party predicted on a solid, theological structure"[6]

The following are guidelines from the PFLP ideology:

- Promote the Palestinian Arab desire for a state to replace Israel, as a component of the worldwide Marxist revolution.
- Liberate Palestine through an armed struggle.
- Establish a Marxist, secular government in Palestine.
- Oppose any political settlement of the Palestinian conflict, including the 1993 Oslo Accords.

The PFLP's new political strategy consists of several objections:[7]

1. Liberation from Israeli occupation.
2. Construction of a democratic society.
3. Recognition that the Palestinian people are an integral part of the Arab Nation.
4. Recognition that the Palestinian struggle is part of the international, democratic struggle towards liberation, progress, democracy, and social justice.

## SELECTED LEADERSHIP

### Dr. George Habash[8]

The founder and former leader of the group, Dr. Habash held the title of Secretary General. He continues to call for the destruction of Israel, despite whatever accords PA Chairman Yasser Arafat signed with the government of Israel. During the 1993 PFLP Congress, a new executive body was elected, with the following members:

Dr. George Habash
Abu Ali Mustafa (Mustafa Zibri)
Abdul Rahim Lallouh
Abu Ahmed Fuad
Saber Mohieddin
Taysir Kubaa
Omar Kutaish

In addition, are several more members who are operatives in the disputed Territories who remain anonymous so as not to be targeted by Israel. In April 2000, Habash resigned as head of the PFLP and was succeeded by Abu Ali Mustafa in July 2000.

## Abu Ali Mustafa (Mustafa Zibri)[9]

Mustafa was one of the founders of the PLO and a member of its ruling Executive Committee. After the 1967 war, he fled from his native town of Arraba in the West Bank to Syria and Jordan. Israel allowed Mustafa to return to the Palestinian territories in 1999, following the reconciliation between Fatah and the PFLP. Mustafa was elected as the new leader of the PFLP in July 2000. In an interview on *Al-Jazeera*, shortly after he was elected, Mustafa stated that "We believe the Palestinian people have the right to struggle, because we think the conflict is constant, while the means and tactics are the variables."[10] In August 2001, Mustafa was killed in an IDF missile attack on his offices in Ramallah. In response to the assassination, PFLP leader Rabah Muhana, stated that "after this crime, every Israeli citizen and every Israeli leader must feel he is a target. The assassination of a Palestinian leader, an Arab leader, will not pass without punishment."[11] His successor is Ahmed Sadat.

## Ahmed Sadat

Sadat is a member of the Political Bureau of the PFLP in the West Bank. He was elected as the Secretary General following the assassination of Abu Ali Mustafa in August 2001. Sadat opposes the Oslo Accords and is loyal to the original PFLP guidelines. During the current Intifada, he has stood out as one of the organization's terrorist initiators. Choosing Sadat as the Secretary General expresses the radicalization of the movement away from the DFLP idealism of a pragmatic solution and engagement in negotiations with Israel. In April 2002, Sadat was sentenced by a PA court to one year in jail for collaborating in the assassination of Israel's Tourism Minister in October 2001. In June 2002 the Palestinian Authority High Court ordered Sadat's release from prison, but continuous Israeli threats against the PA deterred the Authority from releasing Sadat.

## FINANCIAL SOURCES OF SUPPORT

The PFLP receives most of its financial assistance and military support from Syria and Libya. In addition, the PFLP has earned money through front companies and legitimate business ventures. In 1982, Israeli Defense Forces discovered that the PFLP owned and operated a metal works plant in Sidon, Lebanon, worth at least 2 million dollars. In May 1999, Iranian president, Mohammed Khatami pledged to continue funding Palestinian opposition groups such as the PFLP, PFLP-GC, Islamic Jihad and Hamas.[12]

## AREAS OF OPERATION

Israel, West Bank and Gaza Strip, Lebanon, Syria, and Europe.

## HEADQUARTERS

Damascus, Syria.

## MEMBERSHIP

Approximately 800 members.

## TACTICS

In the 1970's, the PFLP gained an international reputation for its ruthless and large-scale attacks and hijacking against civilian targets. Included in the organization's methods of attacks are shooting, stabbing, and use of grenades. From 1970 to 1977, the PFLP was responsible for a number of international terrorism attacks. In the 1980's the majority of their attacks were small scale against Israeli security forces and civilians. In the 1990's the PFLP was active in southern Lebanon and carried out a number of attacks against IDF soldiers. The group also runs a training camp in the Bekaa Valley in eastern Lebanon.

During the Al-Aqsa Intifada, the PFLP has been very active and has claimed responsibility for several car bombings within Israel's pre-1967 borders and the assassination of Israel's Tourism Minister.

## ENDNOTES

[1] For more information see Alexander and Sinai, op. cit., p.40.

[2] Yodfat and Arnon-Ohanna, *PLO Strategy*, p.144.

[3] http://members.tripod.com/~freepalestine/

[4] The full quote reads, a "Marxist interpretation and dialectical materialism in its understanding and analysis of social reality." http://www.pflp-pal.org.about.html

[5] These findings were published in the Israeli newspaper, *Yediot Achronot*, September 4, 2001.

[6] Rubinstein, Elyakim (ed.), *Documents of the Popular Front for the Liberation of Palestine*, Texts for the Seminary of Dr. Yehoshafat Harkabi, (Jerusalem: Hebrew University 1971), pp.3–69 (quoted. in Ely Karmon's, "Fatah and the Popular Front for the Liberation of Palestine." www.ict.org.il)

7   www.pflp-pal.org
8   www.palestinehistory.com
9   www.wpb.be http://www.ict.org.il/articles/articledet.cfm?artcleid=145
10  http://news.bbc.co.uk/hi/english/world/middle_east/newsid_1511000/1511739.stm
11  http://news.bbc.co.uk/hi/english/world/middle_east/newsid_1511000/1511515.stm
12  http://www.ict.org.il/spotlight/det.cfm?id=263

# CHAPTER 3

# POPULAR FRONT FOR THE LIBERATION OF PALESTINE—GENERAL COMMAND

## ALSO KNOWN AS

PFLP-GC
Jabahat al-Shaabiya il Tahrir Falistin al-Qiyadat al Ama

## BRIEF HISTORY

Shortly after the Popular Front for the Liberation of Palestine (PLFP) was established in 1968, Ahmed Jibril and some supporting members broke off from the organization and formed the PFLP-GC. Part of their discontent with the PFLP was claim that the organization was too focused on political issues, and rather needed to concentrate more on violent opposition to Israel. Jibril also disagreed with the PFLP's Marxist-Leninist ideology and the emphasis on class conflict. However, the group still maintained membership in the "rejectionist front"—ten organizations (including the PFLP) that violently opposed the Fatah overtures with Israel.

After splitting from the PFLP, the group continued its violent opposition to Israel by staging (much like the PFLP) some of the most highly dramatic terror attacks of the 1970s. Particularly, the mid-air bombing of a Swissair flight headed for Tel-Aviv in 1970, and the shooting attack of an Israeli school bus packed with children in 1975 are among the organization's most dramatic operations. The PFLP-GC itself split in 1977 when Abu Abbas, Jibril's former second in command, left and formed the Palestine Liberation Front (PFL).

In the early 1980's, the PFLP-GC took an active part in the Lebanese civil war, and attacked US Marine peacekeeping troops stationed in Beirut. Reportedly, a number of PFLP-GC members have been tied with the hijacking and bombing of a TWA passenger plane that blew up over Lockerbie, Scotland in 1988, but none have been convicted to date.

In 1993, following the signing of the Oslo Peace Agreements between Israel and the Palestinian Liberation Organization (PLO), Jibril along with the PFLP, the Democratic Front for the Liberation of Palestine (DFLP) and other group leaders, called for further attacks on Israel and Israeli citizens in order to derail negotiations. Towards the late 1990s, the organization was suspected of collaborating with Hamas and the Palestinian Islamic Jihad (PIJ) in planning suicide attacks on Israeli targets.

Since the beginning of the al-Aqsa Intifada, the PFLP-GC has not been substantially involved in terrorist attacks and has not claimed responsibility for any attacks carried out in Israel. However, the group is still active in Lebanon, and members there continue to run bases in the Bekaa Valley. In May 2001, PFLP-GC members were involved in a smuggling operation of 40-tons of armament from Lebanon to the Palestinian Authority. In addition, members are believed to operate cells in Western Europe. Through 2002, the PFLP-GC has remained on the US State Department list of terrorist organizations.

In May of 2002, PFLP-GC military wing leader and son of current Command leader, Jihad Ahmed Jibril, was killed in a car bomb explosion in West Beirut. Though no official claims were made for the attack, Command members hold Israel responsible for the bombing. In response, Omar Shehabi, a member of the PFLP-GC stated that "the response for the assassination will be on the same scale, but the time and circumstances will decide the nature of the operation and its timing."

## SELECTED LEADERSHIP

### Ahmed Jibril

Born in Jaffa in 1928, his family moved to Syria shortly after he was born. He became an officer in the Syrian army and was later promoted intelligence captain. He established a small PLO office in Syria in 1959 and joined forces with Dr. George Habash to found the PFLP in 1967. After the breakup in 1968, Jibril remained pro-Syrian. Jibril was also involved in the release of 1,150 Palestinian prisoners from Israeli jails in exchange for three Israeli soldiers in the mid 1980's.

### Jihad Ahmed Jibril

Jihad, son of Ahmed Jibril was head of the PFLP-GC military wing and the future leader of the organization. In 1987 Jihad Jibril was behind one of the most dramatic terrorist attacks against Israel involving a hang glider assault on an Israeli Defense Forces (IDF) base in northern Israel. He was killed by a car bomb in May 2002.

## FINANCIAL SOURCES AND OTHER SUPPORT

Syria is the PFLP-GC's most substantial supporter and provides the group with military and logistical support to the group. Libya also financially contribute to the PFLP-GC until the mid 1980's when Jibril shifted his support base from Libya to Iran. The PFLP-GC soon became the major channel between Iran and Palestinian movements such as the Hamas, PFLP, and the DFLP.

## AREAS OF OPERATION

Israel, West Bank and Gaza Strip, Egypt, Lebanon, Syria, Iran and Europe.

## HEADQUARTERS

Damascus, Syria.

## MEMBERSHIP

Several hundred.

## TACTICS

The PFLP-GC is well known for its conventional military expertise, and has well developed air, land and naval infiltration capabilities. The group has carried out militia raids in various refugee camps in Lebanon, and has built tunnels connecting these camps to allow PFLP-GC fighters greater maneuverability during raids.

# CHAPTER 4

# DEMOCRATIC FRONT FOR THE LIBERATION OF PALESTINE

## ALSO KNOWN AS

DFLP

Al-Jabha Al-Dimuqratiyah Li-Tahrir Filastin

## BRIEF HISTORY

The Democratic Front for the Liberation of Palestine (DFLP) was founded by Nayef Hawatmeh after separating from the Popular Front for the Liberation of Palestine (PFLP) in 1969. Shortly after its establishment, a number of leftist Arab organizations joined the DFLP, making it the third largest PLO faction.[1] Initially the group called itself the Democratic Popular Front for the Liberation of Palestine, but formally dropped the word "Popular" from its name in 1975.

Ideologically, the DFLP is a Marxist-Leninist organization that maintains that only a popular working class revolution can achieve Palestinian goals. During the group's early years, members saw themselves as Marxist Leninists fighting against Israel, viewing the Jewish state as imperialistic and racist, and regarding the Arab regimes as "petty bourgeois."[2] In 1969, the DFLP advocated the establishment of a "popular democratic state" for Arabs and Jews, but by mid-1973 the organization had altered its stance and supported a Palestinian state alongside Israel.[3] During the 1977 Palestinian National Council, it endorsed the idea to create a Palestinian state on any territory liberated from Israel. Throughout its existence, the DFLP has carried out numerous attacks on Israeli military and civilian targets.

Traditionally, the DFLP leadership has been critical of the PLO's peace negotiations with Israel. Towards the late 1980s, however, tensions rose between leaders of the organization after a DFLP leader, Yasser Abed Rabbo, supported PLO Chairman Yasser Arafat's initiative for peace with Israel. In 1991, tensions climaxed when Rabbo was elected Secretary General and joined the peace initiative. As a result, Rabbo and his followers split from Hawatmeh's camp. In 1993 Abed Rabbo dropped the

PFLP name and formed the Palestinian Democratic Union (FIDA) based in Ramallah. In 2000, he participated in the Camp David peace talks as part of the Palestinian delegation.

The Hawatmeh-run DFLP continued to refuse any contacts with Arafat. In 1992 Hawatmeh's camp, along George Habash's PFLP and other anti-PLO and Arafat forces, set up an umbrella organization in Damascus, Syria. Calling themselves the "Damscus Ten," these groups continued to oppose any negotiations with Israel and challenged Arafat's Fatah group for the leadership of the Palestinian cause.

After the collapse of the former Soviet Union in the early 1990's, the DFLP along with other leftist oriented groups lost Moscow's funding and prestige. They were pushed aside while groups such as Hamas and the Palestinian Islamic Jihad (PIJ) increased in power and popularity in the Palestinian "street."

In 1999 the DFLP reconciled with Arafat and hinted that it might recognize Israel in the event of a signed peace treaty. As a result of this apparent modification, the U.S. State Department withdrew the DFLP from its list of terrorist organizations on October 10, 1999.

During the al-Aqsa Intifada, the DFLP has initiated a number of terrorist attacks, mainly targeting IDF soldiers in the Occupied Territories.

## IDEOLOGY AND OBJECTIVES

Nayef Hawatmeh's DFLP stated ideology and objectives include the following elements:

- The Palestinian national goal cannot be achieved without a revolution of the working class.
- Revolutionary change in the Arab world, especially in the conservative monarchies, is a necessary precursor to the achievement of Palestinian objectives.
- An international stance must be taken that places the Palestinian struggle within a general world context of liberation in the post-colonial world.
- Elite members of the movement should not be separated from the masses. Lower classes should be educated in true socialism in order to carry out the battle of liberation.
- There must be "hostility and resistance" to U.S. policy in the Middle East, its support for the nonaligned bloc, and its solidarity with all national liberation movements that fight against "imperialism" and "racism."
- The situation in the Middle East must be upgraded to an armed conflict against Israeli soldiers and civilians in the Disputed Territories.

On the other hand, Yasser Abd Rabbo's DFLP (FIDA) promises these goals:

- An end to Israeli "occupation."
- The establishment of Palestinian independence.
- Repatriation of Palestinians abroad.
- Protection of social and democratic interests of various classes and popular groups.
- The "right" to wage "all forms of struggle" against Israeli targets.
- The further development of "mass uprisings (Intifada) and mass action."

## ORGANIZATIONAL STRUCTURE

The DFLP's structure consists of numerous units within local organizations determined according to location, section, and profession. This structure allows full participation of all members and organs in a democratic manner by reviewing policies and electing committee members. Local bodies are directed by the general policy guidelines set by the DFLP leadership. Regional organizations have greater independence from the central office, enabling them to tend to local needs. The central organization is comprised of five different committees: the General National Congress—the highest political and legislative authority which convenes every five years; the General National Conference—similar authority as the Congress but more limited aganda and is called upon when necessary; the Central Committee—held four times a year and is elected by the General Congress; the Political Bureau—the highest executive leadership of the Central Committee; and the Control Committees—responsible for the participation of local organizations.[4]

## SELECTED LEADERSHIP

### Nayef Hawatmeh

The original founder and leader of the DFLP, Hawatmeh was the first PLO leader to openly advocate the foundation of a Palestinian state in the Occupied Territories, and not in all of Israel. He has called for increased violence against Israel to force an end to its presence in the West Bank and Gaza. Hawatmeh is a Jordanian, and currently resides in Syria where he continues to direct the DFLP's activities.

### Yasser Abd Rabbo

Until 1991, Abd Rabbo was the Assistant Secretary General and second in command of the DFLP. He has been a member of the PLO Executive Committee, headed the Information Department, and led dialogues with the United States in the late 1980's. In 1991, Abd Rabbo was elected Secretary General of the DFLP and split from Hawatmeh. In 2000, Abd Rabbo participated in the Camp David peace talks as part of the Palestinian delegation. As of early 2003, Abd Rabbo holds the title of Minister of Culture and Information in the Palestinian Authority.

## MEMBERSHIP

It is estimated that the DFLP has 500 members.

## FINANCIAL SOURCES OF SUPPORT

Most of the financial support for the DFLP comes from Syria and Libya. In the past, the DFLP also received weapons from the former Soviet Union.

## AREAS OF OPERATION

Israel, the West Bank, the Gaza Strip, Syria, and Lebanon.

## HEADQUARTERS

Syria and Lebanon.

## TACTICS

In the 1970's, the DFLP carried out numerous bombings, grenade attacks, kidnapping to negotiate exchange for Arab terrorists held in Israel, and other operations. From 1988 until the Israeli withdrawal from southern Lebanon in 2000, the DFLP changed its focus from civilian aimed terrorism to small-scale border raids against Israeli forces in southern Lebanon. The DFLP has been less active in the 1990's but has renewed activities in the West Bank and the Gaza Strip in light of the Oslo Peace Agreement, signed in 1993. The DFLP has initiated a number of shooting attacks against IDF soldiers during the al-Aqsa Intifada.

## ENDNOTES

[1]   These groups include "The Leftist Revolutionist Palestinian League" and the "Popular Organization for the Liberation of Palestine." In http://www.alhourriah.org/dflp_e.asp

[2]   Alexander, and Sinai, *op. cit.*, p.42.

[3]   Ibid.

[4]   http://www.alhourriah.org/dflp_e.asp

# SELECTED PALESTINIAN PROPAGANDA AND PSYCHOLOGICAL WARFARE EFFORTS

In the months leading up to the onset of the Al-Aqsa Intifada, in the fall of 2000, news agencies and Palestinian media watchdogs reported a significant increase in anti-Israeli and anti-Semitic propaganda, disseminated through the Palestinian Authority's official communication outlets. This form of psychological warfare and propaganda efforts intensified during the current Intifada. As chairman of the Palestinian Authority and the Fatah organization, Yasser Arafat has permitted such incitement to persist, despite his ratification of the Wye River Memorandum, which stipulates a cessation of incitement to violence.[1] The following section includes examples and statements communicated by the Fatah leadership and PA-sponsored media.

## EXAMPLES OF INCITEMENT WITHIN THE PALESTINIAN CHRISTIAN COMMUNITIES

July 23, 2000 broadcast of "Good Morning Jerusalem" on PA Television, featuring an artist explaining his painting of Jesus between two IDF soldiers:[2]

"... Our struggle today against the other [Israel] is an eternal one. It can be said that it started 2,000 years ago and continues until today. I demonstrate this through the figure of Jesus, who came to the world with a message of justice, and the other [Israel] side did what they did to him. The Palestinian demands that same right and is being treated in the same manner. In this painting I demonstrate the following idea: the Israeli soldiers are wearing army uniforms while Jesus has nothing except for the truth. When they searched him at the entrance to Jerusalem, they found a stone, a piece of bread and fish and he was cuffed. This is the Palestinian from the beginning of the struggle until its end—if it will ever end. ....".

"Christian prayer" published in the Fatah-operated daily paper Intifada:[3]

> "O my Radiant Sir, who was betrayed by the contemptible treasonous kiss. Descend upon us from the towers of heaven, and call upon the Glorious Supreme gazing down upon us, that He may wipe from Your face the tears of the masses, and read aloud Your tidings . . . would that it only be that the youth among us will enter now, by the Damascus Gate [of Jerusalem's Old City], chanting their psalms to the Via Dolorosa. But they shall not turn the other cheek, rather they shatter the cross off their backs and throw down the their thorny crowns. They cast their eyes to the heavens which praise [their Creator] for the glory of the fluid of the heart that washes the Via Dolorosa of the dust of [Israeli] soldiers who march alone to the Golgotha [The mountaintop crucifixion site]. Then shall rise up the voices of the mass of the living and the doves from every alley, and the chimes and the subdued yearns. O Son Of The Virgin, they cannot overcome you twice, go Thee slowly into the light-less meekness, and may the angels defend you."

## EXAMPLES OF URGENCY

A well-known song among Palestinians, it had not been broadcast on television or radio for several years. Sung amidst a video collage of violent clashes, the airing is known to be a call to arms and protest among Palestinians:

> "Where are the masses?
> Where is the Arab nation?
> Where is the Arab anger?
> Where is the Arab honor?"[4]

"Fatah announced a general call-up in its ranks as a preparation for the next stage. The movement announced the opening of registration for boys until the age of 16, for weapons training."[5]

## INCITEMENTS EXPRESSED BY YASSER ARAFAT, CHAIRMAN OF THE PALESTINIAN AUTHORITY

- "We are all potential martyrs, the whole Palestinian people."[6]
- "I am willing to sacrifice 70 martyrs to kill one Israeli."[7]

Arab Television Channels Interview Arafat
*Arafat granted interviews to leading Arab television channels. Following are excerpts from these interviews.*[8]

Interview With Al-Jazeera[1]

Arafat: "They decided to take me as a prisoner, a deportee, or to kill me. No. I say to them [that I will be] a martyr, a martyr, a martyr, and a martyr. . . .'And they will be in the front line until Judgment Day' . . . and 'one of their martyrs [who falls in the battle for Jerusalem] is worth 40 martyrs'[2] . . . Allah, give me martyrdom in . . . [Jerusalem], the place from which the Prophet Muhammad ascended to the heavens, and the place our lord Jesus was born . . . I may be martyred, but certainly one of our boys or one of our girls will wave the flag of Palestine over the walls of Jerusalem, over the minarets of Jerusalem, and over the churches of Jerusalem. 'They think it is distant, but we know it is imminent, and we are right' . . . 'They will enter the mosque as they entered it for the first time'[3] . . . This is the path I have chosen . . . Allah, give me martyrdom . . ."

"We defend not only Palestine, the Arab nation, and not only the holy Islamic and Christian places . . . but also all men of freedom and honor in the world. This is our destiny. This is a divine decree . . ."

"Let those far and near understand: None, among the Palestinian people or the Arab nation, will be willing to bow and surrender. But we ask Allah to grant us martyrdom, to grant us martyrdom. To Jerusalem we march . . . martyrs by the millions. To Jerusalem we march . . . martyrs by the millions. To Jerusalem we march . . . martyrs by the millions. To Jerusalem we march . . . martyrs by the millions."

"This is a call to the Arab and Islamic nations and to all the Christians in the world. This is the sacred land called in the West 'Terra Sancta,' Holy Land. We defend these holy places . . ."

"We said to the Americans: You must act. Where are you going? Don't you know this will shake the Middle East? I say to our Palestinian people: 'Oh mountain, the wind will not shake you.' I say to our Arab nation: 'To Jerusalem we march . . . martyrs by the millions.'"

Question: "Mr. President, Sharon said in his press conference that you have become an enemy, that you are not a partner for peace, and that Ramallah has become a den of terrorism. How do you respond to that?"

Arafat: "Isn't he [Sharon] a den of terrorism? The occupation is not a den of terrorism? The F-15 and F-16 warplanes are not a den of terrorism? The tanks that place me under siege are not a den of terrorism? Bombing civilians is not a den of terrorism? Forty-seven thousand Palestinian martyrs and wounded in this Intifada are not a den of terrorism? Destroying the institutions of the Palestinian people is not a den of terrorism? Destroying all the farms of the Palestinian people is not a den of terrorism? . . ."

Question: "Is it possible that the Israeli forces will try to assassinate you?"

Arafat: "They are more than welcome. I seek martyrdom. Allah, grant it to me. Am I better than that heroic youth Fares Odeh? We are seekers of martyrdom. We are all seekers of martyrdom. The entire Palestinian people is a seeker of martyrdom . . ."

Question: "Mr. President, do you think that this extensive invasion by the occupation forces is in response to the Netanya operation,[4] or a response to the Arab initiative at the Arab summit?"

Arafat: "No. It is a response to the Arab summit in Beirut . . .to Crown Prince Abdullah's initiative . . . This is an Israeli response to all the peace attempts because they do not want peace. They do not want peace!!! (sic) We must remember these things. These extremist elements murdered my partner Yitzhak Rabin. Why did they murder him? Because they do not want peace."

"Why do they distort Camp David? They ask why we did not accept Camp David. Should I surrender Jerusalem to them? Who can accept such a thing? Tell me, who can accept such a thing? . . . They are the plunderers, the murderers, the real terrorists in the entire world, in the entire world. We are the only people in the world under occupation. We put our hand in your [the Israelis'] hand . . . If this is the response to the Arab initiative, what does it mean? Who are the terrorists? The Palestinians? The Arabs? The Muslims? The Christians? Did we bomb the statue of the Virgin Mary [in Bethlehem]? The entire world turned upside-down because of the Taliban's attempt to destroy the statue of Buddha . . . is the statue of Mary not sacred? Is she not the only woman mentioned in the Koran? Is there not a Koranic chapter bearing her name?"

Question: "Sharon says that now there is a war without geographical borders. How do you assess the situation?"

Arafat: "By Allah, we consider all possibilities. Nobody is shaken, nobody is scared, nobody is retreating. To Jerusalem we march . . . martyrs by the millions." Interview With Egyptian TV[5]

Arafat: "I want to tell you something: The world went wild because of what the Taliban did to the statue of Buddha. But when they destroyed the statue of the Virgin Mary, who is the only woman mentioned in the Koran, no one in the world says a word . . . We defend these holy places: To Jerusalem we march . . . martyrs by the millions."

Question: ". . . What do you plan to do while the tanks are two meters away . . ."

Arafat: "What two meters?!! They are bombing me. Can't you hear the bombing?"

Question: ". . . Actually, we hear it from a distance . . ."

Arafat: "They attacked positions within the leadership compound."

Question: ". . . The question was, what will you do in this situation? How can the Palestinian leadership calm the situation?"

Arafat: "We are all seekers of martyrdom. We will not hesitate and will not retreat . . . As I told you: To Jerusalem we march . . . martyrs by the millions."

Question: "Is this a specific response to the Netanya operation?"

Arafat: "Great! All this in response to the Netanya operation? . . ."

Question: "It is obvious that the sympathy and enthusiasm of the Arab street is not enough. What do you demand now from the Arab leaders?"

Arafat: "To act in the international and global sphere with all the leaders in the world, in order to stop this international and global terrorism led by Sharon. Don't talk to me about terrorism in Kandahar, don't talk to me about Taliban terrorism, and don't talk to me about terrorism anywhere. The most important and most dangerous terrorism is the terrorism going on in the sacred land . . ."

Question: "Mr. President, we are following [events] with you and we see the Israeli tanks approaching . . . We are with you in our hearts and souls and we pray for your safety and the safety of the Palestinian people."

Arafat: "Man, don't wish me safety! Pray for me to attain martyrdom! Is there anything better than being martyred on this holy land? We are all seekers of martyrdom . . ."

Interview With Abu Dhabi TV[6]

Arafat: "Allah, grant us martyrdom in defense of the Christian and Muslim places holy to you . . . We are in the front line, and this people is defending these holy places . . ."

"True, he [Sharon] besieges us . . .True, he uses all the weapons prohibited by international law. True he uses depleted uranium, true he uses toxic gases . . .but we are steadfast . . . 'And they will be in the frontline until Judgment Day' . . ."

[1] *Al-Jazeera TV/Palestinian Authority TV*, March 29, 2002.
[2] This is a reference to a Koranic verse.
[3] This is a reference to a Koranic verse.
[4] The March 27, 2002 bombing of a Passover Seder held at a Netanya hotel.
[5] *Egyptian TV/Palestinian Authority TV*, March 29, 2002.
[6] *Abu Dhabi TV/Palestinian Authority TV*, March 29, 2002.

*An interview with the Kuwaiti Daily Al-Rai 'Al-'Am on December 12, 2001:*[9]
Arafat spoke of a conspiracy concocted by Prime Ministers Sharon and Barak to bring about a change of government in Israel:

"Barak could have stayed in power for another two and a half years, but the agreement between him and Sharon—following which Sharon went to visit the Al-Aqsa Mosque, which caused the well known massacre of the Friday prayers, as a result of which the Intifada broke out—that agreement [and all of this] was preplanned."

"When Sharon came to power, he asked the Israelis to give him a hundred days to get rid of the Intifada. The hundred days ended and he asked them: 'Give me [an] additional hundred days to carry out my military plan, 'Operation Hell,' and he is still carrying it out . . .'"

Arafat boasted that despite Israeli pressure "no one [amongst the Palestinians said] 'Ahh' [i.e., no one sighed] . . . Let me give you an example . . . do you know what a mother of a martyr does when she is informed of the martyrdom of her son? She goes out to the street with cheers of joy saying 'Allah be praised, my son, that you married Palestine rather than your cousin.' This is the Palestinian people."

In the interview, Arafat also stated that "they say that there are half a million Jews in Afghanistan whom [the Israelis] want to bring to the West Bank and to the Gaza Strip."

Arafat continued by stating: "The extremist forces in Israel killed my late partner Yitzhak Rabin who made peace with me, peace of the brave. This raises doubts about the behavior of some [amongst the Palestinians] who are putting in danger the interests of the Palestinian people and at their head the establishment of an independent Palestinian state with Jerusalem as its capital . . . we have declared a state of emergency because there are some who want to annihilate the Palestinian people."

> "There is a conspiracy against the Palestinian people. Therefore, we have to take a few strong steps and apply a tough policy against those who do not abide by the voice of reason and who do not respect the interests of the Palestinian people."

> "We began with those who carry out those operations that harm and damage the Palestinian cause and the Palestinian image."

> "These people could not find better timing [to carry out martyrdom operations] except the very moment when Sharon went to meet with President Bush with no cards in his hands. They gave Sharon these operations as a present . . ."

> "The Prophet Muhammad was defeated in the Battle of Uhud when a few Muslims came down from the mountains [the battle site] in order to collect the spoils of war. I tell these people: 'Don't let the spoils and support you are getting from the East and West turn into a weapon that hits us and our cause . . .'"

Yasser Arafat, 18 December 2001, in a speech in Ramallah reported in Ma'ariv:[10]

> "We with the help of God will meet next time in Jerusalem, because we are fighting in order to bring the victory to our prophets, every baby, every child, every man, every woman, and every older person, and all the youngsters, we will sacrifice ourselves for our holy places, and we will establish the guard on them, and are prepared to give 70 of our martyrs for every martyr of theirs in this campaign, because this is our holy land. We will continue to fight . . ."

Excerpts from an address given by Palestinian Authority Chairman Yasser Arafat at the headquarters of the Palestinian Workers' Association in Gaza City, October 27, 2001:[11]

". . . The tanks, planes, and missiles will never subjugate our
people, because it is at the forefront [of the battle], until
Judgment Day . . . Oh mountain, the wind cannot move you;
thus it is with our people, no one can move it . . ."

"We are now at a crossroads, but I say that the Palestinian
caravan is on its way to the first direction of prayer [i.e.
Jerusalem], to the third holiest place [Jerusalem], to the place
from which the Prophet Muhammad ascended to heaven
[Jerusalem, according to Koranic tradition], and the cradle of
Jesus's birth [sic]. To noble Jerusalem, the capital of the State of
Palestine, whether anyone agrees or not [i.e. Israel] . . ."

"Our people turns in this direction with great pride, with
determination, and with courage—despite continued attempts
on the part of whoever thinks he can subjugate the Palestinian
people with his tanks, his planes, his missiles, and his artillery."

Arafat went on to cite the *Hadith* [Islamic tradition]: "'There is still a
group of people of our nation who cling to the truth and defeat their enemies whose opponents cannot harm it . . . The Prophet was asked, Who
are [these people] and where are they? He answered: In Jerusalem and
its surroundings, and they are at the forefront [of the battle] until Judgment
Day . . .'"

"This is the grace of Allah, to be at the forefront. And therefore
all must know that we, 104 years after the First Zionist Congress
in Basle [in 1897]—in which the false claim of 'a land without
a people for a people without a land' was made—are today on
our land, and we are fighting, struggling, and confronting, with
firm will, strength, and faith, and I would like to stress that this
people will win, and it will win . . ."

"My brothers, you represent this principle [*Qaida*], and the
strong foundations of this people, who struggled and waged
Jihad; I have great hope in you and in your heroes, because we
believe that we have in us the firm, solid, reliable, and sound
principle [*Qaida*] . . ."

"[We have undergone] a major phase of Operation Oranim
[according to Arafat, an IDF operation], called [also] Operation
Hell . . . But this mass killing only intensifies our stubbornness,
our faith, and our perseverance; we will persevere, Allah willing, on this path until every boy of the boys of Palestine, and
every girl of the girls of Palestine, raises the Palestinian flag over
the walls of Jerusalem, its mosques, and churches—Jerusalem,
the capital of the State of Palestine . . . This is the will and these
are the aspirations of our Arab nation and of all the free men

and men of honor throughout the world; they are watching you and yearning for you to realize this dream for them . . ."

"I say these words so all will hear them, from Sharon to Netanyahu, to the last of the [listeners] in America, Japan, Indonesia, South Africa, Russia, in the North and in the South: 'The Palestinian people will determine its victory whether anyone agrees or not' [i.e. Israel]; 'they see this as far [from coming about], while we see it as soon to come, and we have patience' [Koran], 'and they shall enter the mosque, as they entered it the first time' [Koran]. Allah will not break his promise, Allah will not break his promise . . . Out of our commitment to Allah, to the homeland, and to the Christian and Muslim holy places over which we are custodians, we shall conclude the journey, we shall conclude the journey, we shall conclude the journey . . ."

March 1999 "Fatah" conference Arafat stated:[12]

"We will continue our struggle until . . . our flag [waves] on the walls, mosques, and churches of Jerusalem, the capital of our independent state, whether some people are happy about it or not. He who doesn't like it may drink the water of the Dead Sea . . . the 'Fatah' movement is ready to fight . . . if anyone tries to diminish our legitimate rights and our right to declare a state."

## INCITEMENT FROM RELIGIOUS SERMONS

A Friday sermon delivered by Palestinian Authority Imam Sheikh Ibrahim Madhi at the Sheikh 'Ijlin Mosque in Gaza City, broadcast live on April 12, 2002 by Palestinian Authority television:[13]

". . . Oh, beloved of Allah. [In the Friday sermon] two weeks ago, I bore in your name a blessing of love to the crowns upon our heads, [that is] to the Arab and Muslim rulers. Among other things, I said: 'Oh crowns upon our heads: If Sharon spat in your faces, what would you do?' Today I apologize for these words, because Sharon has not only spat on the heads of the nation, but also trampled us underfoot."

"We are convinced of the [future] victory of Allah; we believe that one of these days, we will enter Jerusalem as conquerors, enter Jaffa as conquerors, enter Haifa as conquerors, enter Ramle and Lod as conquerors, the [villages of] Hirbiya and Dir Jerjis and all of Palestine as conquerors, as Allah has decreed . . . 'They will enter Al-Aqsa Mosque as they have entered it the first time . . .'"

"Anyone who does not attain martyrdom in these days should wake in the middle of the night and say: 'My God, why have you deprived me of martyrdom for your sake? For the martyr lives next to Allah' . . ."

"Our enemies suffer now more than we do. Why? Because we are convinced that our dead go to Paradise, while the dead of the Jews go to Hell, to a cruel fate. So we stand firm and steadfast, in obedience to Allah . . ."

"The Jews await the false Jewish messiah, while we await, with Allah's help . . . the *Mahdi* and Jesus, peace be upon him. Jesus's pure hands will murder the false Jewish messiah. Where? In the city of Lod, in Palestine. Palestine will be, as it was in the past, a graveyard for the invaders—just as it was a graveyard for the Tatars and to the Crusader invaders, [and for the invaders] of the old and new colonialism . . ."

"A reliable *Hadith* [tradition] says: 'The Jews will fight you, but you will be set to rule over them.' What could be more beautiful than this tradition? 'The Jews will fight you'—that is, the Jews have begun to fight us. 'You will be set to rule over them'—Who will set the Muslim to rule over the Jew? Allah . . . Until the Jew hides behind the rock and the tree."

"But the rock and tree will say: 'Oh Muslim, oh servant of Allah, a Jew hides behind me, come and kill him.' Except for the *Gharqad* tree, which is the tree of the Jews."

"We believe in this *Hadith*. We are convinced also that this *Hadith* heralds the spread of Islam and its rule over all the land . . ."

"Oh beloved, look to the East of the earth, find Japan and the ocean; look to the West of the earth, find [some] country and the ocean. Be assured that these will be owned by the Muslim nation, as the *Hadith* says . . . 'from the ocean to the ocean' . . ."

"Oh Allah, accept our martyrs in the highest heavens . . ."
"Oh Allah, show the Jews a black day . . ."
"Oh Allah, annihilate the Jews and their supporters . . ."
"Oh Allah, raise the flag of Jihad across the land . . ."
"Oh Allah, forgive our sins . . ."

Excerpts from an interview given by Sheikh Ibrahim Mahdi praising suicide bombings in Israel. The interview was repeatedly aired on Palestinian television (October 2001):[14]

"All weapons must be aimed at the Jews, at the enemies of Allah, the cursed nation in the Koran, whom the Koran describes as monkeys and pigs . . . We will blow them up in Hedera, we will blow them up in Tel Aviv and in Netanya . . . We bless all those who educate their children to jihad and to martyrdom . . ."

Excerpts from the Friday (August 17, 2001) sermon broadcast live on Palestinian TV from the Sheik 'Ijlin mosque in Gaza. The preacher is Sheik Isma'il Aal Ghadwan:[15]

" . . .It is the duty of the Islamic nation to open the gates of Jihad, where its strength and honor lie. We are a nation that was given Islam and Jihad by Allah . . . S'ad bin Abi Waqqas tells the story of Abdallah bin Jahsh, who wished to launch a Jihad and never come back . . . He was hoping to get early [to Heaven] in order to meet the Prophet when he dies . . . Abdallah bin Jahsh said on the eve of the battle of Uhud: 'Oh Allah, bring me tomorrow an enraged and furious man and I will fight him for Your sake, and he will fight me, overcome me, and chop off my ear and my nose . . .'"

"When I meet with You [Allah] tomorrow, You will say: 'Oh Abdallah, what were your ear and nose chopped off for?' And I will answer: 'Oh my lord, for your sake and for your Prophet's sake.' And You will say: 'You have spoken the truth.'"

"S'ad bin Abi Waqqas said to his sons when the battle was over: 'Oh my sons, what Abdallah bin Jahsh did to spread Islam was much more superior to what I did. By Allah, when the battle was over, I found his ear and nose hanging on a string, and this is what he desired . . . Why? So he could meet Allah and say to Him: 'Allah, I fought the war of Jihad for your sake and for Your Prophet's sake' and when Allah would say to him: 'Show me your proof,' he would answer: 'the [chopped off] ear and the nose are my proofs.'"

"When the enemies of Allah, the Jews, may Allah curse them, mutilate [the bodies], and chop off organs—these organs will serve as evidence for our sons and brothers for whom Paradise in the high heavens is a place of refuge. [Even when] a martyr's organs are being chopped off, and he turns into torn organs that spread all over, in order to meet Allah, Muhammad, and his friends, it would not be [considered] a loss . . ."

"Yes, my believing brother, listen to the words of the Prophet to Jaber bin Abdallah who was sad after the battle of Uhud in which his father was killed . . .: 'Oh Jaber, why are you sad?' [Jaber ]said: 'My father was martyred and left me many children to take care of.' [The Prophet] said: 'Oh Jaber, I will tell you something that will take the sadness out of your heart . . . Oh Jaber, Allah spoke directly to your father without any mediation.' This is the honor given to our martyrs, the martyrs of the Islamic nation, who were killed due to their loyalty to Allah. . . . The martyr is given an opportunity to ask one wish and Allah makes it come true . . ."

"He [Abdallah, the father of Jaber] asked for one thing: to return to this world in order to tell how lucky the martyrs are. In Heaven, he said: My Lord, I only ask to come back to the world and then to be killed [again] for the sake of Allah, [then] go back to the world once again, and be killed again for the sake of Allah, then go back to the world [for the third time] and be killed again for the sake of Allah."

"Allah said to him: 'I have ruled that no one would return to the world.' [Abdallah] said: 'My Lord, is there any good news for the Mujahideen who still follow the Prophet's way . . . ?"

"Allah said to him: '. . . Do not consider those who have died for the sake of Allah as dead, but as alive, and as being provided for by their Lord.'"

"This good news . . . has passed down to our people who still make great sacrifices, defending the honor of the Islamic nation. The sacrifice of convoys of martyrs [will continue] until Allah grants us victory very soon. The willingness for sacrifice and for death we see amongst those who were cast by Allah into a war with the Jews, should not come at all as a surprise . . ."

"Oh believing brothers, we do not feel a loss . . . The martyr, if he meets Allah, is forgiven with the first drop of blood; he is saved from the torments of the grave; he sees his place in Paradise; he is saved from the Great Horror [of the day of judgment]; he is given 72 black-eyed women; he vouches for 70 of his family to be accepted to Paradise; he is crowned with the Crown of glory, whose precious stone is better than all of this world and what is in it . . ."

Excerpts, broadcasted on PA TV, are from the Friday sermon (August 3, 2001) given by Sheik Ibrahim Madhi at the Sheik 'Ijlin Mosque in Gaza:[16]

". . . Oh lovers of Allah. After the leaders of the Jews declared the "Hell" plan, we say: Yes, we accept the challenge, if this is the "Hell" plan. Then our dead [will reach] Heaven and their dead [will reach] Hell, Allah willing. This Jihad activity will continue, whether they like it or if it upsets them. Why do we complicate things. This is Jihad: Either victory or Martyrdom . . ."

"The states called the 'ring-states' [i.e. bordering Israel]— what are they good for? What are they worth? Do they protect us from the Jews, or do they [in fact] protect the Jews from the Mujaheedin in the name of Allah? We have said to them and we keep saying: 'Continue to guard your thrones and bellies, continue to protect your capitals, and let the Mujaheedin saturate this blessed land with their pure and untainted blood. Then, the Jews will see miracles from us.'"

"A young man said to me: 'I am 14 years old, and I have four years left before I blow myself up amongst the Jews.' I said to him: Oh son, I ask Allah to give you and myself Martyrdom . . .'"

"Oh lovers of Allah, we must state clearly: 'There is no difference between the National and Islamic [forces], we are all forces for the sake of Allah. We, the Muslims on this good and blessed land, are all—each one of us—seekers of Martyrdom. We do not know when the bombardments come. If the Jews only knew . . . that if they bombard us, the Arabs would bombard their villages and cities, they would hesitate a thousand times . . .'"

"We must all seek a role in the Jihad and the battle. We said and we still say: 'Even if we, the entire [Palestinian] people, stood in line and signed for the Jews that we want peace, they would not accept it. The Koran is very clear on this: The greatest enemies of the Islamic nation are the Jews, may Allah fight them . . .'"

"The Palestinian people should cure its wounds; we must forget our differences. There is no place for blood-vengeance. Our enemy is very clear. All weapons should be directed towards him. Why do we see weapons that are directed on one another? . . . All spears should be directed at the Jews, at the enemies of Allah, the nation that was cursed in Allah's book. Allah has described them as apes and pigs, the calf-worshipers, idol-worshipers . . . they have said that we are cockroaches and ants and that they should kill us, but we approach them with the words of Allah: '. . . Whoever wants to save himself, should enter to the true religion—Islam—and repent, and then there will be no problems between him and us, our rights will be his and his obligations will be ours. However, he who came to this land as an invader and did not enter the religion of Allah, should go back to the place he came from, or else, our spears will reach him, Allah willing.'"

"Oh beloved, the Jews want to throw us under a wall of despair [and claim] that we are destined to die. We say: 'We accept this challenge. Any one of us who dies, will reach Heaven, Allah willing. I ask Allah that we would meet him as Martyrs for his sake. I ask Allah that our dead will be in Heaven . . .'"

"Whoever can fight them with his weapons, should go out [to the battle]; whoever can fight them with a machine-gun, should go out; whoever can fight them with a sword or a knife, should go out; whoever can fight them with his hands, should go out; This is our destiny. The people who are the most hostile toward the believers are the Jews and the Polytheists . . . The Jews have exposed their fangs. Nothing will deter them, except the color of their filthy people's blood; nothing will deter them except for us voluntarily detonating ourselves in their midst. They have nuclear power, but we have the power of the belief in Allah . . ."

"The Prophet [Muhammad] said: 'The Jews will fight you, and [Allah] will establish you as rulers over them . . .' We blow them up in Hadera, we blow them up in Tel Aviv and in Netanya, and in this way, Allah establishes us as rulers over these gangs of vagabonds. The Jews fight you, but Allah will establish you as rulers over them. Until the Jew would hide behind a stone or a tree, and the stone or the tree would say: Oh Muslim, Oh servant of Allah, a Jew is hiding behind me, come kill him, with the exception of the Gharqad tree which is the tree of the Jews . . .'"

"In several years, Allah willing, we will enter Jerusalem as conquerors, to Jaffa as conquerors. To Haifa as conquerors, to Ashkelon as conquerors. We are certain that victory is near . . ."
"Blessings for whoever assaulted a soldier . . . Blessings for whoever has raised his sons on the education of Jihad and Martyrdom; blessings for whoever has saved a bullet in order to stick it in a Jew's head . . ."

A Friday Sermon on PA TV: We Must Educate our Children on the Love of Jihad . . .' June 6, 2001 on PA TV, from the Sheik 'Ijlin Mosque in Gaza, PA employee, Sheik Muhammad Ibrahim Al-Madhi, called for Jihad education and for turning Jews and Christians into Ahl-Dhimma [protected second rate citizens] under Muslim rule. Following are excerpts from the sermon:[17]

". . . Oh, you who love Allah, in the Koran we read our Lord's words, that we must fight all the polytheists just as they fight all of you . . . Oh, you who love Allah . . . This [Muslim] nation has left the leadership of the human race to a handful of contemptible Jews and their assistants and was satisfied [with its position at] the tail of the convoy . . ."

"The Palestinian people has decided that this blessed Intifada would continue. We sacrifice as many prisoners, martyrs, and wounded as we can; we will continue the Intifada until the land of Palestine is liberated. We will not be satisfied with the mere establishment of a Palestinian state; the Muslim people of

Palestine want to meet Allah and we are the soldiers of the Caliphate, that was announced by the Prophet [Muhammad] . . . Therefore, the Caliphate will be in accordance with the prophecy, in Al-Aqsa, in Jerusalem, and in its surroundings . . ."

"Oh, you who love Allah, the signs of the victory are many . . . Oh, you who love Allah, do not believe the joke of peace. By Allah, do not believe the joke of peace. Even if the Palestinian people here and in the Diaspora will stand in line and sign [on an agreement] with all ten fingers, and even with the toes of their feet, and we will say: 'We all want peace with you'—by Allah, they [i.e. the Jews] do not want peace . . ."

"Even if they slaughter all of the Palestinian people and the only survivors will be one single Palestinian baby girl and one single Palestinian baby boy, the baby boy will marry the baby girl and they will give birth to the one who will liberate Jerusalem from the defilement of the Jews."

"Victory is drawing near, but believe me, there is a secret resolution, decided upon by, unfortunately, many of the Arab and Muslim nations. While they [the Palestinians] sacrifice the last Palestinian child and the last Palestinian fetus, they [the Arab nations] will satisfy themselves with victories on the soccer courts, with music festivals, and with Arab and Muslim summits. Where are the summits, where are their decisions? . . . It was rightly claimed that a thousand verbal shells cannot compare to one shell made of iron. It was rightly claimed that what was taken by force will be regained only by the use of force."

"We must prepare ourselves in accordance with the religion of Allah and the Law of Allah. We must educate our children on the love of Jihad for the sake of Allah and the love of fighting for the sake of Allah."

"We welcome, as we did in the past, any Jew who wants to live in this land as a Dhimmi, just as the Jews have lived in our countries, as Dhimmis, and have earned appreciation, and some of them have even reached the positions of counselor or minister here and there. We welcome the Jews to live as Dhimmis, but the rule in this land and in all the Muslim countries must be the rule of Allah . . . Those from amongst the Jews and from amongst those who are not Jews who came to this land as plunderers, must return humiliated and disrespected to their countries."

"On the other hand, those Jews who are local and who have lived with the Palestinian people and with the locals from amongst the Christians—there is nothing bad with their living [amongst us] in harmony and peace. This is the kind of peace we understand. The Arabs and Muslims must speak, because our choice is the Jihad for the sake of Allah . . ."

"Oh, you who love Allah, there is no alternative to the true return to Allah. Victory will not come from the Kremlin, neither will it come from the White House decisions, or from Arab and Islamic summits. Victory is from Allah . . ."

Later in the sermon, Sheik Al-Madhi focused on the need to refrain from taking credit for terrorist attacks, while using Muslim history as an example to follow:

". . . Oh, you who love Allah, it is our duty to strive so that all our deeds will be [only] for the sake of Allah. Listen to the following precious story:"

"In one African country, a Muslim army was fighting against the Byzantine army. The number of the Byzantines was more than ten times the number of the Muslims . . . The Byzantine commander was Gregorius and his daughter was by his side. Gregorius' daughter said: 'My father, who are these, they are merely a handful, their number is small, no more than 15,000, who are they?' He answered her: 'These are the Arab horsemen.' She said: 'My father, give them to me as spoils.' And he had given her [their property's worth] as spoils, before the battle even took place. However, Allah wanted Gregorius killed in the battle and his daughter to be one of the captives."

"The commander of the Muslim army wanted to know who killed Gregorius, but nobody answered."

"This is how we should also act: Do, do, and do, but without talking."

"Who killed Gregorius? Gregorius' daughter said to the commander of the Muslims: 'I know who killed my father.' And when Abdallh Ibn Al-Zubeir passed next to her she said: 'Oh, commander of the Muslims, this is the man who killed my father.' [The Muslim commander asked him:] 'Oh, Abdallah Ibn Al-Zubeir, why did you conceal this from us?' What did Abdallah Ibn Al-Zubeir say in response? His words still echo in the ear of history. He said: 'Allah knows I killed him.'"

"Allah knows what we do and there is no necessity for humans to know this as well. With such noble values, the [Muslim] nation shall win . . ."

October 2000, Friday sermon in Gaza City:[18]

"The Jews are Jews, whether Labor or Likud, the Jews are Jews. They do not have any moderates or any advocates for peace. They are all liars. They are the ones who must be butchered and killed as Allah the Almighty said: 'fight them.' Allah will torture them by your hands and will humiliate them and will help you to overcome them and will relieve the minds of the believers. Even if a (peace) agreement was signed on Gaza and the West Bank, we shall not forget Haifa, and Acre, and the Galilee, and Jaffa, and the Triangle (Israeli-Arab villages), and the Negev, and the rest of our cities and villages. It is only a matter of time (until we conquer them). Our people must unite in one trench and receive armaments from the Palestinian leadership, to confront the Jews. By Allah, the Jews o brothers in belief do not know, nor have they ever known throughout history, anything but force and Jihad in the path of Allah. The Jews are like a motorcycle pedal, as long as you step on it with your foot, it doesn't move, but if you lift your foot from it, it hurts you and punishes you. This is the case of the Jews. Have no mercy on the Jews, no matter where they are, in any country."

"Fight them, wherever you are. Wherever you meet them kill them. Wherever you are kill those Jews and those Americans who are like them and those who stand with them—they are all in one trench, against the Arabs and Muslims because they established Israel here, in the beating heart of the Arab world, in Palestine. They created it in order that it be the outpost of their civilization and the vanguard of their army and to be the sword of the West and the crusaders hanging over the necks of the Muslim monotheists. The Muslims in this land, they wanted the Jews to be the spearhead for them to impose their greed on the Arab states for Arab petroleum which should be exploited for the sake of (the struggle of) the Palestinian people and for the Palestinian cause. All we want from the Arabs is to open their borders with us, their borders with Palestine, so that the armies of the holy war, from Yemen, from Syria, from Iraq, and other Muslim states, may wage holy war with their brothers the Palestinians."

## PALESTINIAN AUTHORITY INCITEMENTS

At a convention called "Suicide Attacks and the National Dialog" held in Ramallah on 9 June, 2002 the General Secretary of the Palestinian Authority stated:[19]

"Suicide missions are the highest form of struggle of the Palestinian people in the war against Israel for their existence." He also said, "Suicide missions are heroic" and "the arena of these operations should be the conquered territories of '67."

This passage was taken from al Shuhada, a monthly publication issued by the Political Indoctrination apparatus of the Palestinian Border Guard that operates in the Gaza Strip. (issue no.44, November-December 2001): [20]

> "Because of all these, the Jew has no choice but to indulge, in his relations with others, in using any vile means such as theft, deceit, exploitation, fraud and usury. They also authorize him to kill, like Moses did, as described in the Bible and the Talmud, when he killed the Egyptian in a calculated and premeditated act and did not spare his life. Killing a non-Jew, a "Goy" [gentile], according to the Rabbis, is an offering to God, which appeases God and earns the offerer a reward. This is because the non-Jews are enemies of God and the Jews, and they are beasts which one is entitled to kill by whatever means available."

Deputy Commander of "Force 17," Muhammad Dhamrah, A.K.A, Abu Awdh in an interview with Al-Hayat (London, August 17, 2001):[21]

> ". . . Independence will be realized only through sacrificing. We have prepared thousands, tens of thousands, martyrs in order to regain our land and for the return of the refugees. I derive my strength from this people, rather than from the security coordination or from promises made by the CIA. I feel safe, as many others do, among my people. I am not worried. I am very optimistic that victory will come."
>
> "I promise that the number of shootings at the occupation will increase to 500 to 1,000 shooting [incidents] per day . . . The Palestinians have trained themselves to attack the Israeli tanks and explode their bodies that will be loaded with a belt of explosives, as part of the preparations for a possible Israeli attack in the Palestinian territories . . . The current Intifada differs from the previous one because it is armed and the Palestinians are fighting inside their territory and from it . . ."
>
> "We need patience and [have] to continue the struggle [so] we will achieve our freedom in five years . . . The Palestinians have nothing to lose, while the Israelis have a lot to lose. We can live on olives and za'tar [thyme] and continue our struggle until the liberation of our land."

One of the leaders of the "Al-Aqsa Martyrs' Brigades" and its Official spokesman, A.K.A Usama Al-Najjar in an interview with the Hizbuallah weekly, Al-Intiqad, [Lebanon, August 17, 2001]:[22]

"The Al-Aqsa Martyrs' Brigades was established in the first month of the Intifada by groups of Fateh who had been active in the first Intifada of 1987, and especially those who were imprisoned by the occupation and who carried out operations against the traitors. They were released when the Palestinian Authority moved into the West Bank and Gaza in 1994 . . ."

"The activity of the 'Brigades' began with armed confrontations with the occupation soldiers in some places in the West Bank, and its establishment was officially announced on January 1, 2001, during the military parade in commemoration of the establishment of the Fateh movement. The 'Brigades' consider the killing of a Zionist settler near the West Bank village of Jalameh at the beginning of 2001 as its first operation."

"The 'Brigades' believes in the strategy of operating against the Israelis wherever they are. We believe in road-side explosives, armed confrontations, and sniper-shootings. The range for our operations is throughout occupied Palestine, but we do not carry out Martyrdom [meaning suicide] operations because we believe in the importance of protecting the lives of our Jihad-warriors, as much as possible . . ."

"The members of the Al-Aqsa Martyrs [Brigades] are warriors who are not subjected to any political decision and have no relation with the first rank of the PA, although some of its members work in sensitive positions in the PA's civil ministries or its security apparatuses. There has not been any clash between the 'Brigades' and the PA, in contrast to the "[Popular] Resistance Committees" that clashed with the PA and some of whose members were hit in these clashes. The 'Brigades' respect the national interest and [carefully] chose the place and the time to carry out its operations. We killed an Israeli settler and injured others on the first day of the week of "calming." We try to expose the traitors and deliver them to the PA, without killing them, in order to avoid mistakes that were made in the past."

"Recently, the Al-Aqsa Martyrs Brigades have announced that it carries out operations together with the "'Izz Al-Din Al-Qassam Brigades," the military wing of Hamas, and with members of the "Al-Quds Squads," the military wing of the Islamic Jihad in Palestine. One example was the operation that took place on the opening day of the Maccabiya Games, when two members [of the Brigades'] were martyred when they tried to plant a bomb near the stadium. In addition, several shooting operations took place in cooperation with the "Al-Quds Squads.""

"The 'Brigades' do not have a central command and this is the secret of its success. Its people operate separately in each district and decide about their plans."

"The 'Brigades' include hundreds of members, aged between 22 and 52, who were released from Israeli prisons or students in Palestinian universities who operate sometimes with and sometimes without coordination [with each other]."

"The Al-Aqsa Martyrs Brigades will continue as long as the reasons for the resistance exist, i.e. the occupation, the settlements, and the defiling of the holy places. The line of the resistance cannot be forsaken and in the coming days there will be more operations in retaliation for the Israeli massacres."

The Palestinian Information Center: "There Is Serious Thinking about Obtaining Biological Weapons," August 13th, 2001:[23]

"Due to the seriously uneven balance of power in the Israeli-Palestinian conflict, and in light of the escalation of the racist aggression, which elevates to the level of a war declaration, by the Sharon government . . . the Palestinian side is required to use weapons of deterrence that will even the balance of power, at least on the field."

"While the human-bombs [meaning, suicide bombers] may be followed [and maybe stopped by] preventive measures . . . serious thinking has begun for a while about developing a Palestinian weapon of deterrence. This weapon terrifies the Israeli security apparatuses, from time to time, mainly because obtaining its primary components, whether biological or chemical, is possible without too much effort, let alone the fact that there are hundreds of experts who are capable of handling them and use them as weapons of deterrence, thus creating a balance of horror in the equation of the Palestinian-Israeli conflict."

"A few bombs or death-carrying devices will be enough, once they are deployed in secluded areas and directed at the Israeli water resources or the Israeli beaches, let alone the markets and the residential centers. [This will be carried out] without explosions, noise, blood, or pictures that are used to serve the Israeli propaganda. Anyone who is capable, with complete self-control, of turning his body into shrapnel and scattered organs, is also capable of carrying a small device that cannot be traced and throw it in the targeted location."

"What we want to say is that the Israeli security apparatuses take into account such dramatic development in the conflict, although they believe the issue is limited to the possibility of smuggling such weapons from abroad . . ."

"General Mofaz seeks a political future painted with Palestinian blood . . . without considering the level of casualties and economic damage that will be caused to the Israeli society, if the Palestinian people and its leadership are cornered."

## Statements by Heads of Fateh Factions

Deputy Commander of "Force 17," Muhammad Dhamrah, A.K.A, Abu Awdh in an interview with Al-Hayat [London, August 17, 2001]:[24]

". . . Independence will be realized only through sacrificing. We have prepared thousands, tens of thousands, martyrs in order to regain our land and for the return of the refugees. I derive my strength from this people, rather than from the security coordination or from promises made by the CIA. I feel safe, as many others do, among my people. I am not worried. I am very optimistic that victory will come."

"I promise that the number of shootings at the occupation will increase to 500 to 1,000 shooting [incidents] per day . . . The Palestinians have trained themselves to attack the Israeli tanks and explode their bodies that will be loaded with a belt of explosives, as part of the preparations for a possible Israeli attack in the Palestinian territories . . . The current Intifada differs from the previous one because it is armed and the Palestinians are fighting inside their territory and from it . . ."

"We need patience and [have] to continue the struggle [so] we will achieve our freedom in five years . . . The Palestinians have nothing to lose, while the Israelis have a lot to lose. We can live on olives and za'tar [thyme] and continue our struggle until the liberation of our land."

One of the leaders of the "Al-Aqsa Martyrs' Brigades" and its Official spokesman, A.K.A Usama Al-Najjar in an interview with the Hizbuallah weekly, Al-Intiqad, [Lebanon, August 17, 2001]:

"The Al-Aqsa Martyrs' Brigades was established in the first month of the Intifada by groups of Fateh who had been active in the first Intifada of 1987, and especially those who were imprisoned by the occupation and who carried out operations against the traitors. They were released when the Palestinian Authority moved into the West Bank and Gaza in 1994 . . ."

"The activity of the 'Brigades' began with armed confrontations with the occupation soldiers in some places in the West Bank, and its establishment was officially announced on January 1, 2001, during the military parade in commemoration of the establishment of the Fateh movement. The 'Brigades' consider the killing of a Zionist settler near the West Bank village of Jalameh at the beginning of 2001 as its first operation."

"The 'Brigades' believes in the strategy of operating against the Israelis wherever they are. We believe in road-side explosives, armed confrontations, and sniper-shootings. The range for our operations is throughout occupied Palestine, but we do not carry out Martyrdom [meaning suicide] operations because we believe in the importance of protecting the lives of our Jihad-warriors, as much as possible . . ."

"The members of the Al-Aqsa Martyrs [Brigades] are warriors who are not subjected to any political decision and have no relation with the first rank of the PA, although some of its members work in sensitive positions in the PA's civil ministries or its security apparatuses. There has not been any clash between the 'Brigades' and the PA, in contrast to the "[Popular] Resistance Committees" that clashed with the PA and some of whose members were hit in these clashes. The 'Brigades' respect the national interest and [carefully] chose the place and the time to carry out its operations. We killed an Israeli settler and injured others on the first day of the week of "calming." We try to expose the traitors and deliver them to the PA, without killing them, in order to avoid mistakes that were made in the past."

"Recently, the Al-Aqsa Martyrs Brigades have announced that it carries out operations together with the "'Izz Al-Din Al-Qassam Brigades," the military wing of Hamas, and with members of the "Al-Quds Squads," the military wing of the Islamic Jihad in Palestine. One example was the operation that took place on the opening day of the Maccabiya Games, when two members [of the Brigdaes'] were martyred when they tried to plant a bomb near the stadium. In addition, several shooting operations took place in cooperation with the "Al-Quds Squads.""

"The 'Brigades' do not have a central command and this is the secret of its success. Its people operate separately in each district and decide about their plans."

"The 'Brigades' include hundreds of members, aged between 22 and 52, who were released from Israeli prisons or students in Palestinian universities who operate sometimes with and sometimes without coordination [with each other]."

"The Al-Aqsa Martyrs Brigades will continue as long as the reasons for the resistance exist, i.e. the occupation, the settlements, and the defiling of the holy places. The line of the resistance cannot be forsaken and in the coming days there will be more operations in retaliation for the Israeli massacres."

## *A Fatah Official on the Intifada and Its Goals.*

*Sakhr Habash, a member of the Fatah's Central Committee, gave a comprehensive interview to the PA daily* Al-Hayat Al-Jadida *concerning the Intifada and its political goals. Following are excerpts from the interview:*[25]

Roots of the Intifada

"After the Camp David Summit it became clear to the Fatah movement, as brother Abu-Ammar [Yasser Arafat] had warned, that the next phase requires us to prepare for conflict [with Israel], because PM Barak is not a partner capable of complying with our people's aspirations. In light of this estimation, Fatah was the most prepared for a conflict among all other [Palestinian] national movements . . ."

"[The Intifada] did not break out in order to improve our bargaining ability in the negotiations, nor as a reaction to Sharon's provocative visit to Al-Haram Al-Sharif: this was only the spark. It was accumulated in the depths of our people and was bound to explode in the face of Barak's government because of the political problem that was put off for more than a year and a half—the problem of independence. Independence was the core issue of the Intifada that broke out in Al-Aqsa and spread to the rest of the cities, camps and villages in the West Bank and the Gaza Strip, as well as in Palestinian cities and villages within the Green Line [Israel]. The Intifada endorsed the PLO's national plan that reflects the aspirations of our people: the establishment of an independent state with Jerusalem as its capital in the borders of June 4, 1967, and ensuring the Right of Return and compensation for Palestinian refugees—"

Who Controls the Intifada?

Since brother Arafat is busy with many various missions, authority was delegated to leaders in the field, who are on the lowest level of the organizational hierarchy. However, the leadership of the PA remained the source of authority, and it alone was the factor capable of leading the operations of the Intifada throughout the homeland. I can say for certain that brother Abu-Ammar is the ultimate authority for all operations, and whoever thinks otherwise, does not know what is going on—"

"When we declare the establishment of a state and independence, we will have the right to liberate the rest of the occupied land, because this land is not under dispute, as the Israelis claim, but rather it is occupied land which must return to its owners."

Intifada Negotiations

"[At the Camp David Summit] we thought that President Clinton would be able to put pressure on the Israeli government—before leaving the White House—so that Barak would agree to a political solution acceptable to us. But it became clear that the American position coincides with the Israeli position: sharing sovereignty over Al-Haram Al-Sharif with us, and dividing East Jerusalem into four or five parts in order to guarantee Israeli control there—"

"The series of collapsing Israeli governments proves that Israel is still unable to make peace, and at the same time it is unable to defeat the Palestinian decision-making or to diminish our national rights. Our people's steadfastness and the Intifada will continue until the arrival of an Israeli government whose leaders are brave enough to make peace. The Intifada must continue. When the Zionist society has suffered heavy losses, it will demand that its government achieve a peace based on international legitimacy. The continuation of the struggle will also influence American interests and will bring the pressure of the Administration on the Israeli government. Any damage we cause to the Zionist society and to American interests will bring us closer to our goal. Then the Zionist enemy will discover that it cannot break our will, which is the will of international legitimacy. Therefore, we must adhere to the UN resolutions, which are our strongest weapon, although they have not done us historical justice—"

The Armed Struggle

"I am well aware that the balance of power regarding an armed war [with Israel] is not in favor of our people, who cannot carry out an armed war with the Zionist entity. [The will to conduct] a military confrontation is a sort of naivete, and therefore [it is best]—not to fight the enemy where it has an advantage over us; in such a case we would be the losers. Nevertheless, we have weapons that the Zionist enemy does not have. The boy Fares Odeh who attacked an Israeli tank with stones and was killed—is our strongest weapon. He reflects the true image of the Palestinian people for the world which supports us—"

"In the present Intifada, the enemy attacked with helicopters, shot missiles on our posts and caused death and injury to people who have family and friends. The PA cannot limit retaliations which may include use of firearms."

"I do not support an armed war with the enemy, but I support the kind of armed struggle that will shake up the enemy and make the lives of the settlers unbearable. This is what will force them to evacuate our land, which they took by force with the support of the Israeli army—"

Islamists and Nationalists

"The coordination between the national and Islamic forces began years ago—Lately the Islamic Jihad, the Al-Sa'iqa [the Syria based Palestinian Ba'athist faction] and the 'Popular Front—General Command' organization [led by Ahmad Jibril] have joined this [organizational] framework. The coordination is at an especially high level, more so than in the days of the great Intifada of 1987—"

"The national and Islamic forces differ in their influence, presence and size—In order to play a decisive and effective role, they must act in coordination with one another as well as with the PA, so that their decisions do not contradict each other. At the same time, these organizations are not bound by the agreements to which the PA is committed . . . This situation strengthens the PA's position."

"The PA has stood by its people, protected it with force, suffered heavy losses, ended security cooperation with the Israeli government, and released prisoners from the Islamic movement."

Speech by Palestinian Authority Minister of Communications, Emmad El-Faluji, December 5th, 2000:[26]

"Intifada al-Aqsa whoever thinks that this Intifada started as a result of the despicable visit of Sharon to al-Aqsa Mosque is in error—that was merely the straw that broke the patience of the Palestinian people. This Intifada was already planned, ever since the President's (Arafat) return from the last talks at Camp David, at which (Arafat) stood up to President Clinton and firmly rejected the American terms (for the agreement) in the heart of America. Arafat is the first president to unequivocally tell America that he rejects America, when he was still in Washington and Camp David and to state that he will not give in to American terms whatever the circumstances or challenges."

Director-General of the PA Information Ministry, Hassan Al-Kashef, in his daily column in Al-Ayyam, wrote:[27]

"The only way to impose our conditions is inevitably through our blood. Had it not been for this blood, the world would have never been interested in us . . . therefore the continuation of the popular confrontation is an urgent political need . . . the power of the Intifada is our only weapon. We should not toss this weapon away until the Arab emergency summit is convened and until we gain international protection . . . our national duty

is to continue the confrontation, continue the Intifada, continue
to sacrifice our martyrs so that the blood of our martyrs and
injured will not have been spilled in vain . . . so that the Intifada
of Al-Aqsa will be the gate to independence and freedom . . ."

"It's a Woman!" an editorial in the Egyptian Islamist weekly Al-
Sha'ab:[28]

"It's a woman!! A woman, oh men of the [Islamic] nation; a woman,
oh youth of the nation; a woman, oh women of the nation; a
woman, oh those who call for the liberation of the nation's women;
a woman, oh soldiers of the nation; a woman, oh rulers, princes,
and leaders of this nation; it is a woman, a woman, a woman."

"It is a woman who teaches you today a lesson in heroism,
who teaches you the meaning of Jihad, and the way to die a
martyr's death. It is a woman who has inscribed, in letters of
fire, the battle of martyrdom that horrified the heart of the
enemy's entity. It is a woman who has shocked the enemy, with
her thin, meager, and weak body . . . It is a woman who blew
herself up, and with her exploded all the myths about women's
weakness, submissiveness, and enslavement."

"It is a woman who today teaches you, oh Muslim women,
the meaning of true liberation, with which the women's rights
activists have tempted you . . . It is a woman who has now
proven that the meaning of [women's] liberation is the liberation of the body from the trials and tribulations of this world
. . . and the acceptance of death with a powerful, courageous
embrace . . ."

"It is a woman, a woman, a woman who is a source of pride
for the women of this nation and a source of honor that shames
the submissive men with a shame that cannot be washed away
except by blood . . . It is a woman in the spring of her youth
who swore in the name of her God, with every drop of her
blood, with every limb of her body, and with every one of her
cells that turned into coals that burned the hearts of the enemy
with the fire of fear, loss, and pain . . ."

Friday Sermon on PA TV: Calling for Suicide Bombings
Every Friday, the PA television broadcasts a live sermon from one
of the Gaza mosques. On June 8, 2001, a week after the Tel-Aviv suicide
bombing and a few days following Arafat's declaration regarding the
cease-fire, a sermon by Sheik Ibrahim Madhi was broadcast from the Sheik
'Ijlin Mosque. In his sermon, Sheik Madhi preached for 'martyrdom operations' and for the destruction of Israel, the United States, and Britain.
Following are excerpts from the sermon:[29]

". . . I tell you, Oh beloved, that ever since Kamal Ataturk [founder of modern Turkey], this Jew who disguised himself as a Muslim—and there may still be in the Arab nation Jews who disguise themselves as Muslims . . . ever since he announced the end of the Islamic Caliphate in Istanbul—as some contemporary religious sages assert—the era preceding the end [of days] has began—the era of the military rule, the era of revolutionary rule. Allah willing, we are at the end of this era and Allah willing, the Caliphate will return, in accordance with the prophecy, and I pray that we will be among its soldiers . . ."

"Allah is almighty. Had He wanted—He would have beaten them. But He tests you in suffering. We must prepare the ground for the army of Allah that is coming according to the [divine] predetermination. We must prepare a foothold for them. Allah willing, this unjust state will be erased—Israel will be erased; this unjust state, the United States, will be erased; this unjust state, Britain, will be erased—they who caused this people's Nakbah [the 1948 'catastrophe'] . . ."

"Oh beloved, we must be certain that victory will come. Shame and remorse on whoever refrained from raids [against the enemy] or refrained from preaching to himself [to raid]; shame and remorse on whoever refrained from raising his children on Jihad; shame and remorse on whoever hated his Muslim brother while loving one of the infidels; shame and remorse on whoever hid behind excuses that have no basis with Allah . . ."

"Blessings to whoever waged Jihad for the sake of Allah; blessings to whoever raided for the sake of Allah; blessings to whoever put a belt of explosives on his body or on his sons' and plunged into the midst of the Jews, crying "Allahu Akbar, praise to Allah, There is no God but Allah and Muhammad is His messenger."'

"Just as the building collapsed over the Jews in their sinful dancing floor [referring to the collapse of a wedding hall in Jerusalem]—I pray to Allah that this oppressive Knesset will collapse over the heads of the Jews."

"Allah, forgive us our sins,

Allah, show us a black day for the Jews, like the day of 'Aad and Thamud

Allah, turn them into pillage for us

Allah, we strive for martyrdom for your sake . . .

Allah, we strive for your mercy and your paradise . . ."

## INCITEMENTS FROM SCHOOL TEXTBOOKS ISSUED BY THE PALESTINIAN AUTHORITY IN 2000–2001:[30]

- Israel is only mentioned in the context of settlements, the exploitation of natural resources, or fighting and interrogations. There is no mention is made of Israel's borders. The name "Israel" does not appear on geographical maps, which mention only "Palestine."
- A photograph of Jaffa refers to it as a town in Palestine, and the heading above a photograph of the al-Jazzar mosque in Acre reads "Our homeland Palestine."
- Schoolbooks relate to the refugee camps as temporary, until their return to the places that they were forced to abandon. Jihad is a superior value for civilians who wish to protect their homeland. Protecting one's homeland by every available means is a religious precept, and whoever sacrifices his life for the protection of his homeland is shahid—all these appear in a 6th grade schoolbook.
- The Oslo Agreements are seen as a move that enabled the entrance of the Palestinian liberation forces into the territories. Values such as normalization or co-existence are not mentioned at all.

Palestinian summer camps:[31]

Throughout the summer vacation, summer camps are held to give the children semi-military training and inculcate them with anti-Israeli ideology. Messages to the children included the presentation of Israel in general and Israeli residents of Judea and Samaria specifically as murderers. The following is an example of a skit where a father is talking with his boy Salah out in the field:

Salah: "Father, why do the settlers take people's lands?"

Father: "These settlers, we must not trust them. They take away lands in order to build tall buildings for themselves, and we'll go out into the street."

Father (to Muhammad): "What is the goal of the settlers on your land?"

Muhammad: "They want my land that I have plowed and reaped."

Father: "These dogs, the settlers take but they don't give."

The father is then left alone in the field. A group of armed settlers enters, one of them dressed as an Israeli soldier. The father says, "Get off my land! Get off my land! Stop taking other people's property!"

The settlers wave a piece of paper in the air and say, "Listen! It says on this paper that this land is ours!" The father shouts, "This is my property!" and rips up the piece of paper. "I plowed it and reaped it." Pushing and hitting ensue. The father tells them, "Get off my land! I plowed and reaped it." The "settlers" push him to the ground, shoot him and run away. The son Salah returns and says to his father, "Father, Father, what have they done to you? Why are you laying on the ground?" The dying father says to his son, "My son Salah, guard this land because the settlers want to take the land that I have plowed." The show ends.

A collection of Palestinian incitements regarding the Battle of Jenin, April 23, 2002[32]

"Sheikh Jamal Abu Al-Hija, the commander of the Hamas Izz Al-Din Al-Qassam Brigades in the Jenin refugee camp, told the Hamas website in an interview that the members of the various factions, "along with volunteers from the Palestinian security forces," prepared in advance for the Israeli incursion (www.palestine-info.info, April 20, 2002). Sheikh Abu Al-Hija provided more details on the fighting by phone to the Qatari television channel Al-Jazeera, saying, "[We placed] explosive devices on the roads and in the houses; surprises [await] the occupation forces. In several places, there are clashes between the *Mujahideen* and the occupation forces . . . The occupation forces flee in panic from the Jenin camp—but they escalate by using tractors, airplanes, and tanks against the camp. The truth is that the fighting is being conducted from neighborhood to neighborhood, like guerilla warfare. The *Mujahideen* are using automatic rifles, explosive devices, and hand grenades . . ." (*Al-Jazeera* (Qatar), April 8, 2002).

Palestinian Children and School Bags Filled with Explosives
The Islamic Jihad commander in the Jenin refugee camp, Abu Jandal, was interviewed several times by Al-Jazeera during the fighting. In one conversation, Abu Jandal said: "This is the second successive day that the Israeli occupation forces are trying [to enter the camp] with the help of Apache helicopters and tanks. But the steadfastness of the fighters, who swore at the beginning of the battle not to permit [the IDF] to advance towards this camp, defends the honor of the Arab nation from the alleys of the Jenin refugee camp. There were several attempts from several routes, but these were blocked. The truth is that our fighters have switched to an offensive; today we went on the offensive. The Israeli unit commander was killed this morning, 50 meters from the place from which I am speaking to you. I, the commander of the battle of the Jenin camp, have chosen for myself the name 'The Martyr Abu Jandal,' because all

the fighters around me are martyrs. Believe me, there are children stationed in the houses with explosive belts at their sides . . . Today, one of the children came to me with his school bag. I asked him what he wanted, and he replied, 'Instead of books, I want an explosive device, in order to attack . . .'"

Asked how long his men would be able to stand against the Israeli military when all they had were light weapons, Abu Jandal replied: "No. That's not true. We have the weapon of surprise. We have the weapon of honor. We have the divine weapon, the weapon of Allah who stands at our side. We have weapons that are better than theirs. I am the one with the truth, and I put my faith in Allah, while they put their faith in a tank."( *Al-Jazeera* (Qatar), April 4, 2002).

The Egyptian government-sponsored *Al-Ahram Weekly* ran an interview with "Omar," a young, one-armed Islamic Jihad bomb maker known as an 'engineer' who discussed how the Palestinians booby-trapped Jenin, including the participation of women and children in the battles. (www.ahram.org.eg/weekly/2002/582/6inv2.htm)"He is a member of the Islamic Jihad, but says in Jenin all the factions were loyal to only one cause: liberation or death . . .' Of all the fighters in the West Bank we were the best prepared,' he says. 'We started working on our plan: to trap the invading soldiers and blow them up from the moment the Israeli tanks pulled out of Jenin last month.'"

The newspaper explained: "Omar and other 'engineers' made hundreds of explosive devices and carefully chose their locations. 'We had more than 50 houses booby-trapped around the camp. We chose old and empty buildings and the houses of men who were wanted by Israel because we knew the soldiers would search for them,' [Omar] said. 'We cut off lengths of main water pipes and packed them with explosives and nails. Then we placed them about four meters apart throughout the houses—in cupboards, under sinks, in sofas.' The fighters hoped to disable the Israeli army's tanks with much more powerful bombs placed inside garbage bins on the street. More explosives were hidden inside the cars of Jenin's most wanted men. Connected by wires, the bombs were set off remotely, triggered by the current from a car battery."

"According to Omar, everyone in the camp, including the children, knew where the explosives were located so that there was no danger of civilians being injured. It was the one weakness in the plan. 'We were betrayed by the spies among us,' he says. The wires to more than a third of the bombs were cut by soldiers accompanied by collaborators. 'If it hadn't been for the spies, the soldiers would never have been able to enter the camp. Once they penetrated the camp, it was much harder to defend it.'"

"And what about the explosion and ambush last Tuesday which killed 13 soldiers? 'They were lured there,' he says. 'We all stopped shooting and the women went out to tell the soldiers that we had run out of bullets and were leaving.' The women alerted the fighters as the soldiers reached the booby-trapped area. 'When the senior officers realized what had happened, they shouted through megaphones that they wanted an immediate cease-fire. We let them approach to retrieve the men and then opened fire. Some of the soldiers were so shocked and frightened that they mistakenly ran towards us.'"

Sheikh Abu Al-Hija was quoted by the United Arab Emirate (UAE) daily *Al-Bayan* as saying, "After these days of steadfastness and unique resistance, the fighters in Jenin reiterate their motto: 'No surrender—either victory or martyrdom.' Our strength lies in our being true Mujahideen in the face of the new Nazis." (*Al-Bayan* (United Arab Emirates), April 10, 2002).

Unidentified Palestinian sources added, "The ammunition of the fighters in the camp has run out, and they have chosen martyrdom. They are fighting with knives and stones, and blowing themselves up in front of the soldiers of the occupation."(*Al-Bayan* (United Arab Emirates), April 11, 2002).

Haj 'Ali, a commander of the Islamic Jihad's Al-Quds Brigades, said that the Palestinian resistance persists in its intense fighting, and will not permit the soldiers of the occupation to take over the camp.(*Al-Jazeera* (Qatar), April 8, 2002).

## CIVILIANS AND FIGHTERS

Sheikh Abu Al-Hija said, "Even the youths had a significant role in the uprising. They refused to leave the camp before the incursion, and most of them are now under arrest by the occupation forces . . . No one was asked [by us] to stay or go; no instructions were issued to the residents by the fighters, and the choice remained in their own hands. It was necessary for some of the women to remain [in the camp] to provide services for the fighters. The behavior of the residents was honorable; they were determined to remain, to go through everything the *Mujahideen* are going through, and to provide them with services."

" . . .When some *Mujahideen* ran out of ammunition, they leaped onto the tanks in an attempt to grab weapons from the soldiers, who were hiding inside the tanks. As a result, some of them engaged in barehanded combat with the Zionist soldiers. Some of the youths steadfastly filled their school bags with explosive devices; some of the boys remained without food or water for four days. Although the women knew how bad the situation was, a large portion of them preferred to remain, to prepare food for the *Mujahideen*, to risk their lives by bringing water for them, and to raise morale—something that greatly encouraged [their] steadfastness."(www.palestine-info.info, April 20, 2002).

"Abu Ahmad," an Al-Aqsa Martyrs Brigades leader in the Jenin refugee camp, said in a telephone conversation with the Hizbullah weekly *Al-*

*Intiqad*, "The Palestinian resistance will carry out more operations like the martyrdom operation in Haifa, in order to emphasize that it still exists and that it maintains its strength and its capability in spite of the blows [it has taken]. The martyrdom operation by 'Andalib Taqatqah [in Jerusalem's Mahane Yehuda market] is proof of the [Al-Aqsa Martyr] Brigades' capability of striking at the [Zionist] entity any time, anywhere . . . Martyrdom operations were invented during the time when the Zionists occupied the West Bank, and it does not matter much whether the [forces] are in the cities or outside the cities."(*Al-Intiqad* (Lebanon), April 19, 2002).

## ENDNOTES

1. On October 23, 1998 former Prime Minister of Israel Binyamin Netanyahu and PA Chairman Yasser Arafat signed the Wye River Memorandum, a list of further implementations that would be carried out by both sides. Included is the following directive order:

IIA3. Preventing Incitement

a. Drawing on relevant international practice and pursuant to Article XXII (1) of the Interim Agreement and the Note for the Record, the Palestinian side will issue a decree prohibiting all forms of incitement to violence or terror, and establishing mechanisms for acting systematically against all expressions or threats of violence or terror. This decree will be comparable to the existing Israeli legislation which deals with the same subject.

b. A U.S.-Palestinian-Israeli committee will meet on a regular basis to monitor cases of possible incitement to violence or terror and to make recommendations and reports on how to prevent such incitement. The Israeli, Palestinian and U.S. sides will each appoint a media specialist, a law enforcement representative, an educational specialist and a current or former elected official to the committee.

2. Marcus, Itamar, "Rape, Murder, Violence and War for Allah Against the Jews: Summer 2000 on Palestinian Television." *Palestinian Media Watch*, September 11, 2000. http://www.pmw.org.il/report-30.html

3. Intifada, December 13, 2000. Translated by *Palestinian Media Watch*.

4. Ibid. Broadcasted on Palestinian Television on September 10, 2000.

5. *Al-Hayat Al-Jadida*, July 20, 2000.

6. *Washington Post*, March 30, 2002

7. *Israel TV Channel 2*, December 18, 2001

8. Quoted from *MEMRI*, March 31, no.361 http://www.memri.org/bin/articles.cgi?Page=countries&Area=palestinian&ID=SP36102

9. *Al-Rai 'Al-'Am*, December 12, 2001. Quoted from *MEMRI*, no. 317, http://www.memri.org/bin/articles.cgi?Page=countries&Area=palestinian&ID=SP31701

10. http://images.maariv.co.il/cache/ART224713.html, in English at http://www.imra.org.il/story.php3?id=9345)

11. *Al-Hayat Al-Jadida* (Palestinian Authority), October 28, 2001. Quoted from *MEMRI*, no.293, http://www.memri.org/bin/articles.cgi?Page=countries&Area=palestinian&ID=SP29301

12. *Al-Hayat Al-Jadida*, March 20, 1999. Quoted from *MEMRI*, no.132, http://www.memri.org/bin/articles.cgi?Page=countries&Area=palestinian&ID=SP13200

13. *April 12, 2002 by Palestinian Authority television*. Quoted from *MEMRI*, no.370, http://www.memri.org/bin/articles.cgi?Page=countries&Area=palestinian&ID=SP37002

14. *L'Arche*, October–November 2001, p.66, quoted from Wistrich, Robert, S., *Muslim Anti-Semitism, A Clear and Present Danger*, (New York: The American Jewish Committee, 2002), p.17

15. August 17, 2001 by *Palestinian TV.* Quoted from *MEMRI*, no.261, http://www. memri.org/bin/articles.cgi?Page=countries&Area=palestinian&ID=SP26101

16. August 3, 2001 by Palestinian TV. Quoted from *MEMRI*, no.252, http://www.memri. org/bin/articles.cgi?Page=countries&Area=palestinian&ID=SP25201

17. PA Television, July 6, 2001. Quoted from *MEMRI* July 11, 2001, no.240 http://www. memri.org/bin/articles.cgi?Page=countries&Area=palestinian&ID=SP24001

18. *Palestinian Television*, official Palestinian Television, 13 October 2000 broadcast, Gaza Strip

19. Al'Hayat Al'Jadida (9 June 2002), (qtd. from http://www.idf.il/english/announce-ments/2002/june/mazcalreshut.stm)

20. In http://www.intelligence.org.il/eng/bu/march/b2ch2a.doc

21. Al-Hayat, August 17, 2001. Quoted from *MEMRI*, no.260 http://memri.org/bin/arti-cles.cgi?Page=archives&Area=sd&ID=SP26001

22. *Hizbuallah weekly, Al-Intiqad, August 17, 2001.* Quoted from *MEMRI*, no.260, http://www.memri.org/bin/articles.cgi?Page=countries&Area=palestinian&ID=SP26001

23. Al-Manar (PA), August 13, 2001. Quoted from *MEMRI*, no.255, http://www.memri. org/bin/articles.cgi?Page=countries&Area=palestinian&ID=SP25501)

24. Quoted from *MEMRI*, august 22, 2001 no.no.360 http://www.memri.org/bin/arti-cles.cgi?Page=countries&Area=palestinian&ID=SP26001

25. *Al-Hayat Al-Jadida* (PA), December 7, 2000. http://www.memri.org/bin/articles. cgi?Page=countries&Area=palestinian&ID=SP16500

26. Speech by Palestinian Authority Minister of Communications, Emmad El-Faluji, December 5th, 2000 in *Palestinian Violence* 2000–2001, News reports.

27. Al-Ayyam, October 2001. Quoted from *MEMRI*, no.132, http://www.memri.org/bin/ articles.cgi?Page=countries&Area=palestinian&ID=SP13200)

28. *Al-Sha'ab* (Egypt), February 1, 2002. Quoted from *MEMRI*, no.84, http://www.memri. org/bin/articles.cgi?Page=countries&Area=palestinian&ID=IA8402)

29. Palestinian TV, June 8, 2001 Quoted from *MEMRI*, no.228 http://www.memri.org/ bin/articles.cgi?Page=countries&Area=palestinian&ID=SP22801

30. http://www.intelligence.org.il/eng/bu/march/b2ch2b.doc

31. http://www.oslo-war.com/p4_eng.htm

32. Quoted from *MEMRI*, no 90 http://www.memri.org/bin/articles.cgi?Page=coun-tries&Area=palestinian&ID=IA9002

# SELECTED POPULAR FRONT FOR THE LIBERATION OF PALESTINE (PFLP) PRESS RELEASES, COMMUNIQUES, ADDRESSES AND STATEMENTS[1]

**March 21, 2000**
**Jerusalem, the Eternal Capital of Palestine, Welcomes His Holiness the Pope.**

We, the Palestinian people, would like to express our joy in welcoming His Holiness, Pope John Paul II, to Jerusalem, the city of peace, the capital of the Palestinian state; Jerusalem, an Arab city under occupation, is the top priority on the national agenda of the Palestinian people

We welcome His Holiness to Jerusalem, a city which is part of the occupied territories. The Israeli occupation has closed the city, separated it from the occupied territories and turned it into a military camp with soldiers, policemen, and settlers. Israeli flags are raised everywhere in order to prove to you, Your Holiness, and people from every corner of the world, that occupied Jerusalem is a unified city and that the Palestinian people have no sovereignty over it.

The Israeli government's message is one of annexation, isolation, and expulsion. The Popular Front for the Liberation of Palestine (PFLP) would like to send a different message to you, Your Holiness. Arab Jerusalem is, in fact, occupied and there can be no peace without a sovereign Palestinian state with Jerusalem as its capital. In addition, the Palestinian people have a right to self-determination and Palestinian refugees the right of return.

Unified under the flag of the PLO, the Palestinian people alone have the right of sovereignty over the city. It is our right to defend the City in order to ensure and safeguard our existence, our identity, and our Arabic heritage.

Any proposal for peace will be rejected unless Jerusalem is returned to Palestinian sovereignty and the right of return for refugees is secured.

Apologies from the government of occupation are not enough to eliminate the past and present injustices which plague our people. Until such time, we ask you, Your Holiness, and the international community, to provide immediate international protection for the Palestinian people.

We would have liked to welcome you on the occasion of this historic visit to a Jerusalem free of occupation. But, unfortunately, you will see with your own eyes, the suffering of the Palestinian people, the Israeli-imposed siege, and the continuous violation of human rights in Jerusalem.

The Vatican has adopted all international resolutions which declare that Jerusalem is an occupied city. We hope to hear from you, with the clarity of your previous statements, that the Vatican re-affirms its solidarity with the Palestinian people and recognizes their struggle for their legitimate national rights.

We hope that Your Holiness will visit us again very soon when the Palestinian flag will be raised over the mosques and churches in Jerusalem and fly side by side with the flag of the Vatican and other sovereign states.

## May 20, 2000

The PFLP not only condemns these negotiations, but also demands that they be frozen immediately. These talks constitute a real threat to national interests of the Palestinian people. The PFLP calls on all parties to return to the forum of the United Nations which is the only internationally legitimate term of reference for any type of negotiation. Only in this way can the "politics of concession" and unequal compromise be destroyed.

The Israeli occupation hopes to gain even more concessions through these secret talks. In addition, its goal is to enhance the policies of land confiscation and the building of settlements and bypass roads which have been unequivocally condemned not only by United Nations' resolutions, but by the United States as well. (Obstacle to peace.) Last but not least the Israeli occupation government refuses to acknowledge the legitimate rights of the Palestinian people that were recognized by the United Nations, especially resolution 194 which gives all Palestinian refugees the right to return to their homes.

The recent experience with Oslo has proven to be ineffective, at best. Seven years ago, with a wisdom that has since been shown to be correct, the PFLP warned that Oslo, even if implemented, would not bring about a just peace in the Middle East. Now the PFLP is warning again. These negotiations can only serve Israeli interests and their continuing military occupation of Palestine.

The PFLP, standing firm for a just and comprehensive peace, asserts that the Palestinian People will continue their struggle until their national rights are recognized, protected, and preserved.

**May 21, 2000**
**Palestinian prisoners are not and should not be a bargaining chip.**
**It is time for Palestinian prisoners to go home!**

For over two weeks, the Palestinian people have been intensifying their struggle against the Israeli occupation army in all cities, villages, and refugee camps throughout the West Bank and Gaza Strip. They are demanding the release of Palestinian prisoners in Israeli jails and detention camps. In clashes with Israeli soldiers, five Palestinians were shot dead and hundreds injured. Palestinian prisoners began a hunger strike and many solidarity hunger strikes continue in several cities from Gaza to Nablus.

The cry of prisoners reaches every house inside Palestine and even knocks at the door of the international community—a cry demanding that true democratic and progressive forces stand in solidarity and take definitive action. This cry, however, which longs for freedom and peace, is doubtful concerning the current so-called "peace process." The Israeli occupation of Palestinian lands continues. The confiscation of Palestinian lands continues. The building of settlements and their strategic bypass roads continues. The Israeli government refuses not only to dismantle the settlements, but refuses to stop building them as well. The Israeli government simply ignores international resolutions regarding the Palestinian question, especially those regarding refugees and their right to return. At the same time (only a few days ago), Prime Minister Barak is able to welcome with open arms the millionth new immigrant from the former Soviet Union. The four "NO's" of Barak are not only an obstacle to genuine peace which contradict the artificial aura of peace that presently makes headline news, they are also clear evidence that the present peace process is nothing but a facilitator for the establishment of complete Israeli hegemony.

The issue of Palestinian prisoners is a prime example of the inconsistencies within the peace process and reveals the true face of the Israeli occupation that is using prisoners as a tool for political blackmail to extract more concessions from the Palestinian side.

The Popular Front for the Liberation of Palestine (PFLP) recognizes that the issue of Palestinian prisoners is integral to the cause of the Palestinian people. It is not and should not be used as a bargaining chip. The PFLP demands the release of all Palestinian political prisoners and asks all international bodies and organizations to stand in solidarity with these prisoners and to exert as much pressure as possible on Israel to free them immediately.

The PFLP stands for a just solution for the Middle East conflict that can bring a real and comprehensive peace to the people.

Let us work together to bring the Palestinian cause back to the United Nations.

The Popular Front for the Liberation of Palestine

**May 21, 2000**
**There is No Alternative to the Right of Return:**
**Jerusalem and the Independent State of Palestine**

The world was not caught by surprise when the news of secret negotiations were made public. At the same time where Palestinian and Israeli negotiators are meeting in the Middle East and elsewhere, news came out that parallel but secret negotiations are taking place in Stockholm (a repetition of Oslo, but on Swedish ground). This happened at a time when Palestinian people engaged in hunger strikes and bloody clashes with the Israeli occupation forces.

The PFLP states that any negotiations that do not respond to the Palestinian people's need for freedom and independence will fail and will consequently lead only to more violence and bloodshed.

The Palestinian people, who have been struggling for freedom and dignity for the past fifty years, will continue to do so in the future until their legitimate rights are recognized and assured. Any intermediate or final negotiations which neglect this prerequisite will fail, or even worse, will be a success only for the occupier.

The PFLP condemns the way in which the Palestinian Authority and Israel are distorting the Palestinian cause. The PFLP is asking the international community, governments, peoples, and organizations to stand firm with respect to the Palestinian cause. The PFLP believes that only a just solution can bring about a comprehensive peace for the Middle East. This includes the return of refugees and displaced people to their homes. This also includes the right for self-determination and the right to build an independent state with Jerusalem as its capital. Finally, it includes the recognition that ALL settlements are illegal and must be dismantled completely.

The Palestinian people, as any other people in the world, are dreaming to live in a state based on freedom and independence where human dignity, human rights, and democratic values are preserved. The Palestinian people will not agree to live in Bantustans, thus creating and enhancing apartheid in Palestine.

The PFLP calls upon all peoples to stand in solidarity with the Palestinian people and to take a clear stand against all schemes aiming to destroy their unity. The PFLP calls upon all governments to bring back the Palestinian cause to the panels of the United Nations, as the only legitimate reference for peace in the Middle East.

**July 10, 2000**
**The struggle to end the occupation continues**

When the PFLP, in its press release from 2 October 2000, called on the Palestinian leadership to boycott the meetings of Paris and Sharm A-

Sheikh, and warned of their implications, the PFLP was very well aware of the consequences of such meetings. The PFLP knew that they would fail. In addition, the PFLP stated that it was an attempt to undermine the political facts that were created by the Jerusalem Intifada. These facts have buried the policy of capitulation and opened a new road for freedom and independence. The Palestinian leadership should have crowned these facts by declaring the negotiations with Israel dead. These negotiations have always been a cover for the American and Israeli policy that is hostile to the legitimate rights of the Palestinian people; the right for self determination, the right to return and the building of an independent and sovereign state with Jerusalem as its capital.

Accordingly, we in the PLFP reiterate and confirm our positions as follows:

First: We stress that the Intifada and the popular movement must continue until freedom and independence are achieved. We should find all support possible to protect it and its political achievements.

Second: The Intifada of Jerusalem, which spread all over Palestine, had its high price. At the same time it marked the end of the self-rule idea and the beginning of the work towards national independence. For this reason we call for the declaration of the Palestinian State and ask the United Nations and the world community to offer their protection to the Palestinian people.

Third: We highly appreciate and treasure the popular support among the Arab countries and the international community, which expresses itself by the massive demonstrations and calls for more solidarity with the Palestinian people.

Fourth: We renew our call on all Arab countries for an immediate Arab summit, to support our people in their struggle against the Israeli aggression and its unconditional support by the USA.

The Popular Front for the Liberation of Palestine

**October 7, 2000**
**Palestine Communiqué**
**To the Palestinian Arab People at home and in the Diaspora**
**Let all be united in the resistance movement to end the Israeli occupation**

On the dawn of the second week of the popular Intifada (Jerusalem Intifada) and the heroic resistance movement against the Israeli occupation forces, the PFLP states that fight for freedom and independence has been rekindled. Thousands were wounded and dozens were killed to move one step closer to freedom and independence. The Palestinian people all over historical Palestine have been protesting together with millions in the Arab World and Europe. Enough is enough, there shall be no more occupation.

The PFLP calls for the following vital points:

First: Let all Palestinians be united in the resistance movement against occupation. Let all protect, sustain and develop the results achieved by the Intifada until we achieve our legitimate rights. The new national policy should be based on the reality of confrontation.

Second: The release of all political prisoners from the PA prisons. This move is necessary to strengthen the national unity. It is based on the fact that the basic disagreement is with the occupation and its forces.

Third: To consider the national struggle as the uniting factor under the slogan, "(let all be united to end the occupation)," to realize the state of Palestine on the ground with Jerusalem as its capital.

Fourth: To form a popular movement, to boycott all Israeli products and goods that have an Arab or Palestinian substitute until the occupation is over. The PFLP calls on all peoples of the world to boycott Israeli goods until the occupation is over.

We see victory ahead.

## 11 October 2000
## Press Office

*Ramallah:* Following the news about the recent active political movements of the American Administration in the Middle East, the spokesperson of the PFLP declared the following:

1. The recent activity of the American Administration is nothing but an attempt on the part of the United States to reassert its hegemony and monopoly over the region. Furthermore it is a US attempt to be in total control of the political settlement over the peoples in the Middle East. This is done also through the United States' rejection of the formation of an international investigation committee of the crimes of Israel.

2. The claims of the United States to restore the "peace process" are fake. The so-called peace process is nothing but a declaration of surrender and an attempt to impose this surrender on the Palestinian people. The United States is trying to whitewash the Israeli government holding on to a fake peace and ignoring the legitimate rights of the Palestinian people and the numerous resolutions of international legitimacy.

3. This is a clear attempt to contain Palestinian resistance on the national, Arab, and international level. In addition, it aims to sabotage the path to planning an Arab summit that may take decisions considered "unfavorable" to the American administration.

For those reasons we call on all national and international bodies to be alert to these attempts and to stand firm in their solidarity with the Palestinian cause and with the Palestinian people. The PFLP calls on all international bodies to reaffirm the legitimate rights of the Palestinian people: the right to return, the right for self-determination, and the building of a free, independent and sovereign state with Jerusalem as its capital.

Finally: The settlements are illegal and as such must to be dismantled so that the Palestinian people can assume authority over their lands and property in peace and security.

## October, 17, 2000

Following the summit at Sharm A-Sheikh whose results were published on the 17 October 2000, the spokesperson of the PFLP made the following statements:

1. It was a mistake for the Palestinian leadership to participate in this summit, which represents only US and Israeli interests and whose purposes were obvious in advance.
2. The results of the summit show clearly the advantages that the US and the Israeli governments have gained to protect "their" interests. The summit succeeded in turning the meeting to a "security" meeting and in equalizing the victim with the victimizer.
3. The main reason for all the bloodshed and the crisis in the Middle East is caused by the Israeli occupation of the Palestinian lands. "Israel" is solely responsible for this disaster.
4. Forming an investigative committee headed by the United States means only that the United States wants to ascertain again that it determines the terms of reference. Knowing the completely biased position of the United States, this is an obvious attempt to fool international opinion again.
5. All agreements that do not respect the basic rights of the Palestinian people are doomed to fail and will not stop the resistance movement of the Palestinian people against the Israeli occupation.
6. The PFLP reaffirms its position to reject any agreement that aims at stopping the resistance movement of the Palestinian people, thus leading to its surrender.

At present the Palestinian people are engaged in clashes with the Israeli occupying forces in almost all cities, villages and camps, in order to defend their national rights and to demand freedom for thousands of Palestinian prisoners in Israeli prisons and detention camps. At the same time, hidden from the eyes of the world, secret negotiations (parallel to public ones) are taking place in Stockholm between the Palestinian Authority and the government of Israeli occupation. We, as Palestinians, can only be painfully reminded of the Oslo negotiations and the devastating results which were opposed to the interests of our people and our national rights, especially the right to return and to proclaim Jerusalem as our capital.

**October 26, 2000**

The United States Administration and now its Congress continue to address the Palestinian people in an increasingly hostile language. It seems that it is not enough to say that the United States is biased towards Israel. The US is now placing itself in the position of the direct enemy of the Palestinian people and the Arab people in general.

The offensive and amoral resolutions taken by the Unites States deserve an immediate boycott of all US invitations to Arab world leaders. Their sole aim is to impose pressure on the Arab World and to prevent the Arab people and their leaders to redirect the negotiations and their terms of reference to the United Nations and away from the US as the sole decision-maker. The invitation of the United States President to President Arafat to meet in Washington, as Arafat were responsible for all the recent events in the Middle East, is nothing more than an attempt to coerce the Palestinians to accept Israel's terms. The United States is trying again to whitewash Israel.

The Popular Front for the Liberation of Palestine calls on all the Arab people and their leaders to take a clear stand against US policies that have gone too far.

**July 26, 2001**
**Press Office**
**Normalization Equalizes Killer and Victim,**
**Occupation and Resistance Movement**

The recent "normalization" meeting between Yosi Beilin accompanied by a group of Zionist academics and politicians, and a group of officials from the Palestinian Authority accompanied by a contingent of Palestinian business men is a clear violation of the agreement signed by the Islamic and national bodies to boycott all the normalization activities with the Zionist enemies. None of these meetings provide any benefit whatsoever for the Palestinian struggle. On the contrary, they are simply an attempt to promote the policies of Beilin, who refuses to accept the right of refugees to return.

The nature of such meetings only serves to equalize the killer and the victim; the occupation and resistance movement. At the same time, it attempts to distort the core of the Palestinian question and transform the struggle for national liberation into a conflict between two states. The meetings aim to deflect attention from the source of the conflict, the occupation, and to focus on Zionist state security issues.

The PFLP calls on the secretary of the Arab League to demand an account from Hanan Ashrawi, Arab League spokeswoman, for her participation in this meeting. Ashrawi's attendance at the meeting is considered to be a violation of the Arab Follow-Up Committee's decision to end all political contacts with Israel.

It is infinitely more important for the Arab League to demand an account of Palestinians who violate their decisions than to debate whether to freeze Mauritania's membership in the League.

## July 31, 2001
## Press Office

*Ramallah:* The PFLP condemns the two crimes of assassination committed by the Israeli Army in al Far'a and Nablus that resulted in the death of 14 martyrs from Fateh and Hamas. These two crimes represent a basic change in the premeditated policy that the Zionist national government applies against the Palestinian people. In addition, this change is a sign of the real and imminent danger faced by each Palestinian household.

The PFLP believes that the assassination of a number of leaders will not end the struggle of a nation determined to resist the brutal Zionist occupation and regain its legitimate national rights. The Zionist enemy has attempted to implement this policy in the past in Beirut, Tunisia, and other places, but was met with staunch resistance by the Palestinians who are convinced that the Zionists will realize, soon or later, that there is no military solution to the Palestinian question. The enemy will realize also that shelling and bombing and other oppressive measures will not prevent the Palestinians from continuing their Intifada. On the contrary, these tactics will be a motivating factor in the continuation of the struggle until Palestinian legitimate rights are regained—specifically, the right to self-determination and an independent state with Jerusalem as its capital.

The Zionists will never live in security as long as the occupation continues and Palestinian right are being denied.

The PFLP calls on the Palestinian people to continue in their struggle.

The PFLP calls on the Palestinian Authority to establish and arm National Defense Groups in order to fight against the aggressive Zionist attacks.

The PFLP calls on all Arab countries to immediately sever relations with the Zionist state and to allow freedom of expression among the Arab masses in order to protest the ongoing massacres against the Palestinian people.

The PFLP calls on the international community to provide Palestinians with international protection.

The martyrs in al-Far'a and Nablus have not died in vain. Sharon and his settlers and his soldiers will pay for these crimes.

## August 4, 2001
## Press Office

*Ramallah:* The PFLP welcomes the return of the Arab popular solidarity movement due to the Intifada. The movement has been represented by demonstrations that have taken place in Egypt, Jordan, and Qatar.

These demonstrations express the Arab awareness of the dangers presently facing the Palestinian people. In particular, the PFLP appreciates the Jordanian masses in their rejection of the government's decision to prevent public demonstrations and their condemnation of restraint methods of the police forces. These events express clearly the Jordanian national spirit.

The PFLP calls on all Arab governments to remove the restrictions forced on their country's popular movements and to reject American pressure regarding this issue.

The PFLP calls on the Arab popular movement and national parties and bodies to reject the restrictions and to express their opinion freely through public demonstrations.

The PFLP calls on all Arabs to fight for Arab dignity and for the protection of holy places under threat of Zionist control.

The PFLP calls on all Palestinians to remain steadfast in the struggle for their legitimate national rights.

### August 10, 2001
### Press Office

*Ramallah:* The PFLP condemns the Zionist unified government's tank shelling attacks and invasion into Palestinian self-controlled areas. The PFLP also condemns the recently-implemented Israeli policies against Palestinian institutions in Jerusalem, the capital of Palestine. These policies are part of a pre-determined plan, formulated, recognized, and condoned by most Israeli governments. Israel's illegal entry into Palestinian institutions in Jerusalem and the raising of the Israeli flag represents yet another step in the attempt to Judaize Jerusalem. The PFLP interprets this to mean that Sharon's government has launched the battle of Jerusalem on all fronts. What is required, therefore, is that we consolidate our efforts in order to prepare for this battle. Jerusalem, present, past, and future, will remain an Arabic Palestinian city. Not even the barbaric tactics of military occupation can change this fact.

The PFLP calls on all Arab governments to refuse to be controlled by the American administration and to honor their national commitments. The PFLP also calls upon all Arab governments to allow public freedom of expression, including expressed outrage toward the Zionist war against the Palestinian people. Sole responsibility for present and future bloodshed rests on the government of Sharon.

The PFLP also calls on the international community to take responsibility for ensuring that all international resolutions related to the Palestinian question be implemented immediately.

The increase in aggressive attacks against the Palestinian people will never break their will to continue in the struggle to resist occupation and to regain their legitimate rights to freedom and an independent state.

**August 19, 2001**
**Press Office**

*Ramallah:* The secret channel of dialogue between the unified Zionist government and the Palestinian Authority, which were mentioned in recent articles of several newspapers and news agencies, is no more than an Israeli ploy to crush the Intifada. Such channels aim only to pull the Zionist government out of the crisis precipitated by Palestinian perseverance in the Intifada. In addition, it is an attempt to deny the legitimate request for international protection for the Palestinian people and to take the focus away from bringing an end to the occupation.

Peres' statement admitting the existence of such a channel was simultaneously issued with the Israeli announcement that it will continue with its savage attacks against Palestinians, including assassinations and siege over the Palestinian territories. At the same time, the US government announced its plan to veto the Security Council recommendation to provide Palestinians with international protection.

These "secret" channels of dialogue are an integral part of the Zionist government's political attacks against the Palestinian people, including the closure of the Orient House in Jerusalem and the attempt to occupy both Jenin and Khan Younis.

The results of previous secret negotiations channels, such as Oslo and other agreements, served simply to strengthen the Zionist occupation of Palestinian land and to prevent Palestinians from gaining their legitimate right to national independence.

The PFLP calls on the PNA to end immediately its participation in secret channels of dialogue and to actively confront the brutal attacks of the Sharon government against the Palestinian people.

The PFLP calls on all national bodies and the entire Palestinian people to be aware of the danger of such channels, which serve to provide a cover for Zionist aggression on Palestinians.

**August 27 2001**
**Press Office**

*Ramallah:* The Popular Front for the Liberation of Palestine (PFLP) mourns the death of its leader, the general secretary, Abu Ali Mustafa, who was assassinated by the Israeli army on the morning of 27 August 2001. Abu Ali Mustafa, the head of the second largest group within the Palestine Liberation Organization (PLO), was murdered by Sharon and his government. Sharon, however, acts with the full support and backing of the U.S. administration who bears full responsibility for the new escalation in the Middle East, due to its uncritical, unconditional, and blind support of the Israeli occupation of Palestinian lands.

Abu Ali Mustafa was elected general secretary of the PFLP last year, after Dr. George Habash (Al-Hakim) stepped down from the role. Abu Ali, a long-standing comrade of Al-Hakim, was a member of the PFLP since its inception in 1967. Abu Ali held the position of deputy general secretary until the PFLP's Sixth National Conference, where he was elected general secretary.

Born in Palestine in 1938 in Arraba, near Jenin, Abu Ali lived most of his adult life in exile until he returned home in 1999. He was part of the resistance movement against the Israeli occupation and fulfilled his duties from abroad as well as from Palestine.

In representing the PFLP, Abu Ali understood clearly his role and the role of the PFLP in expressing a radical humanistic vision for the Middle East problem. He was adamant and articulate in presenting this vision and loyal to the principles of the party. He defended the Palestinian cause and the inalienable rights of the Palestinian people, foremost among them, the right of refugees to return and the right to establish a sovereign and independent Palestinian state with Jerusalem as its capital. He called for the dismantling of all Israeli settlements and for continuing the Palestinian resistance movement until the Israeli occupation is brought to an end.

He presented the vision of an all-encompassing Palestinian state where people would live together in freedom regardless of their race, religion, or color. He called for a true democratic society where the rights of the majority are protected by the fulfillment of the rights of the minorities. He called the Palestinian resistance movement against the Israeli racist, colonialist occupation, a duty for every Palestinian and for every person who believes in equality, justice, and peace.

Abu Ali Mustafa lived and died defending the Palestinian cause and the rights of the Palestinian people.

As the PFLP, and all the Palestinian people, mourn its leader, the PFLP vows to continue the Intifada and the Palestinian resistance movement until the Israeli occupation is over.

The Life of Abu Ali Mustafa

Abu Ali Mustafa (Mustafa Ali Al-Ali Zabri) joined the Arab National Movement in 1955 and became a member of the Arab National Association in Amman. Together with his comrades and colleagues, he confronted the Jordanian government, calling for the annulment of the Jordanian-British pact and the dismissal of British officers from the Jordanian army.

In April 1957, he was arrested and imprisoned for several months, shortly after the Jordanian parliament was dissolved and the Suleiman Nabulsi government was dismissed. During that time, political parties were banned and Abi Ali was arrested again with many others who were tried in a military court. He was sentenced to five years in Jafer Prison in east Jordan.

After being released from prison in 1961, Abu Ali Mustafa continued his political work with the Arab National Movement and became responsible for the Northern District of the West Bank. He founded and built two organizations, one public, and one underground.

In 1966, Abu Ali was arrested again during a widespread operation organized by the Jordanian government against the Arab National Movement. Abu Ali was imprisoned without trial for several months in Zarka Prison in Jordan.

After the 1967 War, Abu Ali Mustafa joined Dr. George Habash in forming the Popular Front for the Liberation of Palestine. He led the first commandos through the Jordan River inside Palestine and started forming the underground body of the PFLP. The Israelis searched in vain for him while he was hiding out in the West Bank. After several months, he secretly returned to Jordan.

In addition to being responsible for the PFLP in the West Bank, Abu Ali Mustafa became the commando-in-chief of the PFLP military forces (including the period comprising the battles in Amman in September 1970 and the battle of Ajloun in July 1971). Afterwards, he left secretly for Lebanon.

In 1972, at the Third National Conference of the PFLP, Abu Ali was elected deputy general secretary. From 1987 until 1991 he was a member of the Executive Committee of the PLO.

At the PFLP Sixth National Conference in July 2000, Abu Ali was elected general secretary.

**August 27, 2001**
**Address by Dr. George Habash to the Comrades, the Palestinian people, and the Arab masses on the occasion of the assassination of the general secretary of the PFLP, Abu Ali Mustafa**
**To the Palestinian people**
**To the Arab masses**

Today I received with great sadness the news about the assassination of the leader Abu Ali Mustafa by Sharon and his Zionist gang. This heinous crime that has robbed us of our long-standing comrade for over half a century, reaffirms that the Zionist enemy is determined to annihilate the leaders of our revolution and its cadres in order to force us to surrender.

This enemy has apparently not learned the lessons of history. The enemy has not yet learned that the Palestinian people, who have offered hundreds of leaders and thousands of fighters, will not kneel in surrender. On the contrary, we will persevere in the struggle no matter how long it takes to regain our rights and the rights of our nation. We will remain steadfast in the struggle until the Zionist, colonialist project is defeated.

On this day we remember Ghassan Kanafani, Guevara Gaza, Al Amassi, Abu Jihad, Abu Iyad, Faisal Husseini; and before them we remember Al-Qassam and Abd al-Qader Al-Husseini, and countless others who have fallen in the battle for Palestine. Their sacrifice and their memory motivates us to persevere.

As I convey to our people and to the Arab Nation the loss of Abu Ali Mustafa whose determination, courage, and strength distinguished him over so many years, I assure you that the shedding of his blood will not be in vain. His comrades and his people will inhale the strength of his soul and become stronger and more determined to continue the struggle for freedom and independence.

We are proud to remember that until his death, Abu Ali Mustafa proclaimed loudly and clearly that the foul war of Sharon will not frighten us. Neither will it subdue us or force us to deviate the path of revolution—the path to freedom and victory.

Our people, who have lost a teacher and a leader, know that Abu Ali Mustafa was an exceptional man who had the charism of a great leader. Our people will continue to learn from him and from his spirit of resistance—his patience, his determination, his strong will to force out the occupier and fulfill the dream of the right to return and the establishment of an independent, sovereign Palestinian state with Jerusalem as its capital.

On this sad and painful occasion, I turn to all brave comrades of the PFLP and all members of the Palestinian revolution at home and abroad: I call on them to remain faithful, not only to Abu Ali Mustafa but also to all those who have sacrificed their blood for the sake of Palestine and for the Arab Cause. We promise you, dear Abu Ali, that the Popular Front that you helped to establish on the foundation of a spirit of resistance will continue to march on the same road, no matter how long and treacherous it is, no matter how much we will have to sacrifice. The destructive tactics of the enemy will never kill our steadfastness or our will to resist.

## August 29, 2001
## Press Office
## Message to Our Comrades

Dear Comrades,

Yesterday was a sad day in the history of the PFLP. It was also a sad day for the Palestinian people, the Arab World, and the world's internationalists. Yesterday the Palestinian people marched in Ramallah for the last time with Abu Ali Mustafa. More than 50,000 mourners, women, men, and children, joined the procession, making it one of the biggest funerals in Palestinian history. Indeed, many more would have come from all over Palestine, if not for the barbaric restrictions of movement imposed on our people by the Israeli occupation army. Thousands of people in all Palestinian cities, as well as thousands of others in Jordan, Syria, Iraq, and Lebanon, paid tribute to Abu Ali Mustafa by organizing symbolic funerals. Mourning ceremonies to receive condolences took place all over the world. Dr. George Habash, Al-Hakim, addressed the Palestinian people and the Arab masses and offered condolences for the loss of his long-standing comrade and friend.

Israel's assassination of Abu Ali Mustafa is not only a political assassination. It is an attempt to assassinate all the progressive values represented by the PFLP. The reaction of people all over the world to the assassination of Abu Ali Mustafa reveals their tremendous respect for and solidarity with the vision of the PFLP made tangible in the person of Abu Ali Mustafa. The Zionist forces assassinated Abu Ali Mustafa because they realized that the Popular Front is on the right track.

Abu Ali Mustafa knew that he was targeted by the Zionist forces. Recently, he made the statement: "We all are targeted as soon as we begin to be mobilized. We do our best to avoid their guns, but we are living under the brutal Zionist occupation of our lands, and its army is only a few meters away from us. Of course we must be cautious, but we have work to do, and nothing will stop us."

After having lost momentum over the years, the PFLP was strengthened considerably under the leadership of Abu Ali Mustafa who was able to unify the party and renew its energy. He articulated the vision of the Popular Front in a radical, simple language that was accessible to everyone. He emphasized the Arabic depth and the internationalist dimension of the Middle East conflict. He worked for a unified Palestinian strategy to confront the occupation.

Abu Ali Mustafa was a unifying figure not only among the party's own structures, but among the various Palestinian political parties as well. Since his election as PFLP general secretary, the number of members and supporters of the PFLP increased significantly. The most recent poll, conducted shortly before his death, showed that the PFLP enjoys the endorsement of 8.3 % of the Palestinian population. Real numbers would show an even greater percentage of popular support.

Dear comrades! Although the loss of Abu Ali Mustafa seems too great to bear, you should not be discouraged. The PFLP has a solid history, strong party structures, and popular support to sustain it. Our struggle for freedom and independence continues! We will not surrender, and neither should you. Victory is coming!

## September 10, 2001
## Press Office

The Durban Conference reveals the nature of the Imperialism of the West and the complete failure of the Arab regimes in opposition to the popular movement.

The Popular Front for the Liberation of Palestine declared that the final resolutions at the Durban conference fell far short of the expectations and the drafted resolutions of the popular movement represented by over 3000 non-governmental organizations.

The outcome of the conference revealed not only the hegemony of the United States over the United Nations and the European Union but also the nature of the Imperialism of the West and the complete failure of the Arab regimes.

The outcome also showed that the Imperialist West is not free from its own racism, especially when it refused to apologize for its imperialist past and refused the principle of reparations for the slave trade. The results also showed that the United States and Europe are clearly responsible for defending the racist ideology of Zionism and the State of Israel, which makes tangible Zionist, racist principles and practices. Europe's stand illustrated clearly its bias towards the Zionist State which can be interpreted as a regressive step in view of Europe's positions regarding the Palestinian problem.

The PFLP condemns the official position of the Arab regimes who succumbed to US and European pressure.

The PFLP welcomes the stance of all the non-governmental organizations who have formally expressed the will of the people in rejecting Zionism as the racist ideology on which the state of Israel is based.

The PFLP welcomes the stance of all non-governmental organizations who have expressed the will of the people in their affirmation the inalienable rights of the Palestinian people: the right to freedom, the right to an independent state with Jerusalem as its capital, the right of refugees to return.

## September 11, 2001
## Press Office

*Ramallah:* The Popular Front for the Liberation of Palestine declares that it has no connection whatsoever with the attacks in New York and Washington, DC. The PFLP is a political party that is working to regain the national rights of the Palestinian people, including the right of refugees to return and the creation of an independent and sovereign Palestinian state with Jerusalem as its capital.

At this time when the Popular Front declares its commitment to continuing the legitimate struggle against the Zionist occupation, it also declares that the Popular Front is never and can never be against the American people, nor does it bear any hostility to the American people. While it is true that the Popular Front is against the policy of the United States Administration and its blind and unconditional support of the Israeli occupation government, this in no way implies that U.S civilians or any other civilians are a target for the Popular Front.

We look with deepest concern and regret at the attempts of some media organizations, in general, and Israel, in particular, to use this tragic incident to incite the public against the Palestinian people and to distort the image of the PFLP, the Arabs, or the Moslem World. This irresponsibility on the part of the media can only plant the seeds of discrimination and prejudice and lead people to conclude that Islam and the orient are the source of all evil.

As the Popular Front denounces this attack, it sends its sympathy and condolences to the American people.

### September 17 2001

To the Palestinian people:

The end of the first year of Al-Aqsa Intifada is fast approaching. This year has been filled with tremendous sacrifice that you have borne so selflessly—over 700 people have been killed and over 16,500 injured. You have chosen the path of resistance and steadfastness because it is you who are longing for freedom and independence.

Our people have already taught an important lesson to the Zionist enemy. The Palestinian people will persevere in their active resistance and continue to inflict severe losses on the Zionists. We have declared loudly and clearly: the rockets and the tanks will not lead us to surrender. The struggle for freedom and independence has begun and there is no turning back until victory is won.

Despite the international circumstances that followed the tragic incidents in New York and Washington, and despite the US attempt to exploit the tremendous loss of civilians and property, the US is trying to mobilize the international community to increase its hegemony and its aggressive role against the peoples of the world, especially those who are fighting for freedom, democracy, and national liberation. The same atmosphere has been exploited by the Zionist government in order to ensure that it continue its denial of the national rights of the Palestinian people and continue its brutal occupation of Palestinian land. The Zionists have done their best to deceive the world into believing that the legitimate Palestinian resistance movement is a terrorist movement. Israel has increased its military actions against the Palestinian people. It invaded the city of Jenin and followed with the systematic invasion of many other Palestinian cities and towns. It is clear that Israel has used this opportunity, as the world's attention is diverted toward New York and Washington, to commit more and more atrocities against the Palestinian people. Our steadfastness and readiness to defend our homeland, however, will never waver, even as we know that the Zionist occupation will continue in its futile efforts to humiliate us and force us to surrender. Considering this reality, and recognizing the planned response of the international community and its implications for the Arab World in general, and the Palestinian cause, in particular, the PFLP declares the following:

1. The events in New York and Washington, DC, are a product of the universal inconsistencies that were summarized by the Durban Conference against Racism and Discrimination—in particular, the policy of discrimination that increased during the era of globalization and to the hostile policy of the USA toward the peoples and their rights. The international response should be based on drafting policies that would bring peoples closer together and lead to the abolition of all forms of hegemony and slavery and racial discrimination. This international response should lead back to using the international conventions as tools to approve and realize these new policies outside a uni-polar system that determines the fate of the people.

2. At the time when the world is asking for counter-terrorism, we call on all countries, especially those with permanent status in the Security Council, to take immediate measures to implement an international protection plan for our people who are being subjected to a vicious cycle of killing, destruction of homes and infrastructure, uprooting of trees, and bulldozing of lands. This is part of a systematic policy of state terrorism that Sharon and his government are implementing.

3. We call on the Arab Nation not to participate in international alliances under the American slogan of "counter-terrorism" which do not differentiate between terrorism and the legitimate right of the people for self-determination. This is of critical importance so that such policies are not used to subdue popular movements for freedom and independence and ultimately lead to a complete imperialist hegemony over the fate of entire nations.

4. We call on the Palestinian people to unite behind the continuous resistance movement and the Intifada until we gain our legitimate rights. We are aware that the present circumstances are not on our side and will consequently delay our struggle, but it will not stop us as long as we strengthen our will and our readiness and our determination to gain our national rights.

5. We call on the Palestinian Liberation Organization and the National Authority to hasten their response to the call of the Palestinian national forces. This is a call to ensure a wide-based democracy where the masses can participate more actively in political decision-making. We warn the PLO and the PA not to go back to partial and interim negotiations but to demand an end to the occupation in all its forms. We call on the Palestinian Authority and the PLO to reorganize the internal Palestinian agenda and

redraw the administrative, financial, and political priorities in accordance with the option of the Intifada and the resistance movement. We call on the PLO and the Authority to aid in strengthening popular steadfastness, to enhance the role of the emergency committees, and to make available all resources to thwart the Zionist program of brutality.

The Palestinian resistance movement and the Intifada should continue until the occupation is brought to an end and the rights of our people—freedom, independence and the return of refugees—are realized.

## October 3, 2001
## Press Release

*Ramallah:* In order to fill the vacuum created after the assassination of our comrade, the PFLP General Secretary Abu Ali Mustafa, and within the context of the continuing Palestinian resistance movement against the Zionist occupation, the Central Committee of the PFLP convened its full contingency at home and abroad, in an atmosphere of responsibility and democracy, in order to elect new leadership for the PFLP. As a result, Comrade Ahmad Sa'adat was elected as the new General Secretary and Comrade Abdil Rahim Mallouh, as deputy General Secretary.

The Central Committee, together with the newly elected leaders, emphasized the need to persevere in the resistance movement and the Intifada until the Israeli occupation is brought to an end and until our people's legitimate rights to freedom, independence, and the return of refugees, are realized.

At the end of the meeting, the Central Committee stressed that it is of crucial importance to unify all Palestinian forces against the Zionist occupation atrocities that are aiming not only to destroy Palestinian infrastructure but also to destroy the identity of the Palestinian people and to impose conditions of surrender through taking advantage of the current international crisis.

Ahmad Sa'adat, PFLP General Secretary

Comrade Ahmad Sa'adat (Abu Ghassan) was born in 1953 in Al-Bireh. His family origins are in Deir Tarif, Ramleh District. He was graduated from the Teachers' College in Ramallah in 1975 in Mathematics. Abu Ghassan is married and father of four sons.

In 1967, Abu Ghassan joined the National Liberation Movement within the framework of the Union of High School Students. He joined the PFLP in 1969. Between 1969 and 1992, Abu Ghassan was imprisoned by the Israeli occupation army eight times. Since 1993, he has been listed as "wanted" by the Israeli army. The Israeli authorities arrested him three times in 1995 and 1996.

He was elected a member of the PFLP Central Committee at the Fourth National Conference of the PFLP in 1981. He was re-elected to the Central Committee and elected to the Politburo at the Fifth National Conference in 1993. In 1994, Abu Ghassan became responsible for the PFLP's West Bank branch. In the year 2000, he was re-elected to the Central Committee and to the Politburo during the Sixth National Conference.

On 3 October 2001, and after the assassination of Abu Ali Mustafa, Abu Ghassan was elected General Secretary of the PFLP.

Abdil Rahim Mallouh, PFLP Deputy General Secretary

Comrade Abdil-Rahim Mallouh (Abu Sharif) was born in Jaffa in 1945 and became a refugee with his family in 1948. He attended the Jiflik UNRWA school and in 1963 left to work in Kuwait. In 1965, he was part of the Palestinian Liberation Army in Baghdad and finished his schooling in the evenings in Baghdad and participated in several advanced military courses. In 1967 Abu Sharif participated in the creation of the Popular Front for the Liberation of Palestine. He was injured twice during battles with Israel (one of which was the Al-Karami battle in 1968). In 1971 he was injured again in the confrontations with the Jordanian Army. Abu Sharif was detained in Jordan for one year between 1977 and 1978. In 1982 the PFLP gave him the command of the forces in defending Beirut. He became a member of the Palestinian political and military leadership. He participated in several courses in the former Soviet Health Work Committees. Abu Sharif was elected to the Politburo of the PFLP in 1973. He was elected to the Executive Committee of the PLO in 1991. Abu Sharif was elected head of the political department of the PFLP in the year 2000 and elected deputy general secretary of the PFLP in October 2001.

**October 8, 2001**
**Press Release**

*Ramallah:* Within the context of the initiation of the Anglo-American military attack upon Afghanistan—with the support and facilitation of a number of countries in the world and the region—and the threat that this attack will be widened to include other targets, and be drawn out in duration—the Popular Front for the Liberation of Palestine declares the following:

The fact that the United States has ignited the tinderbox of war in the aftermath of the events in New York and Washington, instead of reviewing its hostile policies toward the peoples of the world, contradicts everything that is rational and every endeavor to solve world problems through dialogue and peaceful means through the primary international institution—the United Nations—and on the basis of international law.

The PFLP believes that the American war is only the finishing touch to the imposition of American security hegemony throughout the world, following the supposed imposition of its economic and political hegemony. The future of humanity will show, however, that peace and security cannot be imposed by brute force and aggression. Peace and security will only be achieved on the basis of justice and equality among all of humanity. And the first among the people struggling for justice, peace, and equality is our Palestinian people.

The PFLP calls on the world community, in general, and the American administration, in particular, to take practical steps to stop Zionist state terrorism, which is being practiced in the most ugly fashion; to provide temporary international protection for our people; to compel Israel to implement the resolutions of international law that deal with the Palestine issue; and to end the practice of using double standards in dealing with international problems.

The PFLP also calls upon all the fraternal Arab countries and on the states of the Islamic world not to remain idle as the American aggressive war, that began yesterday, is waged against the people of Afghanistan, with the threat that it will be expanded to include other countries in the region. The PFLP calls on them not to provide any facilities for the operations of the war.

## October 9, 2001
## Press Release

*Ramallah:* Given the unfortunate events that occurred yesterday afternoon in the Gaza region, at a time when the Zionists are escalating their attacks upon the masses of our people, and within the context of the American imperialist attack upon Afghanistan aimed at reinforcing American domination and imposing it upon the peoples of the world, we call upon the masses of our people, their vital political forces, and the Palestine Authority to exercise the highest degree of self-restraint. We call on them to strive to strengthen the bonds of popular and national unity that have been consecrated by the blood of our people's martyrs on the fields of confrontation along the fronts of the Intifada. We call on them to strengthen the resistance movement throughout the whole of our dear homeland. We must not allow the enemies to break the bonds of our internal unity. We in the Popular Front for the Liberation of Palestine, on the basis of our responsibility to our people and their supreme national interests, believe and declare the following:

1. The right of our people to express their opinion and their solidarity with the people of Afghanistan is a sacred right that no one is entitled to violate.
2. The principle that was enhanced by the traditions of our national work and was strengthened by the Intifada, demands that we look

to the logic of responsible, democratic dialogue to solve any manifestation of internal differences.

3. We condemn the choice to resort to the use of weapons in solving problems of internal differences and demand that those who violate this principle be brought to trial.

4. We call on the leadership of the Palestine Authority, the national and Islamic forces, and political and popular activists to work to limit the divisive effects of this unfortunate event and to prevent the occupiers and others from destroying our national unity or the supreme interests of our people.

## October 18, 2001
## Communiqué

*Ramallah:* The significant blow delivered by the military wing of the PFLP to one of the most racist, extremist, and Zionist symbols of Sharon's government, Minister Rehavam Ze'evi, has precipitated widespread national and international reaction. Many countries have described this action as a crime, a political assassination, or an attack against efforts to achieve peace in the region. There is always, however, the other side of this action which politicians in the western world are trying to ignore or forget. The operation of the military wing of the PFLP is a natural reaction to the continuous crimes of the Israeli occupation against the Palestinian people. These can be summarized as follows:

a. the continuation of the occupation of the West Bank and Gaza Strip, and the rejection of the Israeli government to recognize the legitimate rights of the Palestinian people as formulated by international conventions;

b. the criminal siege over Palestinian cities, towns, and villages; the destruction of homes and lands; the military bombardment of a civilian population; the policy of assassination, and the humiliation to which the entire Palestinian population is subject. In the past year, more than 700 Palestinians have been killed and over 16,000 injured.

c. The Israel occupation forces and their security apparatus themselves initiated the policy of political assassination that has resulted in the death of 70 Palestinians. This policy is a clear example of organized state terror.

d. Israel crowned its crimes of targeting Palestinian political leaders when, on 27 August 2001, it assassinated the Palestinian leader and PFLP General Secretary Abu Ali Mustafa. This criminal act has propelled the confrontation to a more critical and dangerous level. It is only natural and legitimate for Palestinians to respond appropriately.

e. The continuation of the Zionist settlement policy in the West Bank, Gaza, and Jerusalem contradicts all decisions of international convention. The Israeli government, under the leadership of Sharon (known for his racism and his massacres against the Palestinian people in Gaza in the seventies and Sabra and Shatilla in 1982), is determined to continue in its racist and aggressive policies. These policies have as their aim the imposition of humiliating conditions on the Palestinian people while at the same time, ensuring the existence of the Israeli occupation, despite the concessions offered by the Palestinian negotiating team. Israel is responsible, through its unjust and inhumane occupation, for all the bloodshed and destruction.

f. The PFLP calls on all organizations and countries around the world to take a firm stand in demanding an end to the brutal Israeli occupation. There can be no security for any force that occupies another people.

## October 22, 2001
### Press Release

*Ramallah:* On 18 October, the Palestinian Security Forces arrested dozens of leaders, members, and friends of the PFLP. This campaign, which continues till today, reflects the response of the PA to Israeli/American conditions and demands that aim to weaken the popular resistance and the spirit of the Intifada. The danger of this step is increased when we consider that Sharon's government is still relentlessly attacking our people, our cities, and our villages, as well as continuing its policy of assassination, rejecting the so-called cease-fire, and continuing its massacres throughout the occupied territories.

The actions of the Palestinian Authority, including the attempt to arrest the General Secretary of the PFLP, are causing grave damage to the Palestinian national and popular unity that has been strengthened by the sacrifice of all our people and all our national and Islamic forces.

Even as the PFLP issues warnings concerning the consequences of this illegal campaign, it places full responsibility on all those leaders within the PA for any harm that may come to the present detainees and demands their immediate release.

The PFLP also calls on those official PA spokespersons who present inaccurate interpretations of PFLP positions and policies, to immediately refrain from doing so, which in the end, does not serve our national interests.

The PFLP values and appreciates the position of the national and Islamic forces who have condemned the policy of political arrest and warn about the consequences.

The PFLP calls on our people at home and abroad, as well as all within the Arab World and all those throughout the world who stand for freedom and peace, to assume their role in stopping this campaign.

The decision of the Palestinian National Security Council, that was taken during the fascist attack of Sharon on our people, is a dangerous decision which ostracizes and declares illegal, the popular resistance movements that arose during the Intifada. This decision, if not reversed, will cause severe damage to our national unity and the continuation of the Intifada and the resistance movement.

We call on the Palestinian Authority and all Palestinian institutions and organizations, especially the Executive Committee of the PLO, the National Council, and the Central Council, to take the initiative in protecting the right of our people to resist occupation and Zionist terror. Furthermore, we demand that these institutions and organizations provide protection for the detained political activists.

The PFLP calls on the Palestinian Authority to release all political prisoners, especially the leaders and members of the PFLP, which is a founding member of the PLO.

We see victory ahead.

## October 23, 2001
### Communiqué

The PFLP recognizes that the decision of the Palestinian Authority to ban the military wing of the PFLP came as a result of tremendous pressure imposed on it by the international community, the USA, and Israel. The PFLP condemns this decision in the strongest terms possible and believes that the present reality of the united resistance movement against the Israeli occupation is infinitely stronger than any decisions or declarations that may be made at an "official" level.

This irrational war, being waged by Israel in order to reoccupy parts of Palestinian cities (Jenin, Qalqiliya, Tulkarem, Ramallah, Al-Bireh, Bethlehem, Beit Jala, Beit Sahour), reveals the bloody plan of Sharon's government. The Israeli government claims that its wide-ranging operation against the Palestinian people comes in retaliation for the assassination of the racist Israeli Tourism Minister Ze'evi. This allegation is completely absurd. First of all, it must be understood that the assassination of Ze'evi came in response to the *ongoing Israeli assassination policy,* which has been responsible for the murder of seventy Palestinians since the beginning of the Intifada, including that of Abu Ali Mustafa, the PFLP General Secretary, on 27 August 2001. In fact, Israel began its policy of assassination in the early 1970s. We remember . . . Ghassan Kanafani, Kamal Nasser, Kamal Oudwan, Yousef Najjar, Majed Abu Sharrar, Abu Jihad, Abu Iyad, Dr. Thabet Thabet, Khaled Nazzal, Abu Al-Houl, Jamal Mansour, Jamal Salim, Fathi Shikaki . . . , and many, many others.

Secondly, and contrary to what Israeli would have the world believe, the Israeli invasion of Palestinian cities did not begin on 17 October, the day Ze'evi was killed. In fact, the invasion began in September 2000, with the start of the Intifada, and continued with the unprecedented incursion into Gaza and Hebron a number of weeks ago, and continues today throughout the occupied territories. The killing of Ze'evi neither precipitated nor justifies Israeli intentions to exert control over the Palestinian people and subdue the Intifada.

Israel's present war against the Palestinian people is one with clear and obvious aims: first and foremost among them is to force the Palestinians to surrender. Secondly, it aims to thwart any attempt or political initiative that would acknowledge the legitimate rights of the Palestinian people: the right to freedom, the right to an independent state with Jerusalem as its capital, and the right of refugees to return.

Sharon's government tries in vain to conceal the facts of the conflict through blinding itself by its own policy of state terrorism. It claims that its military operations are conducted in order to combat Palestinian terrorism. The facts of the conflict, however, reveal that *Israel is a military occupying power* and has been for the last 33 years. It has done everything possible to confiscate Palestinian lands and create "facts on the ground" by building and expanding its settlements and constructing more and more bypass roads. Israel is an occupying power that has not only ignored decisions of international convention, but has also committed gross human rights' violations against the Palestinian people.

The Palestinian people are the ones living under brutal military occupation and their resistance movement is a legitimate response to this reality. Israel and its occupation bear sole responsibility for the bloodshed, grief, and agony in the Middle East. Indeed, Palestinian resistance against Israeli occupation should have been supported and encouraged by the international community years ago.

The international community needs to be honest with itself. No peoples in the world submit to the conditions presently imposed on the Palestinian people. The resistance movement of the Palestinian people is a natural and legitimate means to confront the reality of the Israeli occupation—an occupation which consistently denies Palestinians their basic rights and which refuses to accept international conventions calling for Israeli withdrawal from the occupied territories.

The Palestinian people are not asking for more than what all people have and deserve—to live in peace and security, with freedom and independence.

The present Israeli government insists on rejecting all political initiatives, even those agreements signed by previous Israeli governments. Israel insists on imposing a fake peace on the area while it continues its occupation. Confronted with the Israeli government's racist, extremist, and Zionist policies, the Palestinian people have no other choice than to remain steadfast in their resistance. *Legitimate resistance can never be equated with terrorism.*

We, the Palestinian people, the democratic forces, and the PFLP, have no desire for war or senseless killing. We long simply for our freedom and our right to life.

Within this framework, we call on all peoples of the world and all international bodies to act decisively and seriously to stop the massacres committed by the government of Sharon. The Palestinian people are the ones longing for true peace and security.

We call on all peoples of the world and all democratic structures to exert pressure on Israel to abandon its policy of aggression, to bring an end to the occupation, and to implement all international resolutions relevant to the Palestinian cause.

As one of the historically-rooted political parties within Palestinian society, the PFLP has earned a solid reputation among the population as a whole since its inception thirty-three years ago. We reject all attempts to discredit the PFLP and its legitimacy and interpret them to be a submission to Israeli/American demands which aim to destroy Palestinian national unity.

The PFLP is a political party working toward regaining the legitimate national rights of the Palestinian people which is a necessary first step in establishing a democratic state on the land of historic Palestine—a state where all peoples can live as equal citizens, entitled to basic human rights, regardless of race, religion, color, or sex.

### October 24, 2001
### Communiqué from Comrade Ahmad Sa'adat, PFLP General Secretary

As PFLP General Secretary, and in the name of all our comrades, I believe it necessary to comment on and interpret recent events in order to express concern for the national unity of the Palestinian people and the Palestinian resistance movement that has been persevering in our Intifada for more than a year. Briefly, these events include:

- The developments in our homeland of Palestine since the heroic operation that targeted Rehevam Ze'evi, who was the Minister of Tourism and the head of Moledet, one of the most racist political parties in the Israeli government;
- The continuation of the Israeli occupation's aggression toward and invasion of our cities and villages;
- The continuous killings and assassination of our people and leaders, most recently Ayman Halaweh;
- The recent attack of the Palestinian Authority on the PFLP through its arrest of PFLP leaders and cadres.

Given these events, the PFLP asserts the following:

1. The heroic operation carried out by a special unit of the PFLP and which culminated in the assassination of Rehevam Ze'evi, was not only a legitimate means of exercising our right to self-defense, but also a means to restore self-confidence, respect, and dignity to our people and our leaders. Ze'evi was a racist criminal who called openly for the transfer and killing of the Palestinian people as well as the killing of Palestinian leaders and the destruction of the Palestinian Authority, even going so far as to call for the killing, expulsion, or arrest of President Arafat, the president of the Palestinian state and the chairman of the PLO. As a member of the Israeli government, Ze'evi shared responsibility for the murder of our political leaders, for example, Dr. Thabet Thabet, Jamal Mansour, and our leader, Abu Ali Mustafa.

2. Israeli aggression does not need an excuse to broaden its aggressive operations against our people. The Israeli occupation has never stopped its aggression nor its increasing forceful confiscation and occupation of our lands. The erroneous Israeli claim that the killing of Ze'evi has accelerated the violence serves only to reveal Israel's plan to subdue the Intifada and the resistance movement and ultimately to force the Palestinian people and the Palestinian authority to surrender and to relinquish their national rights and their aspiration to live in peace, freedom, and independence. In other words, the Israelis expect the Palestinian people to mourn Ze'evi as his colleagues and people mourn him.

3. With their initiation of the Intifada in September 2000, our people have regained their national dignity and pride. The Intifada has led to a new articulation of the fundamental terms of reference for our national interests that is based on a broad popular support that refuses to surrender or to return to the humiliating conditions of Oslo and its agreement for slavery. The claim that the killing of Ze'evi has harmed Palestinian national interests must be evaluated accurately and cannot be used as a justification to harass and arrest the cadres of the PFLP. If one is to act honestly in the protection of Palestinian national interests, then all political prisoners must be released immediately.

4. We are aware of the burden weighing heavily on the Palestinian Authority in defending the national interests of the Palestinian people and we stand with the Palestinian Authority, side by side, defending every square centimeter of our homeland. We are also aware of the pressure put on the Palestinian Authority by the international community, the USA, and the Israelis. The appropriate response to this reality, however, is increased national unity in

order to force Israel to comply with international conventions that recognize the right of our people to an independent and free Palestinian state with Jerusalem as its capital, and the right of refugees to return. Genuine national unity is the best response to Israel's continuous aggression and occupation.

5. The difference in opinion concerning the general circumstances that surrounded our cause after 11 September 2001, and the ensuing developments in the international arena also reveal inconsistencies within Palestinian society as well as differences regarding the means and methods to be used to defend our homeland and our people. Our leaders, political parties, and people must listen to reason and engage in a continuous constructive dialogue based on our national unity and our national interests. This will act as the foundation for a comprehensive strategic national program that supports and strengthens our resistance movement not only on the front line, but also at a grassroots level. We must support the resistance movement and the Intifada as well as all democratic structures and behavior in our society as a basis to rebuild the leading popular movements, foremost among them the Palestinian Liberation Organization and its various structures.

Finally, the partnership of the various political parties and their mutual struggle, their common history as well as their common future, the determination to remain steadfast, the longing for freedom and independence and keeping up the resistance movement, force us all to remain united. Neither inconsistencies nor misinterpretations nor "wrong behavior" should sabotage our unity. We must all be patient and wise, while we listen to each other in order to confront the occupation and its aggressive tactics that target everything that is Palestinian. We will be victorious in the end.

## November 3, 2001
## Press Release

*Ramallah:* Within the context of the decision of the United States of America to add the Popular Front for the Liberation of Palestine, the Islamic Resistance Movement, Hamas, the Islamic Jihad Movement in Palestine, and the Hizb Allah Organization in Lebanon to the list of terrorist organizations, and its decision to treat them the same way that it treats the Qa`idah Organization, the Popular Front for the Liberation of Palestine declares clearly that these organizations are national liberation movements. They resist occupation and therefore are not terrorist organizations. They are organizations, indeed, that resist a military, colonial and racist occupation.

Real terrorism is that which is practiced by the government of Sharon and the previous Zionist governments that occupied others' territories, destroyed their houses, expropriated their lands, built settlements on them, expelled the native inhabitants, and scattered them to various countries. Support for such terrorist activity is, in itself, terrorism.

The Palestinian people are the most oppressed people in history. Their country is the last colonial territory. All international law permits this people to engage in all types of struggle in order to rid itself of the occupation and to attain its national independence, armed with United Nations' resolutions, whose implementation America and the Zionist Entity continue to obstruct.

The Popular Front for the Liberation of Palestine is a basic component of the Palestine Liberation Organization which enjoys the recognition of the United Nations as well as the recognition of a majority of the world's countries, and its struggle for national independence enjoys the legality bestowed by such recognition.

The PFLP condemns what US State Department representative David Satterfield said when he described the Palestinian Intifada as "studied terrorism." Such a statement betrays America's absolute alignment with the Zionist Entity and reflects the reality of America's hostile thinking with regard to the cause of the people of Palestine, even though it might cover up that hostility with promises that some imagine are genuine.

The Intifada of the Palestinian people is an uprising of a whole people against occupation and colonization and for self-determination and the establishment of its independent Palestinian state on its national soil, and for the return of its displaced people to their homes, in accordance with international law.

## Statement Issued by Ahmad Sa'adat, PFLP General Secretary

The Zionist political proposals that carry the name "The Peres-Sharon Initiative" have appeared within the framework of attempts to mislead the international community and to cover up the crimes that the Zionist government commits on a daily basis against our people. The most recent examples of outrages, which will not be the last such crimes, are the execution killings of the militants Iyyad al-Khatib, Jamal Mallouh, and Ali Abu Hajlah, and the assassination of the militants Ikrimah Istiti and Majdi Jarradat, in addition to the destruction of Palestinian civil institutions, the bulldozing of fields, and the imposition of a blockade on Palestine's cities and villages. The Zionist initiative is also an attempt to block the way to any attempt that aims to force Israel to stop its aggression against our people and to implement United Nations' resolutions.

The course of what is called the "political initiative" brings with it a clear threat to the will of the international community and to its resolutions concerning the Palestinian problem—resolutions that reject the Israeli occupation of the West Bank, Gaza Strip, and the Jerusalem region, and that demand that our people's refugees are ensured the right to return home.

In view of this, I call upon the international community, and primarily, the United Nations, to put a limit on Israel's determination to challenge the international will. I also call upon the countries taking part in the coalition that have called for a declaration of war on what they label "terrorism," to stand up to the Zionist terrorism practiced against our popular masses, and to provide temporary international protection to our people, in preparation for enabling them to exercise their right to return, self-determination, and the establishment of an independent state with Jerusalem as its capital, in accordance with United Nations' resolutions.

In addition I call on the Palestine Authority to break down the wall of illusion that has come to separate it from sections of our people. These illusions have allowed it to pin its hopes upon international—American and British—initiatives that dovetail with the new Zionist program, and that mark a step down from the level of United Nations' resolutions. I call on the Palestine Authority to act to stop all the steps it has been taking in response to Israeli and American pressure and dictate. I call on it immediately to free all Palestinians detained because of their opinions, or because they resist the occupation, and to proceed to take practical steps in order to build an internal Palestinian home strong enough to respond to the need to develop and escalate the uprising and the resistance, as a prime way to attain the goals of our patriotic people.

Glory to our people and victory to the Intifada and the resistance!

## First Press Conference of the new General Secretary of the Popular Front for the Liberation of Palestine

Saadat: "We have no choice except to continue the intifada." "We refuse to participate in a government of national unity." "Our relations with the Palestine Authority are based on mutual support." The General Secretary of the Popular Front for the Liberation of Palestine, Ahmad Saadat (Abu Ghassan), in his first press conference just after being elected the new General Secretary of the PFLP, called for the continuation of the intifada and resistance to the occupation, no matter how burdensome the hostility of the international environment to the struggle of our people may be. He said that there is no choice before us other than resistance and radicalizing the concentration of the mass and national efforts in order to push our people's cause forward to attain their goals of return, self-determination, and the establishment of an independent Palestinian state with its capital in Jerusalem.

This was said in a press conference held by Saadat in the Hall of the Palestine Information Center in al-Bireh. The conference was attended by the new Deputy General Secretary, Member of the Executive Committee of the Palestine Liberation Organization, Abd al-Rahim Mallouh, and by Member of the Political Bureau of the Popular Front, Ali Jarradat, who declared at the beginning of the press conference that on 3 October 2001 the General Central Committee of the Popular Front held an extraordinary meeting named in honor of the Martyr Abu Ali Mustafa.

Saadat said that the martyrdom of Abu Ali Mustafa—with all his merits, his potential, his history of struggle, and his expertise—left the Popular Front with a loss that will be hard to compensate for. He pointed out that the Popular Front, as a democratic political party, relies on its institutions as the basis for its work, actions, and activity which will be organized and run on this basis.

Regarding the policy of the Popular Front, the new General Secretary affirmed that the Front's policy and positions are determined by the documents approved by the General National Congresses of the Front or documents issued by the Front's central institutions such as the Political Bureau and Central Committee. The General Secretary or the Front's leadership are only expected to translate those documents and resolutions into action in the light of realty and circumstances.

Responding to a question from journalists, the General Secretary said that the call upon the Palestinians to cease fire means, frankly, ending the intifada and resistance. The position of the Popular Front, he said, is to stay committed to the people's resolve that calls for continuing the intifada and the resistance until the occupation is driven away and our national goals are attained.

Relations with the Palestine Authority: Regarding relations between the Popular Front and the Palestine Authority, Saadat said that our relations with the Palestine Authority are not governed by moods, but by the supreme national interest of our people. Therefore the organizing and basic relations now are relations of mutual support and unity. It is natural that different positions and opinions exist in the Palestinian arena and with the Palestine Authority. Saadat emphasized the Popular Front's refusal to participate in a government of national unity. He adddded, "but if there is a new Palestinian political position based on breaking the ties with the yoke of Oslo, and proclaiming the sovereignty of a Palestinian state and putting that sovereignty into practice in the areas that the Palestine Authority manages, while calling on the masses to seize the sovereignty as in the remainder of the occupied areas—that would form the prelude to our principled position of taking part in a government of national unity."

Meeting with Arafat:

Concerning the possibility of a meeting with President Yasir Arafat, Saadat said that meetings between the Front and President Yasir Arafat and the Palestine Authority already take place. The Front has no Party position calling for boycotting such meetings. If there is a need to hold such a meeting with the President, that would be on the top of the agenda of the Palestine situation, in particular as it deals with putting the interior of the Palestinian house in order. For it is not right to call for the continuation of the resistance and intifada while our internal structure is not capable of embracing the tasks of carrying on the intifada, in addition to the general political issues that concern our public such as how to fight back against aggression and provide the wherewithal for steadfast resistance.

Challenges for a General Secretary who is a fugitive from the Israelis:

Saadat explained that his election as General Secretary of the Popular Front was subject to the organs by which the Front governs itself inside the occupied territories and outside. He said that the Central Committee held a meeting with all members present in difficult conditions and in three rounds: one outside Palestine, the second in the West Bank, and the third in Gaza. During their discussion of opinions, proposals, and names of candidates, we came to a conclusion in an internal atmosphere full of democracy and optimism and determination to regain the high regard for the Front that suffered the loss of its General Secretary, the Martyr Abu Ali Mustafa. Saadat added that the "inside" [i.e., the Palestinian territories] is the decisive center for the Front, since the inside represents the general national center of decisive weight, as was determined by the Sixth General Congress of the Popular Front. We implemented that orientation by electing Abu Ali Mustafa General Secretary of the Front just after his return to and entry into the homeland. On the personal level, Saadat said, I treat with this new position as a mission. Before I was General Secretary, I had missions, and my work will continue whether I am General Secretary or not. As to my being wanted by the Israelis, all of our people are wanted by them. For me to belong to a people who are resisting and to the Popular Front which has been determined to resist along side our people—if that is the reason for putting me in a file of wanted persons, then that is an honor for me. I will arrange matters so that it does not affect my work, for every individual and leader among our people faces a challenge—either to persist in his work and activity or to go into hiding. I assure you that I will not hide. I will be among the masses and with the people. I will fight back. If my life is to be the price for that, thousands of martyrs of our people have fallen victim to Israeli perfidy. The Popular Front's response to the assassination of Abu Ali Mustafa:

Saadat said that the response of the Popular Front to the assassination of the late General Secretary will be multidimensional and comprehensive, involving the escalation of our role in confronting the occupation and taking part together with our people and their forces in providing the means for steadfast resistance, and internally by expending more efforts to embrace the condition of the masses who had rallied around the Martyr Abu Ali on the eve of his assassination.

Saadat emphasized that the declarations of the American President George Bush concerning the Palestinian state do not represent a change in the American position. The American administration is clear in its stance of total alignment with Israel. Any new qualitative change presented by America or by any other country that is of benefit to our people will be welcomed by us.

Published in "al-Hadaf" No. 1323, 3 November 2001.

## November 18, 2001
## Statement issued by the Political Prisoners in the prisons of the Palestine Authority

In the midst of the treacherous and continuing aggression against the masses of our Palestinian people, the assassinations, demolitions, and brutal massacres by the forces of the Zionist occupation, at a time of such continuing aggression when it is decidedly necessary to hold fast to the unity of our people and their resistance fighters in the field, when our ranks must stick together to continue the march of our people's struggle toward the achievement, and the establishment of an independent state with Jerusalem as its capital, in precisely these conditions the Palestine Authority continue their arrests of dozens of members of the Popular Front for the Liberation of Palestine and of other national forces whose only sin is their resistance to the occupation, and their rejection of its aggressive and racist policies.

To continue to detain us in the prisons of the Palestinian security while our people continue to be subject to the campaign of killing and destruction is something that is no longer understandable or acceptable.

We loudly proclaim that our arrests are invalid, that they have no legal or legitimate bases. They are nothing more than arrests in conditions of unannounced emergency regulations, which the Palestine Authority enforces against those who have different opinions.

We, the political prisoners detained in the prison of the Palestinian Security Service, have resolved to go on hunger strike beginning on Sunday, 18 November 2001 together with our comrades and brothers in the Central Prison of the Preventive Security who declared their hunger strike.

We consider our hunger strike one of the forms of struggle against the political imprisonment practiced against us for no wrongdoing on our part. We call upon all the national forces, all the free and honorable voices from among our great people, upon the forces, associations, institutions, trade unions, federations, the People' Committees, well-known national and social personalities to declare your solidarity with us, and to put pressure on the Palestine Authority immediately to release us so that we may

return to the ranks of our people and to our homes, so that we may continue, together with you, the struggle against the occupation.

The political detainees in the Prisons of the Palestine Authority
Palestine,

18 November 2001

## 20 November 2001
**Press Statement**

Ramallah:

The Popular Front for the Liberation of Palestine has issued a statement in which it commented on the address by the United States Secretary
of State Colin Powell day before yesterday to the effect that the content
of Powell's address was a rehashed repetition of former American positions in which there was nothing new. The Popular Front's statement said
the Colin Powell's address lacked any practical means for implementation, not to mention its lack of clarity in delineating the character of the
Palestinian state, its capital, its borders, and its sovereignty.

The PFLP statement explained that the new American move aims at
ending the intifada, as it treated Israeli official and organized terrorism,
on the one hand, and the legitimate Palestinian resistance to the occupation, on the other hand, as equal as a fact that makes the American
position one aligned with the occupation.

The statement said that the true test of American policy is its position on the Palestinian demand for the imposition of temporary international protection on the occupied Palestinian territories in preparation for
total implementation of the United Nations Resolutions that call for the
Israeli withdrawal from the lands it occupied in 1967, for the Palestinian
people's right to self-determination, in addition to the implementation of
the Resolutions of the General Assembly providing for the establishment
of a Palestinian state, the return of the refugees to the homes from which
they were expelled and stipulating that the Zionist settlements are illegal.

PFLP Press Office

Palestine

20 November2001

## 20 November 2001
**Letter from Dr. George Habash, Founder of the PFLP**

Dr. George Habash, the founder of the PFLP, demands that the PA
release all political detainees from prison—those leaders and members
of the PFLP, as well as other political parties.

At this time when we are all working together to protect the Intifada
and the legitimate demands of the Palestinian people, we recognize that
the detention of the cadres of the PFLP and other political parties severely
damages our national unity as well as the resistance movement and the
Intifada as a whole. We condemn the negligence of the Palestinian

Authority and its security forces that have failed to keep their promise to release the political detainees, despite their knowing that our comrades in prison are on a hunger strike in protest.

Out of my concern for Palestinian unity, I demand that the Palestinian Authority immediately release all political detainees. The oppressive measures used by the Palestinian security forces, and which are strongly condemned by our people, serve only to support the implementation of Israeli-American dictates.

The continuation of the policy of detention represents a state of confusion within the Palestinian Authority which must not become part of our national heritage. We must put an end to these oppressive measures that are damaging the Palestinian national aspirations upon which the PLO was established. The Palestinian Authority must work together with, rather than against, its people in order to translate their aspirations and vision into reality.

The coming stage demands that all of us consolidate our efforts in order that the Intifada and the resistance movement continue until the Palestinian people regain their freedom and independence.

## 24 November 2001
### Assassination is a Permanent Israeli Policy

The PFLP has said in a statement concerning the latest Israeli assassinations in Khan Younis and Nablus—acts that took the lives of seven martyrs, including five children—that assassination is a permanent Israeli mode of operation in the repression of our people; it is not a matter of retaliation for specific Palestinian actions.

The statement explained that the latest assassinations serve to confirm the uselessness of relying on illusory American promises or on the return of the Israeli Zionist unity government to the negotiations. The killings prove once again that Palestinian laxness only brings on more Zionist repression of our people.

The statement called for the continuation of the resistance and the Intifada. It called on the masses of our Palestinian people to beware of suspicious objects that the occupation forces have strewn about in the Palestinian areas with the intent to kill.

## 27 November 2001

Ramallah:

Ahmad Saadat, General Secretary of the Popular Front for the Liberation of Palestine, has said that the mission of the American team that has come to the Middle East region is merely to treat security problems related to a cease fire and to pressure the Palestine Authority into making more arrests of militants, in return for an Israeli halt to shelling of Palestinian cities and the lifting of the blockade that occupation has imposed on them.

Ahmad Saadat explained that what that means is a demand that the Palestinian people stop their intifada and go back to the negotiating table according to the American preconditions, whose failure caused the outbreak of the intifada in the first place.

Saadat called on America, if it wants to see its mediation succeed, to work politically with the cause of the Palestinian people by pushing the United Nations to guarantee temporary international protection of the Palestinian people as a preparatory step towards implementation of the United Nations resolutions that provide for an end of the occupation, the establishment of the Palestinian State with Jerusalem as its capital, and for the return of the refugees.

Saadat sharply condemned the American demand that the Palestine Authority arrest the activists in the resistance movement whom it labeled terrorists. The PFLP clearly states that it is the legitimate right of the Palestinian people to resist the occupation according to the international resolutions including UN.

Saadat noted that America needs to understand that the Palestinian people do not believe in the American role or in its ability to secure peace, so long as it remains aligned with Israel. That has been established in the course of the experience of the last ten years of fruitless negotiations.

General Secretary of the Popular Front for the Liberation of Palestine
Ahmad Saadat
Palestine
27 November 2001.

**December 1, 2001**
**American Promises require a means for their implementation.**
**Stopping the intifada will only bring on more pressure.**

Ramallah: In a press statement, the Popular Front for the Liberation of Palestine has commented on the call from the Executive Committee of the Palestine Liberation Organization to stop the resistance, and on a series of official statements concerning the mission of the American team of envoys. The PFLP states that this is an attempt to beautify the face of the mission of that American team, despite the fact that it brings with it nothing but ambiguous positions on a Palestinian state, on the Israeli occupation, and on United Nations resolutions.

The Popular Front statement said that the American positions constitute an American attempt to circumvent the achievements of our people, to empty out their contents by stopping the intifada and the resistance struggle, and by returning the Palestine Authority to fruitless rounds of negotiations on the basis of the Oslo Agreements and under the authority of the American Administration. In its statement, the Popular Front rejected the call for a so-called cease fire, and affirmed that it was holding fast to the option of intifada and resistance struggle, as an option that leads to driving off the occupation and compelling Israel to implement UN resolutions.

The Statement also called on the leadership of the Palestine Liberation Organization and the Palestine Authority to cease relying on American promises that lack any practical means for their implementation, and that relegate the Palestinian people to sitting and waiting for the good intentions of America and the Zionists.

The statement repeated the call of the Palestine Liberation Organization to deepen its efforts at rebuilding and reorganizing the Palestinian house internally, reinforcing and strengthening it through the implementation of the resolutions of its last Central Council session, in accordance with the basic rules of the Palestine Liberation Organization.

Additionally it is necessary to hold elections in all local councils and popular organizations, to lay down practical steps that lead to the actual establishment of the Palestinian State, to extending its sovereignty throughout the territories of the State of Palestine, to releasing all political prisoners, and to purging Palestinian institutions of corruption.

Central Information Department Press Office

## December 3, 2001

Rather than declare an emergency, we need a national dialogue to determine a strategy for Palestinian effort Ramallah: The Popular Front for the Liberation of Palestine has commented on the Palestine Authority's declaration of a state of emergency, saying that such a step is impermissible. It restricts public and personal freedoms and gives free rein to further arbitrary decrees at a time when the Palestinian people are living through a real emergency situation in which they need to apply themselves to their concerns and problems.

The statement by the Popular Front explained that the state of emergency declared by the Palestine Authority will have an effect on national unity in the field of confrontation, on the cohesiveness of the national ranks. This will occur even though the most strenuous efforts are made by every group to avoid harming this unity.

The Popular Front in its statement called for a comprehensive and serious national dialogue to define the Palestinian strategy for work in these conditions and in the next stage, for an agreement upon a national collective leadership based on the resolutions that express the national consensus, and for participation in Palestinian political decision making through a national emergency leadership.

The statement also called on the Palestine Authority to beware of meeting American and Israeli conditions, since these might simply bring on more Israeli pressure and dictates and more Palestinian concessions—something that only whets Sharon's appetite for repression.

The Popular Front statement stressed the need to hold fast to national unity in the field, to continue the intifada and resistance as a strategic choice that leads to gaining national independence and to implementing the resolutions of international legality.

Central Information Department
Press Office

## December 4, 2001

In response to the decisions of the Zionist government that are to be considered to be a declaration of war on the Palestinian people and the entire Arab Nation, we in the Popular Front for the Liberation of Palestine affirm that our Palestinian people are united in confronting the occupation that represents the most disgusting types of terrorism and fascism. We also affirm that the struggle and resistance of our people for freedom and independence is a legitimate right guaranteed to them by international law and therefore the recent heroic operations fall within the framework of the natural response to Zionist crimes, and we affirm that resistance is our legitimate right so long as the occupation continues. We call for a declaration of general mobilization and the formation of a united national emergency structure to confront the occupation, for the immediate release of all political prisoners, for a final halt to campaigns of political arrest, and for the cancellation of all steps and decisions that the Palestine Authority has taken in the aftermath of the heroic operations in Jerusalem and Haifa. Enough of betting on useless negotiations! Enough submission to the dictates of the American Administration that gave the green light to the terrorist Sharon to continue and intensify his aggression against our people!

In addition, we call on the Arab peoples to stand beside the Palestinian people in their patriotic struggle and in their resistance to Zionist aggression. The occupation continues . . . the resistance continues! Hail, all hail every military formation that resists the occupation!

We will definitely win!

## December 11, 2001

On the occasion of the Thirty-fourth anniversary of the founding of the Popular Front for the Liberation of Palestine.

The Popular Front for the Liberation of Palestine the patriotic and Islamic Forces paid a visit on the occasion to the tomb of the leader and martyr Abu Ali Mustafa. Wreaths of flowers were laid at the tomb of the martyr. Among the wreaths was one presented in the name of the President of the State of Palestine, Yasir Arafat. There was a wreath in the name of the patriotic and Islamic Forces, and a wreath in the name of the General Secretary of the Popular Front for the Liberation of Palestine, Ahmad Saadat.

A number of speeches were delivered. Ahmad Abdar-Rahman, the General Secretary of the Council of Ministers, gave an address in which he called for the continuation of the struggle along the path for which the leader Abu Ali was martyred. Comrade Abu Layla gave a speech. The Deputy General Secretary of the Popular Front for the Liberation of Palestine, Abdar-Rahim Mallouh, spoke to the meeting about the historical role of Comrade Abu Ali Mustafa in the leadership of the Popular Front since its establishment.

The Popular Front for the Liberation of Palestine
Central Information Office
Press Office
11 December 2001.

## December 13, 2001

At a time of official Arab silence and American pressure on the Palestine Authority, the occupation continues to escalate its savage terrorist aggression against our people and our institutions in a new attempt by it to perpetuate its occupation of our lands and to put an end to our people's legitimate resistance struggle for their freedom and independence.

We in the Popular Front for the Liberation of Palestine and in confrontation with the fascist occupation campaign against our people, our institutions, and our rights, affirm the following:

1. It is only our Palestinian people who decide who their leaders will be and not the terrorist Sharon and his fascist government.
2. The armed resistance is our people's legitimate right as long as the occupation and colonization continue.
3. Confronting the savage pressure and aggression requires that we strengthen our unity, hold firmly to our position and goals, have faith in the energy of our people, and close the book on political arrests. Submitting to dictates is not a way to confront pressure and aggression. We affirm that the international pressure should be directed at the occupation and its practices, since that is the source of the affliction.
4. When the Palestine Authority responds to American and Israeli pressure by encroaching upon the social and political institutions of the Hamas and Jihad movements, this deals a blow to Palestinian unity and resistance, and it weakens our confrontation with the enemy.
5. We demand that the Arab people and the international community move to stop the Israeli aggression against our people.

The Popular Front for the Liberation of Palestine
13 December 2001.

### December 17, 2001

Issued by the Martyr Abu Ali Mustafa Brigades, Forces of the Palestinian Popular Resistance, The Military wing of the Popular Front for the Liberation of Palestine.

In the condition of current political developments when the government of the Zionist enemy still continues to insist on its well-known 'no's to our people's rights; as it pursues on the ground its aggressive policy using warplanes against our unarmed people, storming Palestinian land, bulldozing property and destroying houses—the storming of the town of Bayt Hanoun will not be the last such attack; continuing its assassinations and arrests of our fighters—the crime of assassinating the mujahid Ya`qoub ad-Daqiqi in the steadfast city of al-Khalil [Hebron] this morning will not be the last such act; in these conditions, the leadership of the Palestine Authority has not merged with its people and its National forces. Instead, the Authority's president issued a speech on the day of the Islamic festival Eid al-Fitr to confirm the "state of emergency" and the so-called cease fire that it had recently declared, halting all armed operations against the Zionist enemy and describing those heroic operations as terrorism.

We in the Martyr Abu Ali Mustafa Brigades, in particular, and the Forces of the Palestinian Popular Resistance in general, regard this speech as extremely serious, as will be the results that shall follow upon the pursuit and arrest of resistance fighters and militants of the different armed wings of the national forces throughout the homeland. We affirm the following:

1. The continuation of the armed resistance. Its operations against the occupation will persist as long as the occupation continues squatting on our land, desecrating our holy places, firing at our people from their warplanes, destroying our houses, and storming and occupying our territory.

2. We call on everyone to continue all forms of resistance to the occupation and to the detachments of settlers, and not to comply with the so-called cease-fire order. We warn against any attempt to interfere with our heroic fighters.

3. We call on the functioning leadership of the Palestine Authority to merge with their people, to unite efforts and to cling to the option of resistance; to be done with the policy of going it alone, issuing decrees and relying on the option of the fruitless so-called negotiations on the basis of the authority of the Oslo agreements and under biased American auspices.

4. We call for a halt in the pursuit of the resistance activists and the release from the Palestine Authority's prisons of all those detained for resisting the occupation, and first of all for the release of the

comrade Ali Jarradat and the brothers Ismail Haniya and Abu Shanab.

Martyr Abu Ali Mustafa Brigades
Military wing of the Popular Front for the Liberation of Palestine
17 December 2001.

## December 17, 2001
## Press Release

Issued by the Popular Front for the Liberation of Palestine.

The Popular Front abhors the Palestine Authority's decision to inveigh against our people's armed resistance to the occupation and its escalating aggression against our people. This decision, announced by President Abu Ammar (Yasir Arafat), follows a wave of arrests of our militants, cadres, and leaders of the Hamas and Islamic Jihad movements and the Popular Front, and it represents a loathsome concession to the stance advocated by the European Union, America, and the racist Sharon government.

We in the Popular Front for the Liberation of Palestine—though we affirm the need for unity among our people, their patriotic and Islamic forces, and the Palestine Authority—must regard this development as an unwise and insulting act, which had not secured the barest token of reciprocity, that is, an Israeli guarantee to halt the Sharon government's aggression against our people, our land, and our institutions, much less an Israeli commitment to abide the Fourth Geneva Convention or any other provision of international law regarding the protection of our people.

Given our blood-drenched experience and unending repression, we view the Palestine Authority's action as inviting further demands by the Sharon government, in accord with its insatiable appetite for subduing our people under the false and intrinsically contradictory pretense of security. The Palestine Authority's decision has constituted an unacceptable form of surrender that jeopardizes all the achievements won over fourteen months of struggle, paid for with the blood of countless martyrs and wounded, who set the most admirable example in counteracting the Zionist government's insidious desire to sow discord within the ranks of the Palestinians.

We lament that President Arafat, and the Palestine Authority have not responded to the Popular Front's call for a responsible national dialog between the forces of our people and the national and Islamic institutions, with the intent to devise an effective strategy to wage the patriotic Palestinian struggle in these difficult conditions and to forge a truly inclusive, collective body of leadership committed to basing its decisions on a national consensus.

Since the Palestine Authority's decision-making process appears to have yielded before Zionist and American lobbies, we of the Popular

Front stalwartly reaffirm our commitment to the intifada and resistance, while imploring the Palestine Authority to engage in a comprehensive national dialogue; to announce a general mobilization; to abrogate the legal ramifications of the present state of emergency; to free all political prisoners; to halt the pursuit of militants; and to reverse its closure of institutions run by the Hamas and Islamic Jihad movements.

We reiterate our call for a comprehensive national dialogue, as there is no more vital a necessity in our attempt to build an effective degree of political unity among our people, redoubling their steadfastness to resist the American-subsidized Zionist aggression that aims to humble our people, break our will, and squelch our just yearning for self-determination.

The Popular Front for the Liberation of Palestine

17 December 2001

## December 31, 2001

The American refusal to send General Anthony Zinni back to the Middle East region was expected. His departure from the region a few weeks ago was consistent with his government's support for the Zionist Sharon regime's aggression against the Palestinian people, the Palestine Authority, and its president, brother Yasir Arafat. This action clearly may be regarded as a form of pressure to further subjugate our people, yet our will to resist both the occupiers and their foreign sponsors will not be shaken by such a juvenile manuever.

The American objective to bring the Palestine Authority to its knees before the Sharon government's extortionist security measures—while rending the tissue of the Palestinian domestic front, heightening tensions on the Palestinian street, and transferring the struggle to the Palestinian interior—affront the minimum standard of impartiality, in keeping with Washington's historical allegience to the occupier. As such, we must express both sorrow and consternation regarding the official Palestinian demand for the return of General Zinni, which only whets the appetite of Sharon and his proxies abroad for more, increasingly intolerable demands.

The current Palestinian national interest requires that the Palestine Authority abandon its misplaced hope that America's role in a negotiated settlement will secure the least token of our people's human rights and their uniquely justifiable quest for political self-determination. Our long experience dealing with American negotiators, from the Madrid Conference to today's venues, indicates that their concept of justice only entails moving Palestinian delegates from one tight corner to another in an effort to win concessions based on their durress.

The unbalanced diplomatic struggle faced by Palestinian officials necessitates an abrupt change of tactics: dispensing with the American role in favor of an international authority capable of reigning in the Zionist hostility that negates any meaningful prospect for peace in the region. This would encourage all members of the global family to shoulder their responsibility to compel Israel to uphold resolutions of international law by ending its occupation of territory within the Palestinian state. It also would facilitate our people's repatriation, self-determination, and designation of Jerusalem as the capital of their sovereign homeland.

Meanwhile, the Palestine Authority must terminate the negotiations currently underway with the occupation's foreign minister whose only purpose is to rationalize the Sharon government's escalating military aggression against the masses of our people. It must encourage Palestinian steadfastness and reinforce the domestic front by, in the first place, retreating from all punitive measures taken against those who have been active in resisting the occupation; reopening the Palestinian welfare, cultural, and press establishments; canceling the state of emergency and martial law; and adopting substantive measures to rebuild the Palestinian homeland in the spirit of popular unity, this being the fundamental requirement for continuing the intifada to defend our people and their national rights.

The only legitimate path around the current political impasse must be followed through a Palestinian door, not the door of the White House which only serves as a passageway for the aircraft, warships, tanks, and missiles that ruthlessly enforce our subjugation.

The Popular Front for the Liberation of Palestine
Political Department
International Relations Bureau
31 December 2001
The Popular Front for the Liberation of Palestine
Branch of the Palestinian (West) Bank
31 December 2001.

## December 31, 2001

The Palestine Authority's security agencies have resumed raids on the houses of militants throughout the district of Ramallah and al-Bireh. It has not been satisfied with arresting a number of comrades and friends in the cities of Ramallah and al-Bireh, and with raiding houses and the tents that shelter those whose houses were destroyed by the Zionist occupation forces during their brutal destructive attack on the heroic wounded town of Bayt Rima, scene of a massacre by the occupation. In the last 24 hours the Authority has raided and arrested five supporters of the Popular Front, some of whose houses had already been searched by the occupation forces last week in the villages of Koubar and Berham, and in steadfast Qalandiya refugee camp. Last night the Authority's agencies raided whole districts in the city of Ramallah. At late hours—between midnight and 2:00 a.m.—they searched houses looking for militants wanted by the occupation forces, frightening the peacefully sleeping residents and children.

These agencies have resorted to subjecting prisoners to interrogation, beatings, and abuse. This behavior represents to the masses of our people, their patriotic and Islamic forces, and their democratic organizations a transgression against all legal fundamentals, a brazen violation of the rights of the citizen and the dignity of the homeland, scorn for the values of struggle and national unity, and a stab in the back of the intifada and resistance.

The Popular Front for the Liberation of Palestine, aware that our people and their patriotic and Islamic forces and their organizations are the bulwark of national unity and defenders of the established national goals that are not subject to bargaining, emphasizes again that these practices will not deter the Front, our people, and their patriotic and Islamic forces from pursuing their patriotic alternative embodied in the march of the intifada and the resistance. The Popular Front warns that deep involvement in these doubtful actions and approaches falls within the framework of sparking internal strife, is a blow to the supreme interests of the nation and the citizen, and serves only those who lie in wait to seize the rights and accomplishments of our people. It will only lead to deeper subjugation as the enemy escalates further its conditions and humiliating dictates.

We demand that those concerned stop these practices and put an end to these methods that the consensus of our people and their patriotic and Islamic forces reject. We reaffirm that comprehensive democratic national dialogue, and banning internal violence and fighting, are the only way to treat the differences that exist on the national arena, this is the only way to put our national house in order considering that it is the firm and guaranteed basis for national unity and progress towards our people's goals and their national rights.

The Popular Front for the Liberation of Palestine
Branch of the Palestinian (West) Bank
31 December 2001.

## January 3, 2002

The Popular Front for the Liberation of Palestine esteems and values the position taken by the European Union and its current President, the Spanish government, in rejecting the Israeli request to put the Popular Front on its list of terrorist organizations.

The Popular Front also calls on the European Union to review the position it took on the Hamas and Islamic Jihad organizations, which it labeled as terrorist. The European Union has stood with the Palestinian cause. It took an active part in passing all the international resolutions that have condemned the Israeli occupation of Palestinian lands. It has rejected the "legitimacy" of Israel's settlement building, its expropriation of Palestinian land, its annexation of eastern Jerusalem. It has condemned the Israeli occupation's excesses in refusing to implement resolutions of international legitimacy, and practicing with the cold-blooded repression and killing of children, to the policy of individual and collective expulsions and assassinations, the demolition of houses, and bombing of our people's civil and social institutions.

Because they have taken these positions—which we value—the countries in the European Union will not be deluded or deterred by the policy of the terrorist, racist government of Sharon from seeing the real and essential reason for the continuation of the cycle of violence in the Middle East region, which is none other than the continuation of the occupation and the policy of imposing that occupation by force, ignoring international law and all the documents and laws of international legitimacy.

It is sufficient to understand this fact to see that all the organizations of the Palestinian people, since they are only exercising their right to resist the occupation—a right guaranteed them by the international legitimacy and derived from the United Nations Organization—are indeed wronged when they are described or listed as terrorist organizations.

The Popular Front for the Liberation of Palestine is a Palestinian political organization that struggles against the Israeli occupation and for the liberation of its homeland and the freedom and independence of its people. Its political program is committed to working to implement the resolutions of international legality and to securing the United Nations as supervisor over and guarantor in the Palestine-Israeli conflict and the Arab Israeli conflict. At the same time, the Popular Front is a founding member organization of the Palestine Liberation Organization, the sole legal representative of the Palestinian people, recognized by our people and by the United Nations. The Popular Front always seeks to develop and strengthen the special role of the European Union in the framework of the international role in the effort to compel Israel to end its occupation of Palestinian land and to respect and implement the international resolutions that give our people their right to return, to self determination, and to the establishment of their independent state with Jerusalem as its capital, in order that security, peace and stability may be achieved throughout all the Middle East region, and so that the cycle of violence may be totally eliminated.

The Political Bureau
The Popular Front for the Liberation of Palestine
3 January 2002.

## January 9, 2002

We are now observing two anniversaries dear to our ongoing struggle: the 14th anniversary of the outbreak of the December Intifada, and the 34th anniversary of the founding of the Popular Front for the Liberation of Palestine. These occasions tell stories written in the blood of our sons and daughters—hundreds of martyrs, wounded, and prisoners who have given themselves to the cause of liberation.

These anniversaries evoke great pride as the resolve of our people continues to manifest itself in a heroic resistance movement that has entered its fifteenth month and will continue until the national rights of Palestinians have been irrevocably affirmed.

Our people are demonstrating unflagging resolution, steadfastness, and determination to drive out the Zionist occupiers as the precursor to attaining the national and democratic aims of our cause, which grows greater with each day and every Palestinian fatality. The American-supported occupation poses a relentless, escalating assault, and our intifada remains the target of American collaboration with the Zionists, who are intent on returning our people to the circle of fruitless Oslo negotiations and thus forcing us to yield to Sharon's unacceptable dictates. To further mock our quest for self-determination, our enemies have adopted the strategy of creating derision within Palestinian ranks. Yet our unity has been, must be, and will remain the most indispensable pillar of our people's defiance, and the modus vivendi of our final victory.

We of the Popular Front for the Liberation of Palestine are committed, as avidly as ever, to securing the national rights of our people and upholding our responsibility to our people and their courageous intifada. With unbounded admiration for those Palestinian who have sacrificed themselves in our common cause, we call for the following.

First: To remain steadfast despite the international situation that has evolved in the aftermath of September 11th and in the face of America's declaration of war on Afghanistan and states alleged to support terrorism. This situation entails highly adverse factors for our national struggle, which outsiders condemn as a form of terrorism when they themselves continue to precipitate the conditions which justify our most extreme forms of activism. Therefore, it is imperative that we hold fast to the struggle in defense of our people and our cause, striving for and expanding our national rights and supporting our Intifada.

Second. To abandon all illusions regarding the role of America, which for over half a century has repeatedly proven its commitment to the Zionist aggressors and in recent months has affirmed its devotion to them. We insist that the Palestine Authority not be coerced back into the vicious and self-defeating cycle of negotiations based on the Oslo accords.

Third. For the Palestine Authority and the Palestine Liberation Organization to cease bowing before Israeli and American pressure. We call for a cancellation of the so-called state of emergency, for a halt to the pursuit and arrest of militants, for the immediate release of all the political prisoners detained for their opinions or their resistance to the occupation. We call for a general mobilization of our people and their national forces to confront the escalating aggression of the terrorist Sharon government.

Fourth. For the leadership of the Palestine Liberation Organization, national forces, and popular organizations to begin a comprehensive dialogue to reach agreement for a unified political and combat strategy to safeguard our unity, bolster our people's defiance, and develop their intifada against the Zionist occupation and the many totalitarian injustices that it entails. We call for the agreement between all Palestinian factions to be the basis for building a supreme, collective leadership authority for our people as a step toward the democratic construction of fully independent Palestinian state.

Fifth. For the condemnation of the position of many Arab governments not merely content to observe the Zionist aggression, but insistent upon offering themselves as go-betweens, giving mistaken advice to our people on behalf of the Zionist government's desire for our compliance with American efforts to broker peace at our expense.

Sixth. For the international community to compel Israel, which wields a form of state terrorism against the masses of our people, to comply with and implement international law and the Fourth Geneva Convention, and to provide temporary international protection as a preparation for the implementation by the Zionist government of the resolutions of international legality that give our people their rights to return, self-determination, and the establishment of their independent state with Jerusalem as its capital. This responsibility lies foremost of all with the United Nations General Assembly which, most admirably, has called for all countries with embassies in Jerusalem to remove them.

Finally, we of the Popular Front for the Liberation of Palestine must emphasize that our general secretary has served in the front lines of our people's resistance and thereby set an example for us all. We pledge to our people upon the graves of the fallen that we will carry forth our resistance until all the aims of our national, democratic revolution are achieved.

The Popular Front for the Liberation of Palestine
9 January 2002.

### January 12, 2002

*Ramallah:* The Popular Front for the Liberation of Palestine has commented on the recent statements of US Secretary of State Colin Powell in which he described the savage Israeli aggression against the houses of refugees in Rafah and the destruction of the Gaza Airport as "legitimate defensive action" in response to attempts by the Palestine Authority to obtain weapons. The Popular Front said that these remarks are a reiteration of the American position of support for the Sharon government and its glaring and organized terrorism against the Palestinian people.

The Popular Front condemned the Palestine Authority's resort to arresting brothers whom Israel accuses of being involved in the arms ship operation. The Popular Front calls on the Authority to release those brothers and all the other militants it has detained and to stop cooperating with the mockery of a cease-fire that has only increased the viciousness of the Zionist aggression and the sense of superiority and arrogance of the Sharon government, while reinforcing America's inclination to raise the level of its pressure on the Palestine Authority and increase its scorn for it.

The Popular Front's statement called on all the forces of the Palestinian people to act in self-defense and activate the intifada and the resistance to the occupation army and to the bands of settlers.

The Popular Front for the Liberation of Palestine
Central Information Department
Press Office
12 January 2002.

## January 13, 2002
## Press Release

As the terrorist Zionist Sharon government continues its war of extermination against our people, murdering, destroying, and demolishing with the blessing of its ally the United States of America in a desperate Israeli-American attempt to get our people and their national forces to abandon their firm goals and inalienable rights and their continued commitment to the common national choice, the choice of intifada and resistance, the public security forces and the preventive security forces in the district of Ramallah and al-Bireh continue their feverish campaign against our resistance activists and the supporters of the Popular Front for the Liberation of Palestine, arresting, kidnapping, and torturing them. The number of detainees as of today has risen to 21 resistance activists whose only crime is their participation in the intifada of their people and their heroic resistance.

The Popular Front for the Liberation of Palestine, together with the other national forces, has all along affirmed its position, like a bullet in the chest of the occupation, that these suspicious acts will not reduce its commitment to continuing the resistance so long as the occupation of our land continues. The Popular Front reaffirms that surrender to international developments and to American and Israeli dictates will only yield the same rotten and noxious fruit that has been the result of ten years of compliance with their dictates and endless longing for more negotiations.

We call on our people and their national forces and on all the vital and healthy forces in our Arab nation to take up their role in support for and aid to the course of intifada and resistance, protecting it from the manipulation of those who want to make light use of the honor of the nation and of the citizens and of the national unity that has been embodied in the blood of our martyrs, the torment of our wounded and prisoners, and in the unending suffering our people.

The way out of this current national impasse is not to solve the problems of the occupation forces, complying over and over again with their cunning fascist demands. An honest, responsible, and serious political review is needed through a comprehensive national dialogue, where there is no place for the threats and arrests that have never once succeeded in shutting the mouths of our people and their resistance activists or in putting out the fire of their weapons—fire that is always legitimate in the face of a thieving occupation. No one will convince us with nervous logic and false viewpoints that the unity of our positions, plans, and leadership can be achieved by empty claims that impose their failure upon our national struggle.

Our unity can only be achieved if we seek to win ourselves before we win over the United States, by reordering the interior of our own house, rather than by trying to make our heads fit an Israeli hat. We firmly believe in the ability of our people to impose the priority of comprehensive national dialogue rather than a lust for meetings and talks with the butchers of our people and our Arab nation, who are after our land, our blood, and the very destiny of our people and nation.

Branch of the Palestinian (West) Bank
13 January 2002.
The Popular Front for the Liberation of Palestine
Branch of the Palestinian (West) Bank
31 December 2001.

## January 16, 2002
## Press Release

To set the record straight Declaration issued by the Popular Front for the Liberation of Palestine

To clarify the facts related to the arrest of Comrade Ahmad Saadat, the General Secretary of the Popular Front for the Liberation of Palestine, the Front presents the following information:

1. We in the Popular Front view this as an act of deceit and a total political ambush prepared in advance by the Palestine Authority and its various security agencies.
2. In taking this position we refer back to the stance taken by Abu Ammar (Yasir Arafat) when he spoke to representatives of the patriotic and Islamic forces and to representatives of the Popular Front in a meeting with them last November. At that time he said that the subject of arresting Comrade Ahmad Saadat is not on the agenda.
3. Based on that, during these past months Comrade Ahmad Saadat did not act as a fugitive subject to arrest by the Palestine Authority, although he was out of sight of the occupation and its agents.

4. The meeting that was held in a hotel in the city of al-Bireh yesterday, Tuesday 15 January 2002 between a high-ranking security official in the Palestine Authority and a delegation from the Popular Front led by Comrade Ahmad Saadat took place based on repeated requests made by that official.

5. What took place in the hotel yesterday was a pre-planned brazen political arrest. The greatest proof of the planned nature of the operation was the presence of a large number of armed members of the various security agencies. In no way was Comrade Ahmad Saadat "turning himself in" as claimed by Security Service Colonel al-Tayrawi in a statement published in the newspaper "al-Quds" this morning.

6. We in the Popular Front view all that has happened as a clear act of submission to pressures from the Sharon government, pressures that we know will never end. Therefore, we will not accept this situation that encroaches upon the bases of Palestinian national unity.

Free Comrade Ahmad Saadat and all political prisoners!
The Popular Front for the Liberation of Palestine
16 January 2002.
The Popular Front for the Liberation of Palestine
Branch of the Palestinian (West) Bank
31 December 2001.

## January 17, 2002
## Press Release

By Dr. George Habash, founding leader of the Popular Front for the Liberation of Palestine

Yesterday I was surprised by the arrest, by the Palestinian security agencies, on the direct order of President Yasir Arafat, of Comrade Ahmad Saadat, the General Secretary of the Popular Front for the Liberation of Palestine, while he was holding a meeting with an official in the Public Security Agency in the city of Ramallah, at the agency's request.

This step reflected a great deal of political thoughtlessness, disdain for the feelings of the people, and scorn for the role of the patriotic and Islamic forces that are leading the intifada and continuing the resistance to the racist, Zionist occupation with unequaled courage and heroism.

For the Palestine Authority to resort to a policy of laying traps, trickery, and other contemptible practices in order to arrest the militant Ahmad Saadat, under pressure from the Israeli leadership of Sharon—Eliazar—Mufaz, constitutes nothing but compliance with the plans of the Zionist enemy and its efforts to destroy the basis and foundation of the Palestinian national unity that has been achieved in the field over the course of fifteen months of bitter struggle waged by the Palestinian masses and their patriotic and Islamic forces, side-by-side, against the Israeli occupiers, in an effort to achieve the goals of our people—freedom and independence.

The diligence of the Palestine Authority in carrying forth its policy of acquiescence to Zionist-American conditions and dictates constitutes a very dangerous precedent for internal Palestinian relations. It will gradually lead to aborting the intifada and inflicting the gravest harm on our people's resistance to the occupation. I fear that this step will be the first of many others aimed at destroying the Palestine Liberation Organization as the broad, patriotic Palestinian alliance that, for many long years, we have all struggled to protect and defend.

As we condemn this disgusting step and atrocious crime, and as we denounce the actions of the Palestine Authority and its repressive measures against the Palestinian people's leaders, militants, and fighters, we call on the Palestine Authority and its President Yasir Arafat immediately to free the great militant Ahmad Saadat and all the Palestinian militants and fighters of Hamas, the Islamic Jihad, and the Popular Front for the Liberation of Palestine, out of respect for the blood of hundreds of martyrs and thousands of wounded who have sacrificed everything in the battle of honor, the battle of al-Aqsa, the battle of freedom and independence.

We call on the leadership of the intifada and all the patriotic and Islamic forces and the masses of the Palestinian people to act with utmost speed in exerting every available means of political pressure on the Palestine Authority to end its repressive acts and measures, and to free all the political prisoners, whatever political organization they belong to, and to lead the way for our people and their vital militant forces to continue the path of intifada, the path of struggle and resistance against the Israeli occupiers, in defense of our land and rights in the face of the most revolting, aggressive Zionist practices, so that our people might achieve their goals of return, self-determination, and the establishment of an independent Palestinian state with Jerusalem as its capital.

Dr. George Habash
17 January 2002

## January 18, 2002
## Press Release

Issued by the General Secretary of the Popular Front for the Liberation of Palestine

The Palestine Authority's acceptance of Zionist and American pressure—which we regret—does not avert the need for protection of the Palestinian people and defense of the Palestine Authority.

The declaration of a state of emergency and the efforts to arrest and pursue Palestinian fighters and militants, to impose house arrest on the mujahid Shaykh Ahmad Yasin (the spiritual leader of Hamas), the continuing arrest and detention of the militant member of the Political Bureau of the Popular Front who is responsible for its Central Information Department, Ali Jarradat, and many other members and cadres of the Popular Front—all these acts only serve the logic propounded by the Zionist Sharon government and American imperialism according to which the Palestinian resistance should be treated as terrorism, thereby finding an excuse for the crimes of the occupation—which is the worst and most brazen form of terrorism and is the chief source and reason for the violence in Palestine and the whole region.

Therefore the escalation of the aggression of the Zionist government against the Palestinian people and Authority must be met by a rejection of Zionist and American political and security-related extortion. General mobilization should be declared and a broad national dialogue engaged in to build a national strategy of confrontation that will strengthen the continuing resistance and intifada, and provide for the formation of a collective patriotic and Islamic leadership to serve as the authority for Palestinian national decision making. This would pave the way to rebuilding and reordering the interior of the Palestinian national house on a democratic and patriotic basis, through steps that reinforce national and popular unity and provide the requisites for steadfast resistance and the ability to deter aggression while winning over the logic of the international community to the need for an Israeli commitment to respect international law and the Fourth Geneva Convention, and to guarantee temporary international protection for our people as a preparatory step to international legal resolutions and a guarantee of the rights of our people to return, self-determination, and the establishment of their independent state with Jerusalem as its capital.

The General Secretary of the Popular Front for the Liberation of Palestine
6 December 2001.
The Popular Front for the Liberation of Palestine
Branch of the Palestinian (West) Bank
31 December 2001.

## January 18, 2002
## Press Release "as-Safir" Beirut, Friday, 18 January 2002.
## The Popular Front on the "trick" involved in the arrest of Ahmad Saadat

The Popular Front for the Liberation of Palestine explained to "as-Safir" the facts about the trick played on the Front's General Secretary, Ahmad Saadat that led to his arrest. The Popular Front's representative from the leadership outside Palestine, Mahir al-Tahir, told "as-Safir" that the story began about two weeks ago when the head of the Public Security

Agency on the West Bank, Colonel Tawfiq al-Tayrawi, began to insist that the leaders of the Popular Front arrange a meeting between him and Saadat. During this period the Palestinian President, Yasir Arafat, discussed the matter of Saadat with the deputy General Secretary of the Popular Front, Abd al-Rahim Mallouh. Arafat explained to Mallouh that Saadat was not wanted by the Palestine Authority for anything and that no one was pressuring the Authority to arrest him.

The Popular Front responded to the insistence of al-Tayrawi and agreed to hold a meeting on condition that it be in a public place. A place was chosen for the meeting on this basis—a hotel in the middle of the city of Ramallah. Saadat went to the meeting together with another leading member of the Popular Front, Bashir al-Khayri, who is also a lawyer.

Just five minutes after the meeting began, about 200 men of the Palestinian security forces surrounded the hotel and raided the place where the meeting was underway. An argument then broke out between the Preventive Security Forces under Colonlel Jibril al-Rajjoub, and the Public Security Forces led by al-Tayrawi. Opinions differ at this point about the reason for the argument, whether it was about who would get the "honor" of arresting Saadat or about the arrest itself.

The rival forces were compelled to "seek help" from the Palestinian presidency which accepted the "honor" of the arrest from both of the services. In this way Saadat was brought the headquarters of the Palestinian presidency in Ramallah. At the same time Mallouh arrived at the headquarters of the presidency along with others to meet with Arafat.

Mallouh objected to the arrest of Saadat and demanded his immediate release. But Arafat replied to this request that Saadat was his "guest" and not under arrest and that there is not in fact any order for his arrest.
—"as-Safir"
The Popular Front for the Liberation of Palestine
Branch of the Palestinian (West) Bank
31 December 2001.

## January 24, 2002
### Press Release
Ramallah: Commenting on statements by Qatar's foreign minister in the United States yesterday, the Popular Front for the Liberation of Palestine stated that these are expressions of the decline into which the official Arab regimes have fallen. After the events of 11 September they have yielded to American dictates. The Popular Front stated that the words uttered by Qatar's foreign minister encourage Zionist aggression and American pressure on the Palestinian people, and they constitute an indication of what kind of resolutions the upcoming Arab summit may issue as regards the Arab and Palestinian struggle with the Zionists.

The statement by the Popular Front noted that the deteriorated and divided condition of the official Arab regimes today, requires that the Arab people stand up to resist this condition. It called on the Arab peoples and their political parties and trade unions to move quickly to put a stop to such destructive moral collapse. The statement also called for the convening of an Arab People's Congress, parallel with the session of the Arab summit, that would affirm the Arab nation's resistance to Zionist-American aggression against their land and the dignity of their peoples.

**January 24, 2002**
**Press Release**
**Comrade Jamil al-Majdalawi, member of the Political Bureau of the Popular Front for the Liberation of Palestine, has made the following statement:**
After many comments in the press and elsewhere have been made regarding the alleged "declaration" attributed to the Martyr Abu Ali Mustafa Brigades issued on 23 January 2002, I wish to affirm the following:

1. All of the Front's authorities have confirmed that none of them have issued the above-mentioned "declaration," and that they reject the expressions, denunciations of some people as "traitors," and other epithets contained in the document, all of which are alien to the Popular Front and its political rhetoric and language.

2. We advocate and work for assuring, strengthening, and reinforcing Palestinian national unity so that we can all confront the Israeli aggression of the criminal Sharon government against our people and holy places.

3. The continuing detention of Comrade General Secretary Ahmad Saadat, to the extent that it inflicts great damage on Palestinian national unity and relations, gives an opportunity to the enemies of our people, to the frustrated seekers of revenge, and to anyone who wants to fish in troubled waters to cause still more harm to our unity and to the cohesion of our people's ranks. It allows them to spread discord in the ranks of the people and their militant forces. For this reason we have turned and we are turning to everyone, and in particular to Brother President Abu Ammar (Yasir Arafat) that he may issue his order immediately freeing Comrade Ahmad Saadat, so that we might together and irrevocably close the gates of evil and block the way to all such miserable attempts at sowing discord.

**January 25, 2002**
**Press Release issued by the General Secretary of the Popular Front for the Liberation of Palestine**

In response to reports that political and security sources in the Palestine Authority present my arrest as part of an attempt to discover the location of the heroic comrades accused of killing the racist Zionist minister Rehebam Ze'evi, I am distressed that such statements have been made. They do not excuse or detract from the true issue of my arrest, which openly affronts all sincere efforts to raise the unity of our people and their political forces in defending themselves in the war waged by Sharon against their existence, principles, and national rights. I affirm the following facts:

First. It is delusional to believe that the Popular Front will entertain the notion of bargaining for the lives and freedom of its heroic comrades, and whoever has succumbed to this way of thinking would be wise to refamiliarize himself with our organization's legacy. The freedom of comrades is not even a matter for discussion in our central bodies. The leaders of the Popular Front will defend the freedom of their comrades at any cost, including their own lives. The Popular Front will remain the spearhead of the mass democratic struggle to safeguard democracy and to end all political arrests and the pursuit of militants.

Second. The Palestinian leadership must understand that its compliance with Israeli-American pressures and dictates only moves it from one narrow corner to an even narrower one. It invites even further pressures being brought to bear against it, leading to an endless and unacceptable series of dictates. It will reverse the achievements won by our people's sacrifices over the nearly sixteen months of intifada and resistance. The policy of tightening the noose on Palestinian militants accommodates the forces of Zionist occupation, but it will not satisfy them, as their appetite for our destruction is insatiable.

Third. The amelioration of our people's plight and the promotion of their national cause require utilizing all the resources at our disposal, contained within various political forces, to reorder the internal Palestinian situation and its institutions on patriotic and democratic bases. The objectives also require drawing up a strategic political program for continuing the intifada and the resistance in defense of our people and their firm principles. Therefore, it is the obligation of all patriotic and Islamic forces to wage the democratic struggle to safeguard our people's unity and tighten their ranks while expanding the scope of that struggle to social, as well as political, realms. Democracy is the wall that protects our unity, increases our strength dozens of times over, and provides the best method for opposing the aggression of the racist, Zionist Sharon government.

The General Secretary of the Popular Front for the Liberation of Palestine while under the detention of the Palestinian Authority
25 January 2002

**January 30, 2002**
**Press Release**

*Ramallah:* The Popular Front for the Liberation of Palestine has commented on the Zionist government's plan to isolate Jerusalem from the rest of the Palestinian territories. The Popular Front said that these are steps that lead to the practical annexation of the City of Jerusalem. In addition, this plan also involves expanding the area to be isolated in accordance with the old plans for the old, yet new, Greater Jerusalem scheme.

The Popular Front pointed out that although this plan is being pursued under the camouflage of its being for security purposes, it nevertheless imposes political facts on the ground that dispel all the prevalent illusions in the policy of the Palestine Authority about Jerusalem being a subject for negotiations with the Zionist government. This plan confirms that the Zionist government is continuing with its plan to gobble up our land, colonize it, and Judaize it, without regard for any agreements.

The Popular Front stressed that these steps by the Zionist government must serve as a new lesson for the Palestine Authority about the possibility of negotiating with the Zionists or of even reaching partial agreements on this subject.

The Popular Front believes that the Zionist government decision contravenes international resolutions concerning Jerusalem, and it calls on the international community to shoulder its responsibility regarding this matter. The Front also calls on the Arab and Islamic states and their peoples to act, for Jerusalem is not only a Palestinian issue, it is an Arab and Islamic issue. The Front called on the Palestinian masses to hold fast to the choice of resistance and intifada, and to continue with them and not bet on any of the illusions that still find a place in the approach of official Palestinian policy. The Popular Front said that Jerusalem will remain Arab Palestinian land in spite of all the arbitrary steps that the terrorist Sharon government may take.

Central Information Department
Press Office—Palestine
30 January 2002.

**February 1, 2002**
**Press Release**

In light of the fact that comrade Ahmad Saadat, the General Secretary of the Popular Front for the Liberation of Palestine, continues to be detained under arrest by the security agencies of the Palestine Authority for nearly three weeks, on the basis of a political decision by the Authority's leadership—something that constitutes a qualitative precedent in Palestinian national relations and an encroachment upon the unity and legitimacy of the Palestine Liberation Organization, the sole legal representative of our people wherever they are located, since the Popular Front for the Liberation of Palestine is a basic and founding organization in the PLO and the second organization in it in accordance with a resolution of the Palestine National Council,

And after we have for three weeks given an opportunity for the brothers on the Palestinian and Arab stage, in particular the leaders of the patriotic and Islamic forces in Palestine and the members of the National and Central Councils, to make sincere efforts and to play their role in securing the release of the comrade General Secretary, the Palestinian leadership has not responded to all of these sincere attempts. Therefore, we have resolved, in protest against the decision to arrest the comrade General Secretary. To suspend the participation of the Popular Front for the Liberation of Palestine in the activity of the Executive Committee of the Palestine Liberation Organization until the comrade General Secretary is released.

The release of comrade Ahmad Saadat and of all political prisoners constitutes the necessary basis for strengthening our steadfastness and unity in confrontation with the occupation and aggression. Actual practice has shown that our steadfastness and our hold on our rights in the intifada and resistance is the basis for implementing the pertinent resolutions of international legality and for carrying out the program of the Palestine Liberation Organization, the program of national consensus— the return, self-determination, and an independent state with Jerusalem as its capital.

We view as extremely dangerous the detention of the comrade General Secretary and a number of heroes of the intifada and the resistance, because it comes in compliance with the American pressure and Israeli extortion that have no limits, because it inflicts tremendous harm on the intifada of our people in confrontation with the occupation, and whets the appetite of Sharon and his government for putting on more political and military pressure to weaken the Palestinians subjectively, with the aim of imposing conditions of surrender upon them.

From our position in the Palestine Liberation Organization, and in the Palestinian national liberation movement, we call on our brothers in the patriotic and Islamic forces, on the movements and prominent members of our people, on all Palestinians in the homeland and dispersal to undertake their responsible role to work and struggle to close the file on political arrests, to cancel emergency regulations, and to ban political arrests in order to protect the supreme national interests of our people and to safeguard their unity and steadfastness in confrontation with the occupation and aggression.

We approach President Arafat personally, the leading responsible person and the one who has political decision-making power, to release immediately comrade Ahmad Saadat, the General Secretary of the Popular

Front for the Liberation of Palestine, and we call on the Executive Committee of the Palestine Liberation Organization to play its desired role in freeing the comrade General Secretary and all the Palestinian political prisoners in the prisons of the Palestine Authority and to shoulder its responsibility during this critical stage of the life of our people's current revolution to deny the enemies of our people any chance and to hold fast by the people's aims of return, self-determination, and establishment of a Palestinian state with Jerusalem as its capital.

The Political Bureau
The Popular Front for the Liberation of Palestine
1 February 2002.

**February 5, 2002**
**Press Release**
**The Popular Front for the Liberation of Palestine rejects the description of our people's resistance as "terrorism" and the encroachment on our established national principles.**

Ramallah: Commenting on what President Yasir Arafat wrote in his letter to the New York Times newspaper, the Popular Front for the Liberation of Palestine has said in a statement that it is a cause for condemnation and astonishment that the Palestinian President would describe organizations of the legitimate, defensive Palestinian resistance against the occupation as "terrorist" at a time when American imperialism and the Zionist entity strive intentionally to mix up terrorist acts with the legitimate resistance of subjugated peoples, first among whom are our Palestinian people, whose right to resist is guaranteed by international law and legality. The Popular Front added that such statements merely confirm the extent to which official Palestinian circles have gone in yielding to American-Zionist dictates at a time when our people need to defend themselves, their existence, and their legitimate rights, and to defend the legitimacy of their resistance and to secure an international umbrella for it by carrying out the broadest possible informational and diplomatic campaign to demonstrate that our people are the victims of terrorism.

The Popular Front posed the question: What is the meaning of President Arafat's remark—that he understands the Zionist entity state's demographic concerns as regards the right of our people's refugees to return to the homes, from which they were displaced at bayonet point, in accordance with United Nations Resolution 194? Does that not mean, when translated into political practice, a readiness in principle to bargain over this right? Does it not also mean a readiness to negotiate over the most minimum rights of our people that are expressly provided for by international law? The Popular Front said that such statements represent a violation of national consensus and encroach upon the established principles of the National Program that was agreed upon by the political and social forces of our people who have entrenched themselves to struggle for its realization. The Popular Front affirmed that the right of our people's refugees to return to the homes from which they were displaced has been, is, and will remain the core of the Palestinian cause, the corner stone of the National Program, and a bridge linking this present stage with the ultimate aims of our people in regaining their rights.

The Popular Front concluded its statement by rejecting and condemning these remarks that constitute a danger for our people's struggle, for their rights, and for the unity of their forces. The remarks can start a series of American-Israeli demands and pressures that will not end until they have imposed surrender upon our people. The Popular Front called on the masses of our people, on the resistance activists, to reject these remarks and to continue to hold fast to the established national principles of our people and their legitimate rights, in the first place the right of the refugees to return to the homes from which they were displaced, and to continue to do battle in the intifada and resistance with all their various forms and methods, until the occupation is driven out and our people's rights to return, to freedom, and to full independence are seized back.

Press Office
Palestine
5 February 2002

## February 7, 2002
## Press Release
## The Public Security Agency on the West Bank under Colonel Tawfiq al-Tayrawi continues its kidnappings and torture of the resistance activists.

*Ramallah:* A statement issued by the Popular Front for the Liberation of Palestine states that on the night before last, the Palestine Authority's public security agency on the West Bank under Colonel Tawfiq al-Tayrawi kidnapped Muhammad Abd al-Rasoul Saadat, the brother of Comrade Ahmad Saadat, the General Secretary of the Popular Front. Muhammad Saadat was taken blindfolded to a house in the city of al-Bireh and bound with his hands behind his back for more than two hours. All of this for no reason other than that he is the brother of the Comrade General Secretary.

The PFLP statement added that this is not the first time that this agency has used such methods as kidnapping and denying, for a period of time, that they were holding militants. The practice was employed about a month ago against a social activist that the security agency believed was a Popular Front activist. It was used again four days ago against an employee of one of the health care institutions, the citizen Walid Abu Ras, whose wife and aged mother—who endured the hardship of having to cross the through checkpoints of the Zionist occupation forces that divide the south of the West Bank from its central area—were not allowed to visit him.

The Popular Front statement said that this repressive security agency behavior is reminiscent of the practices of security apparatuses of military juntas in Latin America during the 1970s. It comes at a time when the security situation that our country and society are experiencing is already complicated, filled with incidents of crime, and increasing tribalist, confessionalist, and factionalist tendencies. This is a time when this agency and other agencies of the Palestine authority should take part together with all the patriotic and Islamic forces of our people in providing security and stability for the homeland and the Palestinian citizens, protecting them from being violated by the enemy who is always seeking ways to break down the unity, cohesiveness, and steadfastness of our people to Zionist aggression. This is not an occasion for behavior that could serve the agents of the occupation and their security agencies.

The Popular Front statement added that this resumption of the practice of kidnapping, spiriting people off, torturing them, and denying that the militants are being detained, followed a joint security meeting held by Palestinian security officials with the Israelis. The Popular Front statement concluded by warning the Palestinian Public Security Agency and its chief against the dangers inherent in this practice. It could break open gaps in the wall of our people's unity, cohesiveness, and national morale. The Front called on the responsible political authorities in the agency to prevent it from such shortsighted practices with all the dangers that they entail. The statement urged the masses of our people, their patriotic and Islamic political forces, and their social and public institutions to wage the broadest possible democratic campaign against political arrests and the police practices of the security agencies and against crime in the society, as one way to raise the capacity of our people to stand steadfast and resist the Israeli aggression that aims at subjugating our people and imposing its surrender conditions upon them.

Central Information Office
Press Department
7 February 2002.

## February16, 2002
## Press Release
## The PLO Executive Committee Declaration continues the illusion of betting on America to help

Ramallah: The Popular Front for the Liberation of Palestine has commented in a statement on the results of the meetings of the Executive Committee of the Palestine Liberation Organization. They confirm, the PFLP says, that the official Palestinian leadership continues to maintain its illusions about an "American solution" without any justification for such reliance on the US, given the positions that America has taken, both openly and covertly, with respect to our cause.

The Popular Front statement said that the Palestine Authority leadership, despite all the clear American stances that are hostile our people and their aspirations, continues to respond to and comply with American pressures and dictates, continues to yearn for the return of an American representative even though such a representative will come out with proposals that do not differ in any way from those offered by Anthony Zinni. The Popular Front pointed out that the Executive Committee came out with the results of its discussions at the very time of George Tenet's return to the region and in the framework of this activity that only indicates that the US continues to treat this political national cause as a security problem that requires securing more Palestinian concessions and more Palestinian compliance with American-Israeli conditions.

The Popular Front in its statement sharply criticized talk about official Palestinian commitment to the so-called cease-fire at a time of dangerous escalation by Sharon that has taken on new features after the Zionist occupation of the villages of Tammoun, Sayda, Halhoul, and others, and the attempt to construct a security belt in the Gaza district. The Popular Front underlined its position of rejecting the so-called cease-fire, on the grounds that resistance is a legitimate right, granted not only by international law, but by the continued Israeli attacks. The Popular Front's statement also criticized the Executive Committee for failing to mention the right of return in the results of its meeting.

The Popular Front statement called on the Palestine Authority to beware of America's practices in the coming period, in light of its recent campaign against Iraq and Iran, something that will affect our national cause negatively. That campaign points to the possibility that the regional role of the Zionist entity will be reinforced.

The Popular Front also called for continuing to hold fast to the option of resistance and intifada. It called for a halt to pursuit and arrest of militants and for the release of those imprisoned for resisting the occupation, first among them the General Secretary of the Popular Front for the Liberation of Palestine, Ahmad Saadat.

Central Press Department
Press Office
Palestine
16 February 2002.

**February 18, 2002**

**Political Statement—(communiqué)—Issued by the Political Bureau of the Popular Front for the Liberation of Palestine.**

To the masses of our Palestinian people in the homeland and scattered abroad:

The Political Bureau of the Popular Front for the Liberation of Palestine convened a meeting in the first half of February 2002 that dealt with the Arab, regional, and international developments surrounding our national cause. After saluting the steadfastness of our people as they confront the escalation of Zionist aggression supported by the American Administration, the Political Bureau noted the following:

1. The American war program under the signboard of fighting terrorism in order to strengthen the means for imposing imperialist hegemony is continuing. The Arab region occupies the chief place in this program, the aggression against Afghanistan being only one link in its chain. In accordance with this program, US hegemony is not necessarily to be effected only by means of warfare but also by a series of economic, political, and intelligence measures. The low level of global objection by peoples and governments to what took place in Afghanistan has encouraged the American Administration to go further and to direct its threats with rudeness and impudence at the states and forces that stand up against the policy of hegemony (such as Iraq, Iran, North Korea, Hizb Allah, and the organizations of the Palestinian resistance), indicating that the Middle East region faces new aggressive acts.

2. Within the framework of the links between America's plans for this region and the regional role of the Zionist entity in these plans, the Zionist unity government has escalated its aggression against our people qualitatively (tightening the total blockade; destroying houses in Rafah and Jerusalem; increasing the intensity of destructive bombing and shelling of Palestine Authority national security offices; launching incursions into Tulkarm, Bayt Hanoun, Tammoun, Sayda, and Halhoul; and stationing tanks just meters from the headquarters of President Arafat . . .) Probably the state of panic and fragmentation that afflicts official Arab circles, indeed their complicity at some stages, has helped reduce America's caution about returning to a policy of total congruence with the policy of the Zionist entity government, providing political cover for its acts of aggression, and abandoning even the taste (a bribe) of vague support for the establishment of a Palestinian state that the US expressed before the beginning of its campaign against Afghanistan.

3. In light of the above-mentioned international and Arab circumstances, it was absolutely necessary that the highest level of exactness be used in drawing up a Palestinian national strategy for struggle. But the Palestine Authority and its leadership resorted to a policy of counting down, calling for a cease-fire, declaring a State of Emergency, closing down offices, declaring the military wings of some Palestinian organizations to be illegal, labeling the resistance and resistance organizations as "terrorist," going beyond partial political arrests to return to the practice of broad campaigns of sweeping arrests and the serious hunting down of militants and their weapons. These measures, carried out under the slogan of depriving the Sharon government of its excuses, have only led to more Zionist aggression, more American pressures, and to European activity that timidly differs relatively from the American position by opposing the rude impression of American policy, or by urging that the Palestinian struggle against the Zionists not be treated exclusively as a security problem. The decline of official Palestinian policy has gone so far that a return to where things were before the intifada broke out has become their dream, whereas it used to be an Israeli demand. This decline brought back serious signs of shaken faith and frustration to the Palestinian street. It has undermined the unity in the field that grew strong in the battles of the intifada and resistance, setting off warning bells of the worsening of internal contradictions that appeared recently in the outbursts of tribalist, group, and factional feuds in which unfortunately the Authority's security agencies played a role, where they should have been a part of the effort to prevent and treat such occurrences.

In view of this reality, the Political Bureau of the Popular Front affirms and calls for the following:

First. The nature of international circumstances after 11 September, and what they represent as seen in the content of the American imperialist war, do not contain anything that can push the cause of our people forward. The American war against what it calls terrorism involves, among other things, a war against our people's resistance that is based on the resolutions of the United Nations and international law. Therefore Palestinians cannot protect themselves and defend Palestinian goals by trying to get out of the path of the crazed American bull—its rage is studied and intentional and not some emotional reaction. Rather it must be confronted by a policy of self-defense and defense of our rights, by focusing on defending the legitimacy of our people's resistance. International support for the resistance must be secured by waging the broadest possible informational and diplomatic campaign to demonstrate the fact that our people are the victims of the terrorism and the crimes committed by the occupation with such open American political cover that George Tenet, Director of the American Central Intelligence Agency, went so far as to list Hamas, the Islamic Jihad, and the Popular Front for the Liberation of Palestine as targets of American aggression. Tenet ignored the fact that organizations of Palestinian national activity and resistance in general only emerged as a result of the occupation, and with legitimization by international documents and United Nations resolutions. These organizations will not disappear until the occupation ends and the national rights of our people to their return, to freedom, and to independence are attained.

Second. Waging a broad popular democratic struggle, strengthening national steadfastness and unity in the field, and the demanding that the Palestine Authority stop complying with American-Israeli demands—these are necessary conditions for bringing more factors of Palestinian strength to bear on the confrontation with the Zionist aggression that depends on American political cover and the fragmented and impotent state of official Arab regimes.

Third. The need to stand firm in order to stop the collapse of some class strata in Palestinian decision-making circles that have been opposed to the intifada and the renewal of the resistance struggle since the beginning. They applied pressure to gain acceptance of what was proposed at Camp David, and they are pushing now for acceptance of what is called the Abu `Ala'—Peres Agreement and the open statement on the possibility of bargaining over and encroaching upon established national principles, first among them the return of Palestinian refugees to their homes in accordance with UN Resolution 194.

Fourth. The impotence of official Arab regimes does not diminish the importance of the initiative to activate the machinery of Arab national popular struggle, and to participate actively in initiatives on this level.

Fifth. Reasserting the importance of the popular democratic nature of the intifada is a matter of the utmost importance. The armed resistance is a reserve for this side, not a substitute for it. Activation of the mass organizations, popular federations, and peoples' associations must not be limited to energizing their role in the battles being waged on the ground, but must extend to their participation in the effort to build bridges to similar organizations in the Arab world, in this region, and internationally in order to broaden the spheres of support and assistance for our national cause and the right of our people to resist the occupation.

To the masses of our people:

In concluding its political review, the Political Bureau examined the offense committed by the Palestine Authority of waging a campaign of political arrests that culminated in the arrest of the comrade General Secretary Ahmad Saadat.

After expressing thanks and high esteem for all those who have participated in the political, informational, and mass campaign on the Palestinian and Arab levels to secure the release of the General Secretary and to condemn the arrest for the serious political implications that are inherent in it, and the real dangers it poses for national unity, the Political Bureau expressed its condemnation and astonishment at statements by the Palestine Authority and its leadership that link the arrest of our comrade the General Secretary to the effort to arrest the heroic comrades accused by Israel of liquidating that symbol of Zionist extremism, Ze'evi. Such statements go a long way to making internal Palestinian affairs subject to American-Zionist dictates, going so far as to entertain the illusion of demanding that the leadership of the Popular Front turn in those heroic comrades to the Palestine Authority. This matter never was and never will be subject to discussion or deliberation. The Popular Front and its leadership have never been and never will be for political arrests of people for their opinions or for resisting the occupation. It does not share the illusion that leaders of the Palestine Authority entertain that more subservience to and compliance with Israeli dictates and demands is a way to break the blockade of our people or the President Yasir Arafat. The Israeli demands are endless. They are aimed at imposing conditions of surrender on our people.

Therefore the Political Bureau of the Popular Front, as it condemns the arrest of the comrade General Secretary and demands his immediate release together with all those detained by the Palestine Authority, it also rejects the pursuit of the heroic comrades accused of liquidating Ze'evi. The Political Bureau reiterates that it rejects on principle any discussion of the subject of their arrest.

The Political Bureau

The Popular Front for the Liberation of Palestine Palestine

18 February 2002.

**February 20, 2002**
**Press Release**
**The Massacres by the Zionists will not go Unpunished. For the Establishment of Armed National Defence Committees. Let our People dig in and defend themselves.**

*Ramallah:* Commenting on the criminal escalation of massacres by the Zionist unity government in the last two days, and the falling of dozens of our people as martyrs, the Popular Front for the Liberation of Palestine has said in a statement that the fascist massacres will never break the will of our people and its heroic resistance. They will never deter them from continuing the option of intifada and resistance.

Their resistance struggle has recently escalated and taken on qualitatively new features that have put Sharon's choice of using military and security means to stamp out the resistance in a genuinely tight spot and caused him to lose control. The Israeli street understands that Sharon's approach has failed.

The Popular Front statement appealed to the masses of our people to rally more closely around the resistance and its escalation. That is the shortest and the guaranteed path to expelling the occupation and to seizing back our people's rights of return, freedom, and independence.

The statement called on the Palestine Authority to cancel the existing State of Emergency and all the political arrests and closures of offices that have been based upon it. The PFLP calls on the Palestine Authority to declare that it is in confrontation with the Zionist massacres and to take immediate steps to form armed national defense committees for comprehensive national steadfastness now that Sharon's fascism has been unleashed. This will enable our people to dig in to defend themselves and the rights from which they have been robbed.

The Popular Front statement called on the masses of our Arab Nation to move, to pressure the official Arab regimes into shouldering their Arab national responsibility regarding the massacres that are being committed against the people of Palestine. These crimes are aimed at imposing conditions of surrender upon us. The Popular Front statement underlined the call on the United Nations Organization to provide temporary international protection for our people.

Central Information Department
Press Office
Palestine
20 February 2002.

## February 21, 2002
## Press Release

To the masses of our people in the homeland and scattered abroad.

The barbaric massacres by the government of Zionist unity of everything Palestinian are escalating. Our people and their resistance forces are resisting that qualitative escalation of Zionist aggression. The Palestinian resistance is taking qualitative steps forward and putting Sharon's security and military program in a genuine tight spot and knocking it off balance—something that requires more rallying around the option of resistance, the guaranteed path to the success of our national effort, and requires that everyone dig in on the fields of escalating the intifada and resistance.

At this critical time the public intelligence agency in the West Bank under Colonel Tawfiq al-Tayrawi has arrested comrade Ahid Abu Ghulma, member of the General Central Committee of the Popular Front, and comrades Hamdi Qaraan and Basil al-Asmar, accused by Israel of liquidating the symbol of Zionist extremism, Rehebam Ze'evi. This indicates, in fact it confirms, that the Palestine Authority continues to maintain the illusion that it can avoid the blows of the Sharon government by being even more submissive to American—Israeli dictates and by tying internal Palestinian affairs to these dictates. This contradicts the will of our people and their resistance forces and constitutes a grave danger to the unity of our people and the unity in the field that has grown strong among the resistance forces on the battlefields of the heroic intifada.

In this context, we in the Popular Front for the Liberation of Palestine, as we condemn, denounce, and deplore these arrests, we warn the leadership of the Authority of the dangers inherent in encroaching upon those comrades. We hold the Authority entirely responsible for their lives, and the lives of all the political prisoners who have been jailed for their opinions or for resisting the occupation. We demand the immediate release of all the political prisoners whom the Authority holds. We demand that pursuits, man hunts, interrogation, and torture of militants stop. This is the time for defense of the people and the homeland and for all the firmness that requires on the domestic front, so that we can tighten our muscles to provide the basis for steadfastness and resistance in the face of the crimes and continuing and escalating aggression of Sharon and his fascist government that is trying to impose its conditions of surrender upon our people.

The Popular Front for the Liberation of Palestine
Palestine

## February 21, 2002
### Press Release

Dr. Mahir al-Tahir, member of the Political Bureau of the Popular Front for the Liberation of Palestine and person responsible for leadership of the Front abroad, has made a statement in which he said:

At a time when the Palestinian people are being subjected to the most ferocious, terrorist, aggressive attack on their existence, on their present, and their future at the hand of the government of the criminal Sharon,

At a time when the Palestinian people are uniting all their ranks and all their patriotic and Islamic political forces to confront the continuous Zionist aggression, and to defend their land, their dignity, their honor, and their holy places,

At this time precisely, the Palestine Authority continues to pursue its policy of humiliating submission to Israeli dictates and orders. It arrests the Palestinian militants who defend their people and their homeland. An example of this is the arrest by the Palestine Authority's intelligence agency on the West Bank on the morning of 21 February 2002 of the militants Ahid Abu Ghulmah, Member of the General Central Committee of the Popular Front for the Liberation of Palestine, and of Hamdi Qaraan and Basil al-Asmar whom the Zionist occupation authorities accuse of assassinating Rehebam Ze'evi.

The Popular Front for the Liberation of Palestine demands that the Palestine Authority release the prisoners immediately. It holds the Authority, its security agencies, and Tawfiq al-Tayrawi completely responsible for this arrest.

The Palestine Authority and its security agencies practice a policy of torture, abduction, and arrests. They have abducted the brother of the militant Ahmad Saadat, General Secretary of the Popular Front for the Liberation of Palestine.

These repressive and irresponsible practices dangerously threaten Palestinian national unity, since it is impossible to establish national unity when there exist jailers and prisoners.

We call on all the organizations, the patriotic and Islamic forces, and on the masses of our Palestinian people in the homeland and in all the places that they have found refuge and wherever they are scattered abroad to raise their voices in loud condemnation of these practices and for the release of all the political prisoners from the Palestine Authority's jails.

The Popular Front for the Liberation of Palestine warns the Palestine Authority of the consequences that will entail from their measures and practices and their dangerous repercussions within the Palestinian arena.

Press Office
Damascus

## March 8, 2002
## Press Release

Ramallah: Commenting on the latest escalation of massacres and butchery committed by the government of Zionist unity against our people—the most recent examples of which took place in the refugee camps of Tulkarm, Nur Shams, al-Duhaysha, and Ayida, and in the villages of Absan, Khuza`a, Doura, and Halhoul, where dozens of victims have fallen as martyrs in the last two days—the Popular Front for the Liberation of Palestine has issued a statement that said:

These massacres come in the framework of desperate Zionist attempts to subjugate our people and impose surrender upon them. The statement added that the qualitative and courageous operations of the resistance that are carried out by our heroic fighters—most recently the operations in the Jewish settlement of Ariel and the Ghush Qatif junction—have caused the government of the Zionist enemy to lose its senses. They have confirmed the failure of Sharon's choice of military force to confront the intifada and Palestinian resistance. The PFLP statement said: in this connection, the Popular Front affirms and calls for the following:

First. The demand that the Security Council move immediately to insure temporary international protection for our people.

Second. The demand that the Palestine Authority refuse all cooperation with the American emissary Anthony Zinni. The aim of the American Administration in renewing his mission is to back up the Sharon government in its attempts to undermine the intifada and the Palestinian resistance.

Third. The need for all forms of security coordination and political contact with the government of the Zionist enemy to be stopped, especially since the Zionist assassination operations have struck at the highest levels of the Palestinian security forces, most recently with the assassination of Colonel Ahmad Mefraj, Commander of the National Security forces in south Gaza, and the attempted assassination of Marshal Abd al-Razzaq al-Mujayida, Commander of the National Security forces in the Gaza districts.

Fourth. An appeal to the masses of our people, to their patriotic and Islamic forces and their military wings, for greater unity and that they entrench themselves on the field of struggle in self-defense and for the continuation of the option of resistance until the occupation is driven out, and the national rights of our people to return, to freedom, and to independence are seized back.

Press Office
Palestine
8 March 2002.

**March 10, 2002**
**Press Release**
**The Peres—Qurei meeting is against the will of our people and gives a political cover for Sharon's massacres.**

Ramallah: The Popular Front for the Liberation of Palestine has commented about the meeting between Israeli Foreign Minister, Shimon Peres, and Speaker of the Palestinian Parliament, Ahmad Qurei. The Popular Front stated that this meeting constitutes a departure from the will of the Palestinian people and provides a political cover for the crimes, the massacres, and the mass butchery of the government of Zionist unity and for its decision to continue and intensify these crimes against our people, as it also circumvents the option of resistance struggle that has brought Sharon's military program to a real impasse after the qualitative blows of the resistance demonstrated the failure of this program in its confrontation with the intifada and resistance. The Popular Front statement added that this meeting takes place as a result of American pressure and dictate in order to undermine the intifada and resistance. It follows the failure of American policy to convince world public opinion of its description of our people's resistance struggle as "terrorism," and it comes in preparation for the visit of the US administration's Vice President, Dick Cheney, to the region to make the arrangements for expected American aggression against fraternal Iraq.

The Popular Front statement demanded that the leadership of the Palestine Authority stop fantasizing about driving the Sharon government into political negotiations because even if this is accomplished, it will mean nothing more than a return to square one of the fruitless negotiations that brought great suffering to our people when, for a period of ten years, Palestinian time and efforts were wasted for the sake of the Zionist security agenda. The statement said that this meeting constitutes a stab in the side of Arab and international support for our people's choice of continuing to resist the occupation and its on-going aggression, the latest example of that support being the demonstration of fifty thousand people in Rome.

The Popular Front statement called on the masses of our people, on the patriotic and Islamic forces and their military resistance wings not to look to useless meetings such as this, but to continue the option of resistance, the most effective way to drive out the occupation and seize back the national rights of our people to return, freedom, and independence.

Press Office
Palestine
10 March 2002.

## 13 May 2002
### Press Release from Dr. George Habash

On the Anniversary of the Disaster in Palestine

On the occasion of the 54th anniversary of the disaster in Palestine Dr. George Habash, founder of the Popular Front for the Liberation of Palestine and the Arab Nationalists' movement, made the following address to the masses of the Palestinian people in the homeland and disbursed abroad, and to the Arab Nation:

Among all the things in the Palestinian memory of struggle for freedom and independence, we observe today the anniversary of the disaster of 15 May 1948, there having passed since that tragic day 54 years. We hold the international community completely responsible for the occurrence of that disaster. Despite the fact that our unarmed Palestinian people have not put an end to the difficulties they must endure as a result of that disaster, they fearlessly proceed to confront even more difficult and more hideous conditions as a result of the massacres, the sieges, the mass arrests, and the destruction at the hands of the Zionist military machine, the occupation army, and the barbaric Zionist army criminals who planned this aggression against our children women and elderly, afflicting the very life and existence of a whole people under siege.

In what is called the existence of historic turning points there is a transitional path that the Palestinian cause is traversing to confront a serious political massacre after the intifada and legitimate Palestinian resistance struggle had already faced the military massacres. It has become apparent that targeting the resistance and intifada is one of the priorities on the American-Zionist agenda. We face qualitatively new realities that require us to adopt a contemporary viewpoint to understand the meaning of the 1948 disaster.

The historic ability of our people to continue militantly in the resistance movement and intifada has become a source of assuredness. As a result of our great experience in the Palestinian struggle, we do not have the slightest doubt that our people can guard the resistance and intifada with all the power and steadfastness they have been given, that the burning coal of the Palestinian resistance struggle has not been and never will be put out under the ashes, that the Palestinian rising is guaranteed by its Arab national dimension, and that the Arab masses have built bridges to the intifada and steadfastness of the Palestinian people to move from a position of support to active participation in the Palestinian struggle.

A change has taken place in the course of the last fifty years. The disaster represented by the expulsion and forcible exile of a whole people; it is represented by the occupation of the land, by the takeover by Zionist gangs of Palestine, by the Zionist enemy's terrorism in committing massacres in Palestine; it is represented by the international plot to aid the existence of the cancerous settler colonialism in its spread throughout the land of Palestine to establish a false entity under the name of the "Partition Resolution" and other unjust resolutions that left a new reality in the land of Palestine. Thereafter the immoral international plot reached out to turn our Palestinian people into nothing but refugees awaiting their return to their homes. This plot, led by the imperialist colonial countries, has served to perpetuate the plight of the refugees. More than that, imperialist interests have become interwoven, further obstructing the possibility to establish a Palestinian state or to exercise genuine Palestinian sovereignty over the land.

Historically the imperialist countries have worked beside the Zionist entity to expand the sphere of the Arab-Israeli struggle to create a new reality in the genocidal war against the Palestinian people, so that our struggle with the Zionist enemy would become a struggle for existence. The Palestinian resistance struggle has been able, since its inception and until today, to embrace and protect the legitimate rights of the Palestinian people. With the first and second heroic intifadas our people have been able to give concrete form, through their struggle and sacrifices, to a path of securing freedom and independence. They have escalated the struggle to sweep away and eliminate the occupation in order to reach the goal of establishing an independent, completely sovereign Palestinian state with Jerusalem as its capital and with its chief goal being the sacred right to return.

Our Palestinian people are persisting in their choice of liberation despite great wounds and afflictions, despite the siege, despite all the

forms of genocidal war that the butcher Sharon and his American partner Bush have chosen, after the whole world has witnessed the bloody
war into which the Zionist war criminals have plunged with the complete
connivance and planning of the imperialist American administration, and
in the absence of any international legality, after the commission of inquiry
into the massacres in Jenin, Nablus, and elsewhere, was disbanded. Our
people are facing the most ferocious, barbaric American-Zionist power
that is attempting to break the will and steadfastness of the Palestinian
people. But the reply to this has come in unison from our people who
unfalteringly resort to steadfastness as their only option, Palestinian steadfastness with humanist will.

The anniversary of the disaster comes today to teach again the lessons and examples of history so that we can rise to a comprehensive
evaluation of all that has transpired in the Palestinian arena, and all that
is transpiring in the Arab environment both on the level of the people
and on the official level, with the necessities imposed by the nature of
the future militant tasks. We therefore affirm the following:

1. A review of all the recent practices of the Palestine Authority,
   including arbitrary trials and arrests and expulsions of militants,
   and on that basis a demand for clear political rhetoric, opposed
   to squandering the great sacrifices that our Palestinian people have
   made, heedless of the pressures brought to bear upon us.

2. Our great Palestinian people are waiting for a change to take place
   in the leadership, moving toward collective democratic participation in political decisions, eliminating the go-it-alone style of leadership, and bringing the security agencies into account for all the
   offenses and mistakes they have committed.

3. The need for a comprehensive review and evaluation to be made
   of all the errors that threaten Palestinian national unity. I also call
   on the Palestine Authority leadership to depart from the path of
   shame and to act immediately to free the General Secretary of the
   Popular Front for the Liberation of Palestine, comrade Ahmad
   Saadat, and brother Fu'ad al-Shawbaki and to review the cases of
   the four heroic militants who have been arrested on the excuse
   that they eliminated the racist war criminal Ze'evi.

4. National unity must be strengthened in the field and politically to
   confront the Zionist enemy as it expands its aggression against
   the cities, villages, and refugee camps of the Palestinian Bank and
   Gaza District.

On the anniversary of the Disaster, I send my greetings to our steadfast people under siege in Ramallah, Jenin, Nablus, al-Khalil (Hebron),
Tulkarm, and the Gaza District. I salute on this occasion the struggle of

our Arab Palestinian people in Galilee, the Triangle, and the Naqab (Negev) and their participation in operations to bring aid and support to their steadfast brethren in the West Bank and Gaza District. I convey a big salute to the mothers and families of the martyrs and to the prisoners detained in the Zionist jails, and I call on the Palestinian people to be steadfast and confront the continuing Zionist aggression.

Comrade Dr. George Habash Founder of the Popular Front for the Liberation of Palestine and The Arab Nationalists' Movement.

## March 28, 2002
### Press Release
### Resolutions of the Arab Summit indicate submission to American dictates

The Popular Front for the Liberation of Palestine views the resolutions of the Arab summit as a disappointment to the masses of our Palestinian people and our Arab Nation and, therefore, a disappointment to the intifada and resistance struggle. The resolutions have focused on the Saudi initiative as the only option for peace and disregarded all other alternatives. In doing so they have marginalized practical incentives for supporting the intifada and resistance in Palestine. Worse, the Saudi initiative has been transformed into a Pan-Arab initiative based on an unacceptable strategic concession: willingness to consider ending the struggle and normalizing relations with the Zionist Entity—which in turn offers no evidence of its readiness to cooperate, as by abandoning its permanent refusal to implement United Nations resolutions pertinent to the Arab-Zionist struggle.

The Popular Front rejects negotiations on the subject of Palestinian refugees' right to return to the homes from which they were forcibly expelled. We insist that this right be upheld in accord with UN Resolution 194. The resolutions of the Arab summit have highlighted the ineptitude and weakness of the official Arab regimes, as well as their unconscionable submission to American dictates, oblivious to the will of the Arab masses who have taken to the streets in demanding official support for the Palestinian resistance struggle. The official Arab regimes desecrate the legacy of our martyrs by failing to meet the minimum aspirations of the Palestinian people, they insult our people's sacrifices, and they will find no end to our steadfastness in the face of the escalating Zionist aggression.

The Popular Front, while welcoming progress toward a solution to the impasse of Iraqi-Kuwaiti relations, must insist that the Arab Nation encourage officials to take full advantage of every diplomatic, legal, and moral opportunity at their disposal to halt the devastating embargo on Iraq. We also call for the activation of a joint defense agreement to forestall American plans to attack Iraq and, otherwise, to sustain prolonged military and/or economic retaliation.

These declarations, however sincere and passionate, must be tempered by urging the masses of the Palestinian people not to dwell on the many shortcomings evident at official levels but, instead, to focus their efforts on redoubling the intifada and carrying our resistance struggle through to its glorious final objective. We beseech the masses of the Arab Nation to maintain their support for Palestinians' militant heroism, to continue rallying around it, and to pressure the official Arab regimes to break free of their cycle of submission to American dictates.

Press Office, Palestine, 28 March 2002

## May 15, 2002
## Press Release

In regard to the speech by President Yasir Arafat in the Palestinian Legislative Assembly, the Political Bureau of the Popular Front for the Liberation of Palestine affirms the following: First In light of the total aggression to which the Palestinian people are being subjected, and in light of the general experiences of past years, the Palestinian situation demands a radical review of the political and organizational structures responsible for having brought the Palestinian people to where they are today. Second the speech by President Arafat did not contain any mention of the resistance struggle and the intifada, thus insulting the many sacrifices made by our people as they courageously resist Zionist aggression. This omission came at a time when the Palestinian people are waging a diligent campaign of national liberation to earn their long-delayed freedom and independence, to eject the illegal occupation, and to guarantee that the basic necessities of their right to return, to claim self-determination, and to establish a Palestinian state with Jerusalem as its capital. Third the speech by President Arafat did not contain any mention of the Palestine Liberation Organization, which in the past has proved to be the most effective legal representative of the Palestinian people and which must retain this role in the present and future. The PLO provides an all-embracing framework for the Palestinian people, wherever they currently may reside, within the borders of our homeland or outside them as the consequence of being forced to seek refuge. Fourth when President Arafat stated his responsibility for the current situation, he avoided referring to the most controversial issues that have been resolutely condemned by the Palestinian and Arab masses: the militants imprisoned in Jericho under American-British guard and the arrest of Comrade Ahmad Saadat, General Secretary of the Popular Front for the Liberation of Palestine. It is a further disappointment that President Arafat also avoided referring to the prisoners and detainees held by the occupation forces, and the fate of the Palestinians sent into exile after the siege of Bethlehem. Fifth the Popular Front for the Liberation of Palestine has been involved throughout numerous phases of the Palestinian national struggle and previously has called for a comprehensive, radical reform of all Palestinian structures and institutions. It renews this call today when developments are unfolding with profound urgency, anguish, and the perpetual hope that lies at the core of the resistance movement.

The Popular Front calls for the reconstruction of the political and organizational bases of the PLO, and for the establishment of collective leadership mechanisms, drawing together all structures and institutions of Palestinian society, inside and outside the homeland, furthering the principle of free democratic elections, subject to supervision as a means of guaranteeing their impartiality and exemption from external intervention.Sixth.

As regards internal Palestinian conditions in the West Bank and Gaza District, the Popular Front affirms its principled opposition to the practices of the Palestine Authority over the last eight years, which have been characterized by corruption and despotism.

Therefore, the Popular Front affirms its insistence for all Palestinian social problems and issues in the homeland to be dealt with on the basis of local and municipal elections held in accord with democratic and pluralistic ideals. Popular Front for the Liberation of Palestine, Political Bureau, 15 May 2002.

**May 15, 2002**
**Press Release**

We observe the fifty-fourth anniversary of the rape of Palestine and the imposition of the Zionist entity as a dagger in the heart of the Arab homeland, a dagger thrust with the full complicity of the colonial powers before the international community that refused to intervene, betraying its own humanitarian ideals.We join our people in reflecting upon this anniversary that comes in the wake of another fierce Israeli offensive against our cities, villages, and refugee camps, which brought death, destruction, and brutality to everyone found therein.

Our Palestinian people are writing the finest pages of resistance, glory, and steadfastness in their confrontation with the Zionist military establishment; they are producing more virtuous martyrs to ransom the soil of Palestine and its holy places, as one step in attaining their most legitimate, most imperative national rights to return, to claim self-determination, and to establish a Palestinian state with Jerusalem as its capital.

We mark this anniversary at a unique time in Arab history, when events are repeating themselves tragically, leaving the Palestinian people to their fate without adequate support from the official Arab regimes, recalling their inability in 1948 to defend the land of Palestine and to join the people of Palestine in warding off Zionist aggression.This is a unique time in Arab history, when the official Arab regimes are unable to defend pan-Arab security or the security of individual Arab states, and when the

Palestinian people are striving to fulfill this role, defending the honor of the Arab Nation as well as their own.

This is a unique time in Arab history, which demands the official Arab regimes and the Arab peoples and their political forces to review the nature of the Arab-Zionist conflict, paying special attention to its objective, historical characteristics, which can be applied to the review their political programs, their means for taking action, and their national and pan-Arab roles. This painful anniversary comes in the shadow of tremendously complicated and dangerous conditions, in the shadow of an offensive by the hostile Zionist-American alliance, directly waged by Zionists but sponsored by the Americans whose weapons are used to harvest the lives of thousands of martyrs and wounded, destroying the structures and institutions of Palestinian society, with the aim of imposing the dictates of surrender upon the Palestinian people and their militant political forces of vastly differing ideological orientation.

Despite these exceptional conditions in the life of the Palestinian people, the finest epics of struggle, steadfastness, and heroism have been written and in the process have foiled the Zionist-American plan to eliminate and defeat Palestinian memory and consciousness.Our people have confirmed and forever will continue to confirm their decision to maintain every possible means of resistance, struggle, and intifada until their goals of freedom and independence are attained.

On this occasion the Popular Front for the Liberation of Palestine affirms the following:

1. The Palestinian people will continue every form of intifada and resistance until all of their legitimate national rights have been met, from the right of return, to the right of self-determination, to the right of establishing an independent Palestinian state with Jerusalem as its capital. United Nations resolutions substantiate the right of the Palestinian people to resist the forces of occupation until these rights have implemented.

2. The battle being waged by the Palestinian people is a battle for liberation from forces of occupation, and it a battle of both self-defense and the defense of national and pan-Arab rights and honor.

3. The Popular Front for the Liberation of Palestine emphasizes the need to build a solid political foundation to enhance Palestinian national unity and uphold national principles and resolutions determined by national consensus.

4. We must revive and rebuild the institutions of the PLO to confront the next dangerous stage of the liberation struggle equipped with political and organizational expertise and democratic, collective leadership.

5. America is a participant in the aggression against the Palestinian people. There can be neither peace nor compromise until such time that UN resolutions and other documents of international legality are enforced.
6. By its nature the Zionist entity is contrary to the notion of peace. This fact was confirmed yet again at the most recent Likud Party congress, which rejected the establishment of a Palestinian state.
7. We must surmount the risk of internal divisions by rebuilding and reconstructing all the institutions on democratic national foundations; by freeing all political prisoners in the jails of the Palestine Authority; by halting all manhunts, political arrests, and summonses; and by working to free all the prisoners in the jails of the Zionist enemy.

The Popular Front for the Liberation of Palestine pledges to the masses of our Arab people and our Palestinian people, wherever they may reside, that it will remain faithful to the spirit of the martyrs and to the goals for which the Palestinian people have struggled and sacrificed everything dear to them. The Popular Front will continue the struggle in all its forms and in collaboration with all patriotic, democratic, and Islamic forces until the goals of our people are achieved. The Popular Front for the Liberation of Palestine, 15 May 2002.

## May 30, 2002
## The Meeting with President Arafat

In the evening of 29 May 2002, a meeting was held with President Arafat at his invitation. In addition to Comrade Abd al-Rahim Mallouh, it was attended by three other comrades. Discussion centered on the political situation, the internal situation, the prisoners in the Palestine Authority's custody, in the first place, Comrade Abu Ghassan (Ahmad Saadat, General Secretary of the Popular Front for the Liberation of Palestine), and on the formation of the coming cabinet. The President's aim in holding the meeting was to invite the Popular Front to participate in the governmental cabinet being formed. The highlights of the discussion were as follows:

The President spoke about the dangerous nature of the political situation and Sharon's continuing military offensive and his efforts to escalate it to the point of eliminating in practice all the agreements that have been achieved with him on the ground. American cover for him is continuing as evidenced by the fact that visits by Americans and Europeans are limited to opinion research. The international conference is continuing to be postponed and the attempt to empty it of its contents is an indication of this fact. He [President Arafat] personally still cannot leave Ramallah to go abroad for fear that he will be prevented from returning. He complained of the Arab states' non-fulfillment of their obligations, in particular as regards financial assistance, of the stifling financial crisis that the Palestinian situation is suffering at a time when growing unemployment and abject poverty afflict many families. After that they push for meetings with Egyptian, Jordanian, and Saudi officials. Then there is the call on him to take internal measures, and he must make them on his own, for fear that otherwise they will be imposed from the outside in light of the American and European demands for such change, etc. . . . In light of all that and because he knows of the need for such measures, he is going to form a new governmental cabinet, implement changes in the security apparatus, and sign a number of laws, etc. . . . He hopes that the Popular Front will take part in the new governmental cabinet, in view of what the Popular Front represents, and because it is necessary that it participate so that we can work together to confront all of that which faces us, etc. . . .

We stated the following:

We thank him for his invitation and interest. We believe that we are in dire need, after all that has happened and before all else, to carry out a review and evaluation of our policies and our situation. We believe that this is the correct approach to determining how to pursue our struggle against the occupation. In particular since the Israeli "Defensive Wall" operation in actuality put an end to whatever was left of the agreements with Israel. Now the occupation has become a total one of all the Palestinian territories. We believe that the correct approach is to enter immediately into a comprehensive national dialogue in which all the forces, active groups, and individuals inside the homeland and disbursed abroad take part so that all will bear their responsibility and fulfill their role and take part in making decisions and in the responsibility for carrying them out. We do not believe that re-organizing the ministries is the correct approach, although it is important; rather there should be an agreement on a temporary unified national leadership until such time as free and fair elections can be held to build our national institutions and at their heart the institutions of the Palestine Liberation Organization and the institutions of the Palestine Authority. We believe that directly holding elections, in the first place local elections and elections in trade unions, etc. . . must be regarded as of great importance, and the general elections and local elections must be made a battle in confrontation with the occupation in which we unite our forces and the forces of our people. We need a new election law.

At the same time we must be avid in linking the continuation of the intifada and resistance to the occupation with internal reforms. We cooperate with the reform because we regard it as necessary for the continuation of our battle with the occupation. In addition to this, though, we have a problem, for we want to know if we are partners or prisoners. It is very hard to participate in the cabinet while our comrade, the General

Secretary, is in prison. We believe that the mistake of imprisoning him from the beginning has been compounded with other mistakes, bringing us to the present situation. There has been a series of opportunities that have been lost when he and the other comrades could have been released. We have not understood why you refused to make use of those opportunities. We call on you immediately to release him and to treat the problem of the other comrades.

Separately from our stance regarding participation in the cabinet, we call on you to take real and serious measures in the ministries and security agencies with regard to their integrity, to protecting public funds, and to their competence. . . There are some who have sullied their hands with public money at the level of cabinet ministers and in the security apparatus. They must be expelled, and Your Excellency knows who they are. The people need a message of hope after all the sacrifices they have made and still are making.

We have always put our battle against the occupation ahead of any internal differences or contradictions. Once again, we call on you personally to take measures to release the comrades and for serious reform by taking the correct approach that guarantees the participation of all in political decision making and their bearing their responsibility for implementing the decisions.

Afterwards, Abu Ammar (Yasir Arafat) commented as follows:

- With regard to Saadat, he is not a prisoner and I agree with your opinion that we missed opportunities in the past by not releasing him. Do not believe that I do not care for his situation, for he weighs more heavily upon me politically and personally than any other person. I am awaiting the political opportunity to release him and guarantee his security. . . The Popular Front has been a participant at every stage of the struggle and will remain so. I hope you will evaluate the situation. For my personal situation is no different from that of Saadat, and that of our people as a whole. In any case, I am working to solve this problem soon. And I value your stances, in spite of everything.

- Unfortunately, the Arab situation is not helping us. There is weakness in the movements to stand beside us. A long time ago I asked for a meeting of the Follow-Up Committee but have not received an answer. If it weren't for the latest efforts of Crown Prince Abdullah [of Saudi Arabia], there would have been none who asked about us and we were abandoned.

- The assassination of Jihad Jibril was a message to everyone, and particularly to Syria. Information indicates that there were hands inside Lebanon that had a part in that operation.

- I hope that you will reconsider participating in the cabinet. We can leave a seat for you until such time as Saadat comes out.

We reiterated that we declined, stressing both the political dimension of our position and of our viewpoint regarding the nature of the needed reforms, as well as the problem of the imprisonment of Saadat.

## June 3, 2002
## Press Release

Ramallah: The Popular Front for the Liberation of Palestine has issued a declaration in which it hailed the order of the Palestinian Supreme Court of Justice for the immediate release of Comrade Ahmad Saadat, the General Secretary of the Popular Front for the Liberation of Palestine. The declaration stressed that the court ruling,

1. Places President Arafat and the Palestine Authority before a clear and obvious legal obligation which they must enforce,
2. Places the Palestine Authority before a test of the credibility of its decision to ratify the law on the independence of the courts.
3. Places particular responsibility upon all Palestinian forces, institutions, and political and popular bodies to act to implement this court order.
4. The immediate release of Comrade Ahmad Saadat and action to that end constitute a test for all those who call for the rule of law, democracy, human rights, and reform, regardless whether they are Palestinians, Arabs, or people from around the world.
5. The Popular Front affirms that it will end the suspension of its participation in meetings of the Executive Committee of the Palestine Liberation Organization as soon as the Palestine Authority carries out the court order.
6. The Popular Front demands that Palestine Authority respect the court order, and respect its own signature on the Authority's law on the courts; and that it immediately release the Front's General Secretary. This is a matter that constitutes a real test of the intention to bring about reform and change in the Palestine Authority.

The Popular Front also called on all Palestinian forces and personalities to work for the implementation of these rulings.

Press Office
Palestine
3 June 2002.

**June 4, 2002**
**Press Release**

Commenting on the decision of the leadership of the Palestine Authority to continue detaining Comrade Ahmad Saadat, the General Secretary of the Popular Front for the Liberation of Palestine, on its latest act of submission to Israeli dictates, and on its non-implementation of the order of the Palestinian Supreme Court immediately to release Comrade Ahmad Saadat, the General Secretary of the Popular Front for the Liberation of Palestine, a responsible source in the Popular Front stated the following:

1. The decision of the leadership of the Palestine Authority not to release immediately Comrade Saadat constitutes a new act of submission to Israeli dictates and pressures. It makes the freedom of Saadat, and of his comrades and brothers who are being held as prisoners in the Authority's prisons, dependent upon an Israeli decision.

2. The Palestine Authority and its agencies have failed to protect the people, their institutions, and fighters, including the headquarters of President Arafat. The Authority therefore has no right to use as an excuse the need to keep Comrade Saadat and other militants in prison for their protection. The imprisonment of the militants, and in the first place of Saadat, is not the appropriate way to protect them from the violence of the occupation. Protecting them means to set them free, for they and their people are the guarantors of their self-defense.

3. Throwing aside the order of the supreme court to free Saadat immediately indicates the Authority's lack of seriousness about carrying out the needed reforms and its lack of respect for the rule of law, for the highest legal body represented by the Supreme Court of Justice, and for human rights.

4. We call on the leadership of the Palestine Authority to review its decision and to release immediately Comrade Saadat and all the political prisoners and those being held for resisting the occupation. They are better able to defend their persons than are the British and American soldiers.

5. We call on all the forces and organizations that believe in democracy, human rights, the rule of law, and the right of our people to resist the occupation and to live in freedom, to move to force the leadership of the Palestine Authority to implement the order of the Palestinian Supreme Court of Justice that calls for the release of Saadat, and not allow it to drive a big nail into the coffin of

reform and democracy. We must reject the Israeli and American pressures aimed at imposing a police state upon our people in service of American and Israeli interests.

Press Office

Palestine

4 June 2002.

## June 16, 2002
## An Appeal for the Immediate Release of the great leader Abd al-Rahim Mallouh.

We members of the Palestine National Council and the Legislative Council who are rallying with representatives of the patriotic and Islamic forces, and personalities and activists of the civil society, sharply denounce and condemn the arrest of the leader Abd al-Rahim Mallouh, a member of the Executive Committee of the Palestine Liberation Organization and Deputy General Secretary of the Popular Front for the Liberation of Palestine, and an outstanding leader of the popular Intifada.

Of great seriousness is the arrest of our brother, Abd al-Rahim Mallouh, member of the Executive Committee of the Palestine Liberation Organization. It is a serious assault on Palestinian legitimacy and a violation of all international norms, laws, and principles of human rights. It is an attempt to prepare the way for a dangerous political settlement in accordance with Israeli-American plans.

The crime of arresting Comrade Mallouh, one of the leaders in political and mass work, confirms that the occupation and fascist Israeli aggression aim at eliminating the national political leadership of our people, and exposes the falseness of their claim to be fighting terrorism.

We appeal to the masses of our Palestinian people, our Arab nation, the Islamic community, all free people in the world, and all the humanitarian institutions and human rights organizations to undertake the most massive action to secure the immediate release of the brother Abd al-Rahim Mallouh, and of all the detainees and prisoners denied their freedom in the prisons of the occupation, in the first place of the leaders Marwan al-Barghouthi, Jamal al-Tawil, Riyad al-Ali "Abu al-Muntasir," Ali Jarradat, Abd al-Hakim Musalima, and all their heroic comrades. We call on the Arab and Islamic governments to take stands that deter this new Israeli aggression. We call on the masses of our people everywhere they are living in the homeland or disbursed abroad to undertake the broadest actions and mass activities today. We call on the masses of our Arab nation and Islamic community and on all free people to stand in solidarity today with our prisoners and detainees and their right to freedom. This is the basis on which to develop and escalate the campaign of Arab and international solidarity with the prisoners denied their freedom, the symbols of steadfastness and resistance, and to consider the solidarity movement with our heroic prisoners to be solidarity with the intifada and the legitimate right of our people to resist the occupation and fascist Israeli aggression.

We pledge to our courageous prisoners and detainees that we will keep their banner flying, by keeping the intifada and resistance going until our national rights to freedom, independence, and return are attained, and the free flag of Palestine is raised over the walls of Jerusalem, the eternal capital of the independent, completely sovereign state of Palestine.

**June 22, 2002**
**Press Release**

Commenting on remarks by the President of the Palestine Authority to an Israeli newspaper concerning his agreement to the proposals of the former American president Bill Clinton which were tabled at Camp David with the aim of reaching a Palestinian-Israeli political agreement and which the President of the Palestine Authority rejected at the time, a spokesman for the Political Bureau of the Popular Front for the Liberation of Palestine has made a statement in which he said:

The remarks of the President of the Palestine Authority represent a political concession that poses the utmost danger to the basic interests of the Palestinian people and their established and inalienable national rights, because the Clinton proposals clearly confirm the elimination of the right of the Palestinian refugees to return to the land and homes from which they were expelled in 1948 and they completely ignore the United Nations resolutions, in particular Resolution 194 that affirms the right of the refugees to return.

In addition, these proposals are in total violation of the United Nations resolutions that demand a total Israeli withdrawal from the lands occupied in 1967, including Jerusalem. Instead, the proposals perpetuate Israeli sovereignty over the holy city.

The remarks by the President of the Palestine Authority will have the most dangerous effects on the internal situation in the Palestinian arena because the Palestinian people have not commissioned anyone to concede their rights and because the Palestinian people and all the patriotic and Islamic forces will never accept under any circumstances whatsoever this new capitulation and this new surrender.

The Popular Front for the Liberation of Palestine calls on all the patriotic and Islamic forces and organizations to tighten their ranks and unite their efforts to confront this new concession that constitutes an act of complying with and submitting to American and Israeli demands. The Popular Front affirms that it will continue the struggle and resistance until the last Israeli soldier is expelled from our land and our country.

The Political Bureau
The Popular Front for the Liberation of Palestine

**June 23, 2002**
**Press Release**

For a number of months Palestinian resistance activity has been subjected to a fierce attack in the press and in the field aimed at stopping Palestinian resistance action in general and martyrdom operations in particular. New elements have joined this campaign, the most recent of whom are a cocktail of "civilized intellectuals" who have nothing in common except opening the flow of funds from donor countries to their increasingly cramped pockets. Others among them are seeking to use this issue to make a place for themselves in the information media and on the newspaper pages. An appropriate opportunity has now arisen, particularly since it is a step that has the blessings of the Israeli occupation and the western democracies, and as a result taking this position will cost them nothing. On the contrary, they will reap esteem and praise from the Zionists and support from the Americans and Europeans. Concomitantly, however, they have forgotten that they will reap the condemnation and denunciation, and perhaps more than that, from the masses of our Palestinian people who in their majority support the resistance activity against the invading Zionist thieves. In the latest opinion poll carried out by an information gathering body, 86 percent of those surveyed supported the operations in the territories occupied in 1967, including east Jerusalem, even those operations that were against so-called "Israeli civilians." More than 60 percent of them supported these operations. Or is this great majority of the masses of our people made up of barbarians and terrorists, oh honorable civilized intellectuals????

As we condemn and warn against this suspicious campaign by a group of intellectuals and those who cling on to the shoulders of the struggles of our people and their vital forces, we affirm the following:

1. As we affirm the continuation of our course of attacking all that is Zionist in the territories occupied in 1967, and in particular in east Jerusalem, we reserve our right to target Zionism inside the territories occupied in 1948 at any moment that Palestinian civilians are targeted—in particular our children, women, and elderly—by the Zionist thieving invaders.

2. We affirm that delimiting the forms of resistance and the timing of attacks is a prerogative of the patriotic and Islamic resistance forces which they carry out through the formation of a national emergency leadership that takes on the responsibility of setting the general framework for the Palestinian national struggle in accordance with the interests of the vast majority of the masses of our Palestinian people. It is not a prerogative of a group of intellectuals, known to our people as mouthpieces of the propa-

ganda of the western democracies that regard the struggle of our people and their resistance to the occupation as terrorism.

3. We appeal to the brothers and holy warriors and comrades in all the Palestinian military formations to study together the course of targeting all that is Zionist in the territories occupied in 1967, while reserving our right to respond to the Zionists inside the territories occupied in 1948 whenever Palestinian civilians have been targeted. We also affirm that the Zionist military are targets wherever they might be located.

4. We call upon all the intellectuals who stick by our people and their vital forces to organize their ranks and to stand up against this suspicious campaign that is led by "a group of civilized intellectuals" who draw up the appeals and declarations that would have been better directed at condemning the ugly massacres perpetrated by Sharon and his Nazi government.

Shoulder-to-shoulder, together we will continue the fight against the Zionist thieving invaders and those who support them!

## June 24, 2002
## Press Release
## Irish Republican Socialist Party
## IRSP Demand Release of Ahmad Saadat

A spokesperson for the International Department of the Irish Republican Socialist Party dismissed the Palestinian Authority's justification as "transparently false" and "yet another example of caving in to the Zionists' demands."

Ahmad Saadat is the General Secretary of the Popular Front for the Liberation of Palestine. He was arrested by Arafat's Palestinian Authority police for allegedly having ordered the assassination of a right-wing member of the Israeli cabinet. When Zionist troops overran the West Bank, the American and British governments agreed to ensure Saadat was held. Subsequently, the Supreme Court of the PA ruled that Saadat was not guilty and ordered him released. Yet he remains incarcerated, with Arafat claiming this is to protect him from Israeli assassination squads roving the countryside.

The IRSP spokesperson declared:

"In the interests of justice, the IRSP are demanding that the Palestinian Authority immediately release PFLP General Secretary Ahmad Saadat. "The Palestinian Authority is on record as having recently proclaimed the independence of the judiciary must be respected. Yet, despite the Zionists and Western imperialists demanding that the Authority immediately undertake a series of reforms to become more democratic, none of them are insisting that it abide by the ruling of its own Supreme Court. The Palestinian Authority's Supreme Court found no evidence that Ahmad Saadat was guilty of any crime and ordered his release, yet he is still being held in incarceration.

"This demonstrates the hypocrisy of the Israeli government, the United States, the European Union, and others who have taken up the demand for a complete overhaul of the Palestinian Authority as a requirement for the renewal of peace negotiations. They are merely supporting Sharon's attempt to completely reverse the small gains made by the Palestinians under the previous government. As Secretary Saadat himself recently stated, the Israeli violence visited upon the Palestinian people is: 'a military strike aimed at destroying the Palestinian infrastructure, whether that was the infrastructure of the Palestinian Authority, or the political infrastructure of the national movement, or the social and cultural infrastructure. There is a feverish effort now on the part of the American administration, the government of Ariel Sharon, and the staff of Zionist entity to gather the political harvest, by which I mean to exploit the military campaign and impose the Zionist Israeli concept of a settlement on the Middle East region.'

"Similarly they repeatedly denounce so called 'suicide bombers,' but remain mute regarding Israel's killing far more Palestinian civilians. Forty percent of those killed by the Israeli Army have been children, and the Zionists have killed roughly four times as many Palestinians as Israelis have been killed by the Palestinian resistance. Can we expect a condemnation of this genocidal terror from the United States? Probably not, since they killed more civilians in Afghanistan than were killed in the attacks of last September 11th, which were used to justify attacking Afghanistan.

"The Palestinian Supreme Court has found Saadat guilty of no crime and ordered his release. This ruling has been supported by Amnesty International, whose recent report concluded that Saadat should be released immediately, on the grounds that there is no evidence of his having committed any crime. We in the Irish Republican Socialist Party join in demanding the immediate release of Ahmad Saadat and call upon the Palestinian Authority to demonstrate their respect for the independence of their judiciary by abiding by its ruling to release Saadat. Saadat's only crime is his continued opposition to the Zionist state and the threat the PFLP poses by combining the campaign for national liberation with that seeking social justice for the masses of working people within Palestine."

Reflecting a moment, the IRSP spokesperson concluded:

"Ahmad Saadat is the Dessie O'Hare of Palestine. In both cases, the courts have ruled that they should be released and in both cases a government disregards its own courts and manufactures excuses for continuing to incarcerate someone on purely political grounds, displaying absolute disregard for human rights and justice."

## 20 August 2002
## Press Release

"Dr. George Habash, founder of the Arab Nationalists' Movement and the Popular Front for the Liberation of Palestine, condemns the Gaza-Bethlehem First Agreement and calls for continuing the Intifada and resistance.

Dr. Habash has sharply condemned the agreement signed by representatives of the Palestine Authority and the Israeli government known as the "Gaza-Bethlehem First Agreement." He said in a statement to the press that the danger of this agreement lies in the short-term and long-term aims that the Zionist war-criminal government is striving for in the Palestinian arena. In the first place it seeks to light the fuse of internal Palestinian conflict by deputizing the Palestinian security agencies to make every effort to stop the intifada and heroic national resistance against the forces of the racist Zionist occupation.

Dr. Habash stated that the difficult and dangerous conditions that now surround our people as a result of the persistent Zionist offensives do not justify in any way whatsoever submission to Zionist-American pressures, and the granting of more concessions, which inflict the most severe and serious damage to the struggle of the Palestinian people and their right to resist the Zionist occupation in order to compel it to withdraw and recognize the legitimate, established, and historical rights of the Arab Palestinian people.

Dr. Habash concluded by emphasizing the necessity of continuing the Intifada and resistance in spite of all agreements. He called for strengthening the unity in the ranks of all the patriotic, democratic and Islamic forces to confront the imminent dangers and challenges facing the Palestinian national cause in the current circumstances, and to activate all forms of resistance to the Israeli occupiers in order to attain the aims of the Palestinian people: freedom and independence."

Damascus

## 21 August 2002
## Press Release

"Dr. George Habash has denounced the criminal Zionist assassination of our militant comrade Muhammad Saadat, brother of the General Secretary of the Popular Front for the Liberation of Palestine. In a statement to the press this morning, he stressed the link between this loathsome crime and the Gaza-Bethlehem First Agreement, signed just two days ago between the Palestine Authority and the Zionist enemy.

Dr. Habash added, "the submission of the representatives of the Palestine Authority to Zionist dictates and conditions is only another factor that encourages the forces of the Israeli occupation to continue their criminal and aggressive policies and practices against our people, their leaders, their cadres and the bases of the armed Palestinian national resistance to the Israeli occupiers."

Dr. Habash added, "As we announce to the masses of the Palestinian people and the Arab Nation the death of the militant hero Muhammad Saadat, we call on all the patriotic and Islamic forces, the independent patriotic and social personalities, to take more steps in order to block the security agreements with the Zionist enemy and to escalate the struggle of the masses and armed struggle against the occupation army and its settlers, in response to this crime and the series of daily crimes that have been building up against the masses of our people, their institutions, their infrastructure and economic structure, in order to attain the goals of our people: freedom and independence."

## 26 August 2002
## Press Release

"In protest of the continuation of his imprisonment, Saadat declares a hunger strike.

Jericho: Comrade Ahmad Saadat, the General Secretary of the Popular Front for the Liberation of Palestine, yesterday commenced a hunger strike in protest of the continuation of his imprisonment in Jericho. After making this declaration, the General Secretary elaborated that the reasons for his strike are as follows:

1. His continued imprisonment and the non-implementation of the order by the Palestinian Supreme Court that he be released. His continued detention has thus become illegal and Ahmad Saadat demands that the legal status of his continued detention be defined.

2. The continued presence of the Anglo-American team that participates with the Israelis in repression, and his demand that it be withdrawn. This is based on the fact that a ruling from the highest legal authority in the Palestine Authority has been issued for his release. This position is an affirmation and defense of judiciary independence and the binding rule of law, contrary to the Palestine Authority and the openly biased foreigners.

3. The role of the Anglo-American team as an agent of Israel, eager to implement its will, most evidently by increasing measures for

the social and political isolation of Comrade Saadat and our other comrades.

4. The campaign of humiliating measures taken against him and against his comrades and visitors by the Anglo-American in fulfilling Israeli wishes.

Saadat has declared that his hunger strike will last 72 hours until the arrival of an prominent Palestinian official with whom to hold discussions. In light of that meeting and its results he will decide whether to proceed with or cancel his strike.

The Popular Front for the Liberation of Palestine has called on the legal and humanitarian organizations and on the Islamic and Patriotic Forces and the Arab popular forces to intervene to stop the farce of the continuing detention of Comrade Saadat.

The Popular Front also demands that the Palestine Authority implement the ruling of the Supreme Court that Comrade Saadat deserves to be set free."

Press Office
Palestine

## 1 September 2002
### Press Release

"Speech by Abd al-Rahim Malluh, Deputy General Secretary of the Popular Front for the Liberation of Palestine and Member of the Executive Committee of the Palestine Liberation Organization. Made before the Israeli Military Tribunal in Bayt Il, 1 September 2002.

I reject my arrest and trial because my arrest and trial are illegal and unlawful under international law and the Charter and regulations of the United Nations.

My arrest and trial have been carried out by the occupation forces that have forcibly occupied the territory of another. This matter is rejected and condemned by international law and the United Nations, its charter, its regulations, and its resolutions. The Palestinian land and people are suffering from the yoke of the Israeli occupation that is based on military force.

My trial is illegal and unlawful from the standpoint of international law. This is so, in the first place, because the trial is taking place on occupied Palestinian land. It is so, in the second place, because I am an elected member of the highest political body of the Palestinian People, namely the Executive Committee of the Palestine Liberation Organization, which is recognized by our people and internationally as the sole legal representative of the Palestinian people. It is illegal and unlawful, in the third place, because I was kidnapped by the Israeli occupation forces from territory under the control of the Palestine National Authority.

The PLO and its constituent forces, such as the Popular Front for the Liberation of Palestine, have accepted the rulings of international law that are pertinent to the Palestinian-Israeli conflict. It has accepted the establishment of peace between the Palestinians and Israelis on the basis of the implementation of those resolutions. The Palestinian people yearn to live in peace, security, and stability, and to build their future and the future of their children far removed from wars, killing, destruction, and blockades. But they are not ready to concede the rights guaranteed them by the United Nations.

The policy of aggression, blockades, and expropriation of land; the policy of expansion, and settlements is responsible, from beginning to end, for the Palestinian and Israeli blood that has been shed. This policy must be stopped in order to make it possible to preserve the lives of coming generations.

International law and the United Nations with its regulations, charter, and resolutions have guaranteed the right of peoples under occupation to resist it. The Palestinian people have been under occupation for decades and it is their right to resist the occupation. The legitimacy of the PLO and the Palestinian national movement, constituted in part by the Popular Front for the Liberation of Palestine, comes from the Palestinian people and from international recognition of them and the legitimacy of their struggle and their rights, and not from the occupying power.

The occupation forces have arrested thousands, have destroyed our infrastructure, have imposed a blockade, and starved our people, but they have not broken our will. They have not been able to force us to surrender. It has therefore become necessary for Israeli politicians and intellectuals to comprehend this fact. It is also a fact that the occupation has not guaranteed security and stability—not yesterday, not today—and it will fail to do so in the future. What can guarantee security and stability is the recognition of our people's rights to freedom and independence.

The Israeli government has recognized the Palestine Liberation Organization and has concluded agreements with it. But it has come to deny that recognition and has reoccupied regions under the Palestine National Authority, has besieged the headquarters of President Arafat, virtually imprisoning him, for more than nine months. It has undertaken a campaign of arrests affecting thousands, including myself, and I am a member of the Executive Committee of the PLO, and have come here in that capacity. All of this points to the nature of the policy of the Israeli government, and its non-compliance with what it has signed.

It is not I who should be taken to court, but the Israeli leaders who are responsible for the crimes committed against the Palestinians, first among them Prime Minister Sharon, who is, by the way, wanted by the authorities of international justice.

You must understand one thing, and that is that the Palestinian people are clinging fast to their rights for freedom and independence and will attain them, just as the other people of the world have, whether that takes a long or a short time. Let us try to shorten the time, and reduce the period of suffering, for this would be much better for us and for you."

Abd al-Rahim Malluh, Member of the Executive Committee of the Palestine Liberation Organization, Deputy General Secretary of the Popular Front for the Liberation of Palestine.

## 2 September 2002
## Press Release

"The following statement has been issued jointly by Abd al-Rahim Malluh, Member of the Executive Committee of the Palestine Liberation Organization and Member of the Political Bureau of the Popular Front for the Liberation of Palestine, who is presently confined in an Israeli prison; and Taysir Khalid, Member of the Political Bureau of the Democratic Front for the Liberation of Palestine:

The continued occupation, the ongoing Israeli aggression against the Palestinian people, the continued imposition of collective sanctions by the occupation forces as they blockade, strangle, and destroy our access to vital necessities, the escalation of this aggression through the daily perpetration of massacres that affect whole families of Palestian civilians, and the destruction of the houses of innocent citizens all confirm to the whole world that the Sharon government is making war against the existence of the Palestinian people and not merely their rights. The situation reveals that the enemy does not hesitate to use the vilest forms of terrorism to expropriate and plunder the rights, land, and lives of the Palestinian people. Current events undeniably attest that the Sharon government's only strategy is one of aggression and terrorism. It is therefore a waste of time to seek political solutions. This fact must compel the executive leaders of the Palestine Liberation Organization and the Palestine Authority to immediately halt all political, security, and other kinds of meetings or communications with this government.

Instead of deceiving themselves that it is valuable to make endless compromises which breed false hopes throughout the Arab nation and the world at large—hopes that are quickly dashed by Israeli tanks, bulldozers, and warplanes, as well as the Israeli soldiers themselves who seethe with contempt for our people's humanity—these leaders must accept their greater responsibility to tighten the bonds of national unity while adopting a more inclusive leadership model designed to strengthen the resistance movement and the defense of our people's human and national rights.

We demand that the international community stop providing cover for the Israeli aggression. We call on the Security Council to censure the State of Israel for its violation of international and humanitarian law, and for its complete disregard for universally accepted judicial norms. This reality demands that every effort should be made to condemn Israeli abuses and to call for the severest sanctions against the Sharon government, insuring international protection for the unarmed Palestinian people. We demand that the Arab foreign ministers who will meet next Wednesday [4 September 2002] address the dimensions and dangers of Israeli policy and that they renew in the most practical way the resolutions of earlier Arab summit meetings, intended to isolate Israel, sever all contacts with it, and prosecute the war crimes of its leaders before an international tribunal. In addition, international public opinion must be mobilized against Washington's unfailing support for the policies of the Sharon government, as well as its commitment to stock and restock the already overflowing arsenal of the Jewish state. The current American Administration bears undeniable responsibility for the Sharon government's continued perpetration of massacres and its endless other forms of aggression against the rights and dignity of the Palestinian people."

## 6 September 2002
## Megiddo Prison Appeal

"Israeli Prime Minister Sharon has clearly exposed what his official policy is after putting it into practice on the ground, relying on armed force and the Zionist military leviathan. The essence of the Israeli policy is based on denying the rights of the Palestinian people, denying our sovereignty over our own homeland, robbing us of any formal national identity, subverting our institutions and sense of geographical unity, and attempting to force our compliance with the Zionist agenda. Sharon's policy relies on so-called autonomous arrangements for parts of occupied Palestine, while it also nurtures an alliance with the American administration to secure hegemony over the entire region and its resources, and to redraw the map yet again, always to the benefit of occupier.

Like Netanyahu and Barak before him, Sharon has put an end to the Oslo agreements in principle and on the ground, reoccupying areas formerly controlled by the Palestine Authority. The Israelis have imposed a full blockade against the Palestinian people and the Palestinian leadership, and meanwhile they proceed to expand their assassinations, arrests, settlements, and expropriations of our land. These practices blatantly underscore both the impotence and failure of the Oslo agreements, on one hand; and the true aim of the Zionist enemy to free itself of any meaningful obligation, on the other hand.

We are called upon by conscience and self-preservation to confront these policies and their intolerable results for our people. Now Washington is going even further by issuing naked threats to Iraq and any states that either esitate to support American intervention or dare to question its legality. We must recognize and denounce this trend for what it is—the latest phase of Israeli-American aggression directed against the entire Middle East.

Lessons must be drawn from the past stage. We must pool our efforts and unite our forces. The factors leading to the steadfastness of our people must be reinforced. There must be agreement on a political vision and a unified national strategy of action. The draft programmatic document agreed upon in Gaza, after an intense exchange among many political forces, provides a solid basis for this vision, and a fighting political strategy for our people. This will enable us to confront the coming stage and its challenges.

An urgent call for a Palestinian national dialogue must be made repeatedly until it takes place—and remains in place—on a truly comprehensive scale.

All of the political and social forces and activists of our people are called upon to bring this about and to transform it into a detailed blueprint for our militant struggle, based first upon internal organization and then upon coordinating the efforts of our supporters in and outside the region.

Together we will sweep away the occupation! We will triumph, establish an independent Palestinian state with Jerusalem as its capital, and insure the right of the Palestinian refugees to return to their homes!"

Your brother,

Abd al-Rahim Malluh

Member of the Executive Committee of the Palestine

Liberation Organization, Deputy General Secretary of the Popular Front for the Liberation of Palestine.

### 28 September 2002
### Press Release

"Political Statement issued by the Political Bureau of the Popular Front for the Liberation of Palestine on the Occasion of the Second Anniversary of the al-Aqsa Intifada.

At this challenging interlude we pause to commemorate the second anniversary of our people's glorious intifada. Through their many forms of struggle, our people's forces have written the most brilliant verses of heroism and vigor. Holding fast to their legitimate rights and continuing the intifada and the resistance, they have affirmed the certainty that our people and their Patriotic and Islamic Forces will persist in their noble uprising, driven by the unshakable resolve to expel the tyrannical Zionist occupiers, to stablish a fully independent Palestinian state, based on inviolable sovereignty, and to guarantee the right of our people to return to their homeland. Neither Sharon's arrogance nor his American-sanctioned aggression can encroach upon the established rights of our people and their ability to stand solid, cleave together and hold fast to their established principles, rallying in support of a Palestinian legitimacy that extols the virtues of struggle and confrontation while emboldening the stance of the Palestinian masses who reject the occupation, the aggression, and the dictates and crude acts of interference in our internal affairs.

The political, economic, and security repercussions of this intifada have exposed the impotence of the policies of the fascist, racist, and terrorist Israeli government. This heroic intifada has inflicted human, military, economic, and security losses on the enemy, and it has substantiated the power of our people to defeat the military and security plans directed against us. While the balance of power disfavors us, our painful blows against the Zionist enemy clearly have shaken the pillars of its security strategy. The enemy is no longer able to attract more immigrants since it lacks security and is distracted by taking measures against the Palestinian people, their structures and institutions, and their Patriotic and Islamic Forces. The intifada burns ever more fiercely as it gains momentum. The stormy rising against the Zionist assault on Palestinian legitimacy yields infinite proof of our people's vitality and their ability to renew themselves, to hold together, side-by-side and inexhaustible as they march onward along the path of militancy. It shows the utter commitment of our people to make sacrifices and wage the intifada and the resistance as long as necessary.

As the intifada constitutes the front line of defense for the Arab Nation and its masses, it deserves every form of permanent and continuous support and backing from the sons and daughters of this Nation, from their mass movement, from their institutions, their trade unions and professional organizations, from their Arab patriotic and Islamic political parties. We therefore call upon all of these many forces to invigorate their ranks and to reignite the mass movement with the indomitable fire that characterized the early days of the intifada. Holding protests in the streets of all the Arab cities is a patriotic and national duty. So too is sharing every possible form of material and moral support with the resistance and putting pressure on the silent official Arab regimes to shoulder their responsibility to confront Israeli terrorism and arrogance, as well as to denounce America's guilt in supporting the Zionist crimes against our people.

The Arab masses are called upon to exercise their right to impose their will on the official Arab regimes, demanding an escalation of official measures against Israel's practices and its perpetual, bloody, uncivilized aggression against the Palestinian people. As we greet the third year of the intifada, there is no longer any permissible excuse for states to maintain their diplomatic or economic relations with Israel. Arab summit resolutions calling for the political and economic support for the intifada must be followed, renewed, and expanded. Arab unity must be greatly enhanced in order to confront the serious challenges that we face in Palestine and Iraq, and this objective calls for a new Arab summit conference where officials unite without hesitation to consecrate a unified stance and render an overall blueprint to provide for our present and future.

On the Palestinian level, the time has come for the Palestine Authority to understand that it must preserve and strengthen the gains of the intifada by assuming a position that takes heed of what has instigated the mass uprising of our people—the need to defend the legitimacy of our demands and the integrity of our institutions. Enough time has been squandered betting on liquidationist solutions urged by the American Administration, the patron of Zionist terrorism, for these solutions have only increased the aggression and barbarism of Sharon and his government, which has reneged on all its agreements with the Palestine Authority. It must commit itself to the option of continuing the intifada and resistance by halting political and security negotiations with the Sharon government. It must release comrade Ahmad Saadat and his four comrades detained in the Jericho prison. It must present a genuine and open national initiative based on canceling all agreements with the Zionist enemy so that it will be able to empower our people and their Patriotic and Islamic Forces. It must engage in a comprehensive national dialogue to analyze and overcome the difficulties of our national struggle, beginning with a review of our experiences, both positive and negative, and proceeding to develop a national program based on common principles that bring all the Patriotic and Islamic Forces under a single democratic framework and in doing so pave the way for reforms of the mechanisms of the PLO and all Palestinian institutions. Ultimately this process must lead to the establishment of a provisional council for national action to supervise the reforms and energize the Palestinian struggle.

The Patriotic and Islamic Forces must understand that there is no way to rouse our people and to confront Israeli aggression other than through unity and devotion to the only acceptable groundwork for our future: the establishment of an independent Palestinian state with Jerusalem as its capital and the imperative for all exiled Palestinians to be afforded the right of return.

On this occasion we pledge to the masses of our people and our nation that we will be faithful to the martyrs, prisoners, and wounded; that we will abide our commitment to the option our people have chosen of continuing the intifada and resistance. We will ceaselessly defend our right to pursue reform and unity on firm political, organizational, and militant bases, and our right to fight corruption since this is the only trust-worthy response to the sacrifices of our people and their admirable state of combat readiness. We pledge to continue the struggle until the occupation is driven out and an independent state is established and the right to return is guaranteed."

The Political Bureau of The Popular Front for the Liberation of Palestine

Damascus

## 22 October 2002
## Press Release

A spokesman for the Popular Front for the Liberation of Palestine has made the following declaration:

Newspapers and wire services have been reporting the contents of an American plan called a Road Map to a Permanent Solution. President Abu Ammar (Yasir Arafat) told the press last Sunday, 19 October, that the plan had not reached the Palestinian leadership in an official form and that the leadership would study it when they receive it officially and familiarize themselves with its contents. Dr. Nabil Shaath, however, declared that he had discussed details of the plan with members of the Quadripartite Committee and with the American representative, and that he had informed the American representative that the Palestinians have reservations about it. In light of these diverse and unclear positions taken by members of the leadership of the Palestine Authority, we in the Popular Front for the Liberation of Palestine affirm the following:

First: The American plan amounts to brazen interference in Palestinian internal affairs in all areas, beginning with how the Palestinian constitution should be formulated, and going on to how the cabinet ministers should be constituted, to how elections to the legislature should be organized, and leading finally to the formation of security agencies and determining what party that would supervise them.

Second: In accordance with this disreputable plan, the end of the intifada and resistance and of "all forms of violence against the Israelis everywhere" constitutes the first and most basic step in this plan. This amounts to open surrender to Israeli dictates and conditions.

Third: This American plan is based on a denial of United Nations resolutions which demand Israeli withdrawal from the Palestinian and Arab occupied lands and provide for the right of our people to return and self-determination, and to establishing an independent state. The plan returns us once again to the useless and harmful cycle of negotiation about everything, including borders, Jerusalem, the Refugees, the Jewish settlements, all without any points of reference and authority.

Fourth: A detailed study of this American "map" and its numerous stages reveals clearly that it is a rehash of the well-known Sharon plan called a "long-term temporary solution."

In light of that, we in the Popular Front for the Liberation of Palestine call on the masses of our people to reject this poisoned American plan. We call on the Palestinian leadership to reject it and to hold fast to the United Nations resolutions that affirm the right of our people to return and to national independence. We also appeal to the Palestinian leadership not to meet with the American envoy, in light of the declared and clear American position of not cooperating with and not meeting with President Abu Ammar.

The report that a Palestinian delegation has been selected to meet the American envoy Burns constitutes submission to the American position. It facilitates their interference in Palestinian internal affairs and their effort to determine the choice of Palestinian authorities so that they will be agreeable to America.

It is impermissible for the people of the intifada to accept or condone this.

The Popular Front for the Liberation of Palestine

## 9 November 2002
## Press Release

Commenting on United Nations Security Council Resolution 1441 concerning Iraq, which was issued yesterday, 8 November 2002, a spokesman for the Political Bureau of the Popular Front for the Liberation of Palestine has made the following statement:

The Security Council Resolution devoted to disarming Iraq comes as a result of intense and continuous pressure applied by the American Administration over the last few weeks. In spite of the changes that were introduced by some members of the Security Council, the essence of what the American Administration wants from the resolution is that it prepare a path for comprehensive military aggression against Iraq, targeting its oil wealth and other potentials, as a first step on the path to redrawing the entire map of the region.

The decision to attack Iraq has been taken by the American Administration, but it wants an international cover for its aggression—the pretext of eliminating Iraqi weapons of mass destruction—although everyone knows that Israel possesses all forms of mass destruction weapons—thermonuclear, atomic, biological, and chemical.

Israel occupies Palestinian territory and practices all forms of terrorism, killing, and crime against the unarmed Palestinian people. It refuses to implement UN General Assembly and Security Council resolutions concerned with the Palestinian issue. Despite that, the world does not call it to account, nor does the American President or the British Prime Minster threaten it with painful consequences. On the contrary, they provide it all kinds of support and assistance in its aggressive war against the Palestinian people and the Arab Nation.

There is no doubt that the double standard, the injustice, the preparation of the path to aggression against Iraq, and the escalation of the Israeli war against the Palestinian people are steps aimed at subjugating the whole Arab Nation and threatening the heart of Arab national security.

Therefore, the Popular Front for the Liberation of Palestine appeals to the Arab peoples and their governments to grasp the danger of what is taking place, to protect the land and people of Iraq, and to prevent the aggression threatened by the American Administration from occurring. The Popular Front calls on the Arab Nation to grasp the danger of what is taking place, and of the escalation of Zionist aggression against the Palestinian territories that will take place, and which is a part of the comprehensive plan drawn up for the region.

We call on everyone, before it is too late, to protect Iraq and Palestine, to protect Arab National security and future Arab generations.

The Popular Front for the Liberation of Palestine Press Office—Damascus

## 11 December 2002
### Statement by the founder, Comrade Dr. George Habash on the 35th Anniversary of the Launch of the Popular Front for the Liberation of Palestine.

I come before you on the occasion of the 35th Anniversary of the launch of the Popular Front for the Liberation of Palestine, a patriotic, democratic, and progressive detachment that has, with its long struggle, written the finest verses of heroism, sacrifice, and vigor. Over the course of its three and a half decades of struggle, it has affirmed its resolve to cling to the legitimate rights of the Palestinian people while displaying the greatest determination to continue the intifada and resistance struggle until victory and the return [of exiled Palestinians].

I address you on this glorious occasion and send you and to the people of the intifada my truest, warmest, most heartfelt greetings—to you and to the heroic activists, to all the patriots, free people and progressives in our Arab Nation and the world. In particular, I greet our militant comrade, the General Secretary of the Popular Front Ahmad Saadat who languishes with his beloved comrades in a prison of the Palestine Authority in Jericho under Anglo-American supervision and control. I say to you today with the inspiration of this occasion that the Popular Front for the Liberation of Palestine will continue to have a free will, and a free resolve that cannot be broken. It will continue its militant march until victory and liberation. The difficulties linked to the imprisonment of the General Secretary and his deputy and of dozens of leaders and hundreds of cadres and members, and the sacrifices of one constellation of martyrs after another, are finally destined to increase the Front's firmness and strength.

Heroic masses of our people, the anniversary of the launch of the PFLP comes this year in the shadow of gathering challenges on many levels, and of the increase and worsening of the threats against many quarters from the circle of American-Zionist aggression against the Palestinian people and their glorious intifada, and against the steadfast, noble Iraqi people. This is occurring in the shadow of unlimited political, financial, and military support by American imperialism to the Zionist enemy, and in the shadow of its great and increasing pressures upon the official Arab regimes in the framework of what it calls a battle against terrorism. Here we must say, unfortunately, that American political pressure has found fertile ground in the Arab world because of the state of impotence in which the official Arab regimes find themselves. I am certain that if America succeeds in waging its treacherous aggression against noble Iraq that this aggression will not stop until it has seized total control over Iraq's oil and the oil of the entire region, until it has subjugated the whole Arab Nation, suppressed the Palestinian people's intifada, and aborted the whole effort at Arab revival. It will reinforce the Zionist deluge of the region economically and culturally, enabling the further imposition of its hegemony throughout the region.

Here the legitimate question arises, What will Sharon do? Will he implement the plans to "transfer" the Palestinians out of Palestine? Will he implement the "Road Map" that is based on the political vision of George Bush and has received the blessings of the Quadripartite Committee and internationally? Or what? Or will he simply return to the long-term "temporary plan" that is based on establishing the facade of a Palestinian state on 40 percent of the West Bank and 75 percent of the Gaza Strip according to purely Sharonist specifications and criteria, and without the remotest connection to the true rights, interests, and goals of the Palestinian people? Whichever path he takes, the plans of Sharon will not succeed. I say this, deeply understanding that the current balance of forces is overwhelmingly in favor of the enemy camp. But Palestinian steadfastness backed by the Arab National depths will enable the intifada and the resistance struggle to attain the goals of freedom and independence. Therefore, there is no alternative to the continuation of the intifada and resistance. They lift the Palestinian national liberation struggle upwards. They must return to their true course and true identity.

Here I appeal to all leaders of groups dedicated to patriotic action, and affirm to them the need to understand that for the intifada to attain its supreme national goals, it must fly on two wings—one wing of escalating the resistance struggle against the occupation and the other wing of putting the Palestinian house in order. The responsibility here falls especially on our brothers in Fateh and on their militant and mujahid vanguard to stand with others in living up to this revolutionary national task, to address the need to regin in destructive criticism of the intifada, to reject any inclination to seek harmony with American-Israeli plans. We are in favor of the kind of constructive criticism that promotes national unity and paves the way toward freedom and independence.

The current Palestinian political situation, in spite of all its difficulties and complications, demands that we take a serious look at the factors that urge us to surrender, at the calls of frustration that urge us to give up in despair. These arise from divisions and splits within the Palestinian condition as a result of the intensity of the unjust war being waged against the masses of our people. We must understand that the American Administration is structurally afflicted with the madness of being the greatest (most powerful) empire, and this affliction gives shape to all of the many forms of American imperialism. The events of 11 September served simply to increase the barbarism of the current American administration and to increase the extent to which its policy coincides with the policy of the terrorist, racist Zionist entity, with the purpose to rationalize a strike against Iraq and the intifada. Because of this, the region faces tempestuous political and military storms that could strike at the end of this current winter season or the beginning of next spring. They bring with them enormous and dangerous demands. It is therefore incumbent upon the forces and organizations of the Palestinian movement to undertake a comprehensive, bold, and critical review of the current stage of the Palestinian national struggle by way of a comprehensive national dialogue. A strategy is needed for the resistance. The current unity of the forces in the field must be deepened and reinforced.

The reality of the current international situation in the shadow of American terror shows that there can be no protection for Arab interests, and neither can occupied territories be won back unless the solidarity of the Arab peoples with the intifada is redoubled to counteract America's arrogance, steeped in its lust for power and appetite for tyranny. All the vital and noble forces in this Arab Nation, with their different orientations and political and ideological inspirations, are called on to take up this role.

Honor cannot be protected, rights cannot be defended, and the future cannot be built unless we understand how to confront the challenges and demands of the present. I believe that these fundamentally can be attained by our unity, the source of our strength, and by coordinating our efforts and seriously cooperating with all the militants, progressives, and honorable people around the world.

Finally, I am deeply convinced that the American-Zionist policy will never succeed in falsifying the realities of Arab geography and history. The Palestinian, who has resisted the Zionist enterprise for more than a century, and has resisted Israelization for 54 years inside the borders of the part of Palestine occupied in 1948, will never give up his national dreams, his goals of return and self-determination.

On this glorious anniversary, I extend my profound greetings to the prisoners in the jails of the Zionist occupation, esteeming their sufferings, sacrifices, and tortures and those of their loved ones, knowing that they are the heroes of freedom and independence.

I extend my greetings to the mothers and families of the martyrs and the injured from whose wounds blood has flowed on the path of freedom and independence.

Dr. George Habash,

Founder of the Arab Nationalists' Movement, and of the Popular Front for the Liberation of Palestine.

## 11 December 2002
## On the Occasion of the Thirty-Fifth Anniversary of the Launch of the Popular Front for the Liberation of Palestine.

On the eleventh of December 1967, from the heart of the sufferings of the heroic Palestinian Arab people, the Popular Front for the Liberation of Palestine emerged as one of the most dramatic and necessary responses to the defeat of the fifth of June. Today we light the thirty-fifth candle on the path of its triumphant and ongoing struggle for the liberation of Palestine. Over these thirty-five years it has been an honor for the Popular Front to shed waterfalls of blood and to offer caravans of martyrs and prisoners in defense of the most just and most sacred cause of this age.

The Popular Front has affirmed through its glorious militant march that it is a party of martyrs and of leaders willing to sacrifice their dearest possessions for their homeland and people. The blood of the heroic leaders—the Guevara of Gaza, Ghassan Kanafani, Basil al-Kubaysi, and Abu Amal—has drenched the soil of Palestine, affirming the determination of the people of Palestine to continue the struggle and resistance until all Palestinian national rights have been reclaimed.

At every point in the continuing intifada, the Popular Front has adorned the firmament of Palestine with constellations of martyred leaders. Chief among them is the knight of the martyrs, the great Palestinian and Arab leader Abu Ali Mustafa, the former General Secretary of the Front. The Front also has bid farewell to the mass leader Comrade Ribhi Haddad who defended his heroic city: proud, steadfast, defiant Nablus.

The Popular Front for the Liberation of Palestine affirms to the masses of our Palestinian people and our Arab Nation that it will remain faithful to its Palestinian and Arab national principles, values, and aims as they were embodied by the first leaders of our party, in the first place by our leader and founder Dr. George Habash and the outstanding martyr Abu Ali Mustafa.

On this occasion that is dear to our hearts and to the hearts of all those struggling for freedom, democracy, and social progress in our Arab Nation and around the world, the PFLP affirms that it will continue its

184 • *Palestinian Secular Terrorism*

just struggle using every militant technique at its disposal. It affirms its intent to continue the march of the intifada and the resistance and to defeat the continuing American-Israeli efforts against our people. It will use every means to defend and strengthen our militant national body. We appeal to all honorable people in our Arab Nation and throughout the world to continue to support our just and legitimate struggle against the occupation and its exterminationist plans to uproot our people.

The Palestinian cause and Arab national security now face immense dangers and enormous challenges as the American Administration prepares for total aggression against fraternal Iraq, using the least credible pretexts and justifications, aiming to take possession of Iraq's resources and oil and to gain complete control of the region in an attempt to eliminate the Palestinian cause and the national rights of the Palestinian people.

The Popular Front for the Liberation of Palestine appeals to the Arab Nation and the Islamic Community, their peoples and governments, to reject the plans of aggression against Iraq. It affirms its stance entirely on the side of Iraq in its confrontation with the current U.S. policy of aggression and arrogance, for this policy cannot be separated from Washington's unflagging support for the Zionist Entity, as evidently and purposefully contrary to the interests of the Arab Nation.

The Popular Front for the Liberation of Palestine flatly and unequivocally rejects what is called the American "Road Map" that aims to eliminate Palestinian national rights. It reiterates its firm condemnation and total rejection of the so-called Sari Nuseibeh Document that openly and shamelessly calls for abandoning the right of Palestinian refugees to return, and which abandons the City of Jerusalem. The PFLP calls on our people to resist the policy of concessions and suspicious calls to halt the intifada and armed operations against the Zionist occupation.

We call on the masses of our people and on all of their patriotic and Islamic forces, on our Arab Nation, and all free people of the world to raise their voices loudly for the release of the militant Ahmad Saadat, the General Secretary of the Popular Front for the Liberation of Palestine, whose incarceration is no longer acceptable by any legal or moral standard whatsoever, particularly after the decision of the Palestinian Supreme Court calling for his release. We call on all the forces supporting welfare, freedom, and progress in the world to raise their voices to join together in demanding the release of more than nine thousand captives in Zionist prisons, in particular the militant Abd al-Rahim Mallouh, Deputy General Secretary of the Popular Front for the Liberation of Palestine.

The Popular Front for the Liberation of Palestine renews its call for the reordering of the Palestinian agenda by way of a comprehensive Palestinian national dialog including all Palestinian forces without exception in order to regain Palestinian national unity and to rebuild the institutions of the Palestine Liberation Organization along more dynamic political and organizational lines. The document considered in the Gaza discussions forms a promising basis for this objective, as well as the need to guarantee the fruition of comprehensive Palestinian national unity and to guarantee the construction of a real democratic civil society that puts an end to all forms of corruption and despotism.

On the thirty-fifth anniversary of the launch of the Popular Front for the Liberation of Palestine we renew our pledge and commitment that we will remain faithful to the blood of the martyrs Ra'id Nazzal, Muhannad Ismail Mahdi, Muhammad Saadat, Ribhi Haddad, Wadi Haddad, Abu Amal, Khalil al-Wazir, Fathi al-Shiqaqi, Abu Ali Mustafa, and to all the martyrs of our Palestinian people and Arab Nation. The banner will never fall and the intifada and resistance will continue until the last Israeli soldier has been expelled from the soil of our country.

**21 January 2003**
**Press Release**

Yesterday evening the delegation of the Popular Front for the Liberation of Palestine headed by Dr. Mahir al-Tahir, the Front's top man outside of Palestine, arrived in Cairo where it held talks with the brothers in Egypt. It sought from them an invitation to the brothers in the Popular Front for the Liberation of Palestine—General Command and the brothers in the Vanguards of the People's Liberation War al-Sa`iqah Forces to participate in the dialogue. This is necessary to ensure that a comprehensive Palestinian national dialogue take place that includes all the organizations under the Palestine Liberation Organization and the Islamic Forces. The PFLP delegation affirmed its position that the resistance must continue and the intifada must continue. It also affirmed that the armed resistance is a legitimate right of the Palestinian people until the last Israeli soldier is expelled from our land.

Press Office
Damascus

**23 January 2003**
**Press Release**

The Zionist occupation forces have arrested Mrs. Ablah Saadat, the wife of the General Secretary of the Popular Front, Comrade Ahmad Saadat, who is being held in prison in Jericho. She was arrested as she was crossing into Jordan on her way to Brazil to participate in a solidarity conference there and was sentenced to five months administration detention.

The Popular Front for the Liberation of Palestine holds the occupation forces completely responsible for the results of this arrest and warns of the consequences of any harm that might be done to or any suffering that might be inflicted upon Mrs. Ablah Saadat.

The PFLP demands her immediate release and appeals to human rights organizations and to all concerned parties to intervene at once to secure the freedom of Mrs. Ablah Saadat.

The Popular Front for the Liberation of Palestine
Press Office

## 29 January 2003
### Press release concerning the results of the elections to the Zionist Knesset.

A spokesman of the Popular Front for the Liberation of Palestine has made the following statement:

The results of the Zionist Knesset elections reveal the truth about the racist, aggressive nature of this entity that clings to its illegal occupation and policy of war crimes. The spokesman added that the election results reproduce the very crisis in which the Israeli society and Sharon government found themselves beforehand. This fact brings the Palestinian people and their patriotic and Islamic forces face-to-face with their primary task to continue steadfastly in carrying forth the intifada and resistance, seeking national unity through the formation of a provisional national leadership capable of ordering internal Palestinian affairs and rebuilding the Palestine Liberation Organization on genuinely democratic and thereby militant bases. This is the only way to deepen the security, economic, and social crises afflicting the occupation. This is the only way to achieve the goals of the intifada and resistance—the return of Palestinian refugees, the end of the occupation and Jewish settlements, and the establishment of a fully sovereign, independent state with Jerusalem as its capital.

From its inception the Popular Front has called for democratic national reform to guard our people from all harmful, corrupt, and debilitating obstacles along their militant path. It now re-amplifies this call and expresses support for the continuation of a dialogue that builds on the previously laid foundations, including the recent Cairo meetings, in order to arrive at a national unification program of common denominators. This process establishes a solid basis on which to forge unity and to continue the resistance on the Palestinian and Arab National levels, as well as to prompt the international community to accept its responsibility to counteract the Zionist-American excesses wrought against our people and to insist on an unbiased commitment to upholding international law and UN resolutions.

The Popular Front spokesman called on the Arab peoples and governments to view the election returns as further proof of the need to discard any illusions about what the Americans and Israelis refer to as a peace process.

The Popular Front for the Liberation of Palestine

# SELECTED PEACE EFFORTS

## TRILATERAL STATEMENT ON THE MIDDLE EAST PEACE SUMMIT AT CAMP DAVID
## JULY 25, 2000

### PRESIDENT WILLIAM J. CLINTON
### ISRAELI PRIME MINISTER EHUD BARAK
### PALESTINIAN AUTHORITY CHAIRMAN YASSER ARAFAT

Between July 11 and 24, under the auspices of President Clinton, Prime Minister Barak and Chairman Arafat met at Camp David in an effort to reach an agreement on permanent status. While they were not able to bridge the gaps and reach an agreement, their negotiations were unprecedented in both scope and detail. Building on the progress achieved at Camp David, the two leaders agreed on the following principles to guide their negotiations:

1. The two sides agreed that the aim of their negotiations is to put an end to decades of conflict and achieve a just and lasting peace.
2. The two sides commit themselves to continue their efforts to conclude an agreement on all permanent status issues as soon as possible.
3. Both sides agree that negotiations based on UN Security Council Resolutions 242 and 338 are the only way to achieve such an agreement and they undertake to create an environment for negotiations free from pressure, intimidation and threats of violence.
4. The two sides understand the importance of avoiding unilateral actions that prejudge the outcome of negotiations and that their differences will be resolved only by good faith negotiations.
5. Both sides agree that the United States remains a vital partner in the search for peace and will continue to consult closely with President Clinton and Secretary Albright in the period ahead.

Source: http://www.mfa.gov.il/mfa/go.asp?MFAH0hnl0

Sharm El-Sheikh Fact-Finding Committee, (Mitchell Plan)
April 30, 2001

## SUMMARY OF RECOMMENDATIONS

The Government of Israel (GOI) and the Palestinian Authority (PA) must act swiftly and decisively to halt the violence. Their immediate objectives then should be to rebuild confidence and resume negotiations.

During this mission our aim has been to fulfill the mandate agreed at Sharm el-Sheikh. We value the support given our work by the participants at the summit, and we commend the parties for their cooperation. Our principal recommendation is that they recommit themselves to the Sharm el-Sheikh spirit and that they implement the decisions made there in 1999 and 2000. We believe that the summit participants will support bold action by the parties to achieve these objectives.

The restoration of trust is essential, and the parties should take affirmative steps to this end. Given the high level of hostility and mistrust, the timing and sequence of these steps are obviously crucial. This can be decided only by the parties. We urge them to begin the process of decision immediately.

Accordingly, we recommend that steps be taken to:

## END THE VIOLENCE

The GOI and the PA should reaffirm their commitment to existing agreements and undertakings and should immediately implement an unconditional cessation of violence.

The GOI and PA should immediately resume security cooperation.

## REBUILD CONFIDENCE

The PA and GOI should work together to establish a meaningful "cooling off period" and implement additional confidence building measures, some of which were detailed in the *October 2000 Sharm el-Sheikh Statement* and some of which were offered by the U.S. on January 7, 2001 in Cairo (see Recommendations section for further description).

The PA and GOI should resume their efforts to identify, condemn and discourage incitement in all its forms.

The PA should make clear through concrete action to Palestinians and Israelis alike that terrorism is reprehensible and unacceptable, and that the PA will make a 100 percent effort to prevent terrorist operations and to punish perpetrators. This effort should include immediate steps to apprehend and incarcerate terrorists operating within the PA's jurisdiction.

The GOI should freeze all settlement activity, including the "natural growth" of existing settlements.

The GOI should ensure that the IDF adopt and enforce policies and procedures encouraging non-lethal responses to unarmed demonstrators, with a view to minimizing casualties and friction between the two communities.

The PA should prevent gunmen from using Palestinian populated areas to fire upon Israeli populated areas and IDF positions. This tactic places civilians on both sides at unnecessary risk.

The GOI should lift closures, transfer to the PA all tax revenues owed, and permit Palestinians who had been employed in Israel to return to their jobs; and should ensure that security forces and settlers refrain from the destruction of homes and roads, as well as trees and other agricultural property in Palestinian areas. We acknowledge the GOI's position that actions of this nature have been taken for security reasons. Nevertheless, the economic effects will persist for years.

The PA should renew cooperation with Israeli security agencies to ensure, to the maximum extent possible, that Palestinian workers employed within Israel are fully vetted and free of connections to organizations and individuals engaged in terrorism.

The PA and GOI should consider a joint undertaking to preserve and protect holy places sacred to the traditions of Jews, Muslims, and Christians.

The GOI and PA should jointly endorse and support the work of Palestinian and Israeli non-governmental organizations involved in cross-community initiatives linking the two peoples

## RESUME NEGOTIATIONS

In the spirit of the Sharm el-Sheikh agreements and understandings of 1999 and 2000, we recommend that the parties meet to reaffirm their commitment to signed agreements and mutual understandings, and take corresponding action. This should be the basis for resuming full and meaningful negotiations.

## INTRODUCTION

On October 17, 2000, at the conclusion of the Middle East Peace Summit at Sharm el-Sheikh, Egypt, the President of the United States spoke on behalf of the participants (the Government of Israel, the Palestinian Authority, the Governments of Egypt, Jordan, and the United States, the United Nations, and the European Union). Among other things, the President stated that:

The United States will develop with the Israelis and Palestinians, as well as in consultation with the United Nations Secretary General, a committee of fact-finding on the events of the past several weeks and how to prevent their recurrence. The committee's report will be shared by the U.S. President with the U.N. Secretary General and the parties prior to publication. A final report shall be submitted under the auspices of the U.S. President for publication.

On November 7, 2000, following consultations with the other participants, the President asked us to serve on what has come to be known as the Sharm el-Sheikh Fact-Finding Committee. In a letter to us on December 6, 2000, the President stated that:

The purpose of the Summit, and of the agreement that ensued, was to end the violence, to prevent its recurrence, and to find a path back to the peace process. In its actions and mode of operation, therefore, the Committee should be guided by these overriding goals . . . The Committee should strive to steer clear of any step that will intensify mutual blame and finger-pointing between the parties. As I noted in my previous letter, "the Committee should not become a divisive force or a focal point for blame and recrimination but rather should serve to forestall violence and confrontation and provide lessons for the future." This should not be a tribunal whose purpose is to determine the guilt or innocence of individuals or of the parties; rather, it should be a fact-finding committee whose purpose is to determine what happened and how to avoid it recurring in the future.

After our first meeting, held before we visited the region, we urged an end to all violence. Our meetings and our observations during our subsequent visits to the region have intensified our convictions in this regard. Whatever the source, violence will not solve the problems of the region. It will only make them worse. Death and destruction will not bring peace, but will deepen the hatred and harden the resolve on both sides. There is only one way to peace, justice, and security in the Middle East, and that is through negotiation.

Despite their long history and close proximity, some Israelis and Palestinians seem not to fully appreciate each other's problems and concerns. Some Israelis appear not to comprehend the humiliation and frustration that Palestinians must endure every day as a result of living with the continuing effects of occupation, sustained by the presence of Israeli military forces and settlements in their midst, or the determination of the Palestinians to achieve independence and genuine self-determination. Some Palestinians appear not to comprehend the extent to which terrorism creates fear among the Israeli people and undermines their belief in the possibility of co-existence, or the determination of the GOI to do whatever is necessary to protect its people.

Fear, hate, anger, and frustration have risen on both sides. The greatest danger of all is that the culture of peace, nurtured over the previous decade, is being shattered. In its place there is a growing sense of futility and despair, and a growing resort to violence.

Political leaders on both sides must act and speak decisively to reverse these dangerous trends; they must rekindle the desire and the drive for peace. That will be difficult. But it can be done and it must be done, for the alternative is unacceptable and should be unthinkable.

Two proud peoples share a land and a destiny. Their competing claims and religious differences have led to a grinding, demoralizing, dehumanizing conflict. They can continue in conflict or they can negotiate to find a way to live side-by-side in peace.

There is a record of achievement. In 1991 the first peace conference with Israelis and Palestinians took place in Madrid to achieve peace based on UN Security Council Resolutions 242 and 338. In 1993, the Palestine Liberation Organization (PLO) and Israel met in Oslo for the first face-to-face negotiations; they led to mutual recognition and the Declaration of Principles (signed by the parties in Washington, D.C. on September 13, 1993), which provided a road map to reach the destination agreed in Madrid. Since then, important steps have been taken in Cairo, in Washington, and elsewhere. Last year the parties came very close to a permanent settlement.

So much has been achieved. So much is at risk. If the parties are to succeed in completing their journey to their common destination, agreed commitments must be implemented, international law respected, and human rights protected. We encourage them to return to negotiations, however difficult. It is the only path to peace, justice and security.

## DISCUSSION

It is clear from their statements that the participants in the summit of last October hoped and intended that the outbreak of violence, then less than a month old, would soon end. The U.S. President's letters to us, asking that we make recommendations on how to prevent a recurrence of violence, reflect that intention.

Yet the violence has not ended. It has worsened. Thus the overriding concern of those in the region with whom we spoke is to end the violence and to return to the process of shaping a sustainable peace. That is what we were told, and were asked to address, by Israelis and Palestinians alike. It was the message conveyed to us as well by President Mubarak of Egypt, King Abdullah of Jordan, and UN Secretary General Annan.

Their concern must be ours. If our report is to have effect, it must deal with the situation that exists, which is different from that envisaged by the summit participants. In this report, we will try to answer the questions assigned to us by the Sharm el-Sheikh summit: What happened? Why did it happen?

In light of the current situation, however, we must elaborate on the third part of our mandate: How can the recurrence of violence be prevented? The relevance and impact of our work, in the end, will be measured by the recommendations we make concerning the following:

- Ending the Violence.
- Rebuilding Confidence.
- Resuming Negotiations.

## WHAT HAPPENED?

We are not a tribunal. We complied with the request that we not determine the guilt or innocence of individuals or of the parties. We did not have the power to compel the testimony of witnesses or the production of documents. Most of the information we received came from the parties and, understandably, it largely tended to support their arguments.

In this part of our report, we do not attempt to chronicle all of the events from late September 2000 onward. Rather, we discuss only those that shed light on the underlying causes of violence.

In late September 2000, Israeli, Palestinian, and other officials received reports that Member of the Knesset (now Prime Minister) Ariel Sharon was planning a visit to the Haram al-Sharif/Temple Mount in Jerusalem. Palestinian and U.S. officials urged then Prime Minister Ehud Barak to prohibit the visit. Mr. Barak told us that he believed the visit was intended to be an internal political act directed against him by a political opponent, and he declined to prohibit it.

Mr. Sharon made the visit on September 28 accompanied by over 1,000 Israeli police officers. Although Israelis viewed the visit in an internal political context, Palestinians saw it as highly provocative to them. On the following day, in the same place, a large number of unarmed Palestinian demonstrators and a large Israeli police contingent confronted each other. According to the U.S. Department of State, "Palestinians held large demonstrations and threw stones at police in the vicinity of the Western Wall. Police used rubber-coated metal bullets and live ammunition to disperse the demonstrators, killing 4 persons and injuring about 200." According to the GOI, 14 Israeli policemen were injured.

Similar demonstrations took place over the following several days. Thus began what has become known as the "Al-Aqsa Intifada" (Al-Aqsa being a mosque at the Haram al-Sharif/Temple Mount).

The GOI asserts that the immediate catalyst for the violence was the breakdown of the Camp David negotiations on July 25, 2000 and the "widespread appreciation in the international community of Palestinian responsibility for the impasse." In this view, Palestinian violence was planned by the PA leadership, and was aimed at "provoking and incurring Palestinian casualties as a means of regaining the diplomatic initiative."

The Palestine Liberation Organization (PLO) denies the allegation that the intifada was planned. It claims, however, that "Camp David represented nothing less than an attempt by Israel to extend the force it exercises on the ground to negotiations," and that "the failure of the summit, and the attempts to allocate blame on the Palestinian side only added to the tension on the ground . . ."

From the perspective of the PLO, Israel responded to the disturbances with excessive and illegal use of deadly force against demonstrators; behavior which, in the PLO's view, reflected Israel's contempt for the lives and safety of Palestinians. For Palestinians, the widely seen images of the killing of 12-year-old Muhammad al Durra in Gaza on September 30, shot as he huddled behind his father, reinforced that perception.

From the perspective of the GOI, the demonstrations were organized and directed by the Palestinian leadership to create sympathy for their cause around the world by provoking Israeli security forces to fire upon demonstrators, especially young people. For Israelis, the lynching of two military reservists, First Sgt. Vadim Novesche and First Cpl. Yosef Avrahami, in Ramallah on October 12, reflected a deep-seated Palestinian hatred of Israel and Jews.

What began as a series of confrontations between Palestinian demonstrators and Israeli security forces, which resulted in the GOI's initial restrictions on the movement of people and goods in the West Bank and Gaza Strip (closures), has since evolved into a wider array of violent actions and responses. There have been exchanges of fire between built-up areas, sniping incidents and clashes between Israeli settlers and Palestinians. There have also been terrorist acts and Israeli reactions thereto (characterized by the GOI as counter-terrorism), including killings, further destruction of property and economic measures. Most recently, there have been mortar attacks on Israeli locations and IDF ground incursions into Palestinian areas.

From the Palestinian perspective, the decision of Israel to characterize the current crisis as "an armed conflict short of war" is simply a means "to justify its assassination policy, its collective punishment policy, and its use of lethal force." From the Israeli perspective, "The Palestinian leadership have instigated, orchestrated and directed the violence. It has used, and continues to use, terror and attrition as strategic tools."

In their submissions, the parties traded allegations about the motivation and degree of control exercised by the other. However, we were provided with no persuasive evidence that the Sharon visit was anything other than an internal political act; neither were we provided with persuasive evidence that the PA planned the uprising.

Accordingly, we have no basis on which to conclude that there was a deliberate plan by the PA to initiate a campaign of violence at the first opportunity; or to conclude that there was a deliberate plan by the GOI to respond with lethal force.

However, there is also no evidence on which to conclude that the PA made a consistent effort to contain the demonstrations and control the violence once it began; or that the GOI made a consistent effort to use non-lethal means to control demonstrations of unarmed Palestinians. Amid rising anger, fear, and mistrust, each side assumed the worst about the other and acted accordingly.

The Sharon visit did not cause the "Al-Aqsa Intifada." But it was poorly timed and the provocative effect should have been foreseen; indeed it was foreseen by those who urged that the visit be prohibited. More significant were the events that followed: the decision of the Israeli police on September 29 to use lethal means against the Palestinian demonstrators; and the subsequent failure, as noted above, of either party to exercise restraint.

## WHY DID IT HAPPEN?

The roots of the current violence extend much deeper than an inconclusive summit conference. Both sides have made clear a profound disillusionment with the behavior of the other in failing to meet the expectations arising from the peace process launched in Madrid in 1991 and then in Oslo in 1993. Each side has accused the other of violating specific undertakings and undermining the spirit of their commitment to resolving their political differences peacefully.

Divergent Expectations: We are struck by the divergent expectations expressed by the parties relating to the implementation of the Oslo process. Results achieved from this process were unthinkable less than 10 years ago. During the latest round of negotiations, the parties were closer to a permanent settlement than ever before.

Nonetheless, Palestinians and Israelis alike told us that the premise on which the Oslo process is based—that tackling the hard "permanent status" issues be deferred to the end of the process—has gradually come under serious pressure. The step-by-step process agreed to by the parties was based on the assumption that each step in the negotiating process would lead to enhanced trust and confidence. To achieve this, each party would have to implement agreed upon commitments and abstain from actions that would be seen by the other as attempts to abuse the process in order to predetermine the shape of the final outcome. If this requirement is not met, the Oslo road map cannot successfully lead to its agreed destination. Today, each side blames the other for having ignored this fundamental aspect, resulting in a crisis in confidence. This problem became even more pressing with the opening of permanent status talks.

The GOI has placed primacy on moving toward a Permanent Status Agreement in a nonviolent atmosphere, consistent with commitments contained in the agreements between the parties. "Even if slower than was initially envisaged, there has, since the start of the peace process in Madrid in 1991, been steady progress towards the goal of a Permanent Status

Agreement without the resort to violence on a scale that has character-ized recent weeks." The "goal" is the Permanent Status Agreement, the terms of which must be negotiated by the parties.

The PLO view is that delays in the process have been the result of an Israeli attempt to prolong and solidify the occupation. Palestinians "believed that the Oslo process would yield an end to Israeli occupa-tion in five years," the timeframe for the transitional period specified in the *Declaration of Principles*. Instead there have been, in the PLO's view, repeated Israeli delays culminating in the Camp David summit, where, "Israel proposed to annex about 11.2% of the West Bank (excluding Jerusalem) . . ." and offered unacceptable proposals concerning Jerusalem, security and refugees. "In sum, Israel's proposals at Camp David pro-vided for Israel's annexation of the best Palestinian lands, the perpetu-ation of Israeli control over East Jerusalem, a continued Israeli military presence on Palestinian territory, Israeli control over Palestinian natural resources, airspace and borders, and the return of fewer than 1% of refugees to their homes."

Both sides see the lack of full compliance with agreements reached since the opening of the peace process as evidence of a lack of good faith. This conclusion led to an erosion of trust even before the perma-nent status negotiations began.

Divergent Perspectives: During the last seven months, these views have hardened into divergent realities. Each side views the other as hav-ing acted in bad faith; as having turned the optimism of Oslo into the suffering and grief of victims and their loved ones. In their statements and actions, each side demonstrates a perspective that fails to recognize any truth in the perspective of the other.

The Palestinian Perspective: For the Palestinian side, "Madrid" and "Oslo" heralded the prospect of a State, and guaranteed an end to the occupation and a resolution of outstanding matters within an agreed time frame. Palestinians are genuinely angry at the continued growth of settlements and at their daily experiences of humiliation and dis-ruption as a result of Israel's presence in the Palestinian territories. Palestinians see settlers and settlements in their midst not only as vio-lating the spirit of the Oslo process, but also as an application of force in the form of Israel's overwhelming military superiority, which sustains and protects the settlements.

The Interim Agreement provides that "the two parties view the West Bank and Gaza as a single territorial unit, the integrity and status of which will be preserved during the interim period." Coupled with this, the Interim Agreement's prohibition on taking steps which may prejudice permanent status negotiations denies Israel the right to continue its illegal expan-sionist settlement policy. In addition to the Interim Agreement, custom-ary international law, including the Fourth Geneva Convention, prohibits

Israel (as an occupying power) from establishing settlements in occupied territory pending an end to the conflict.

The PLO alleges that Israeli political leaders "have made no secret of the fact that the Israeli interpretation of Oslo was designed to segregate the Palestinians in non-contiguous enclaves, surrounded by Israeli military-controlled borders, with settlements and settlement roads violating the territories' integrity." According to the PLO, "In the seven years since the [Declaration of Principles], the settler population in the West Bank, excluding East Jerusalem and the Gaza Strip, has doubled to 200,000, and the settler population in East Jerusalem has risen to 170,000. Israel has constructed approximately 30 new settlements, and expanded a number of existing ones to house these new settlers."

The PLO also claims that the GOI has failed to comply with other commitments such as the further withdrawal from the West Bank and the release of Palestinian prisoners. In addition, Palestinians expressed frustration with the impasse over refugees and the deteriorating economic circumstances in the West Bank and Gaza Strip.

The Israeli Perspective: From the GOI perspective, the expansion of settlement activity and the taking of measures to facilitate the convenience and safety of settlers do not prejudice the outcome of permanent status negotiations.

Israel understands that the Palestinian side objects to the settlements in the West Bank and the Gaza Strip. Without prejudice to the formal status of the settlements, Israel accepts that the settlements are an outstanding issue on which there will have to be agreement as part of any permanent status resolution between the sides. This point was acknowledged and agreed upon in the Declaration of Principles of 13 September 1993 as well as in other agreements between the two sides. There has in fact been a good deal of discussion on the question of settlements between the two sides in the various negotiations toward a permanent status agreement.

Indeed, Israelis point out that at the Camp David summit and during subsequent talks the GOI offered to make significant concessions with respect to settlements in the context of an overall agreement.

Security, however, is the key GOI concern. The GOI maintains that the PLO has breached its solemn commitments by continuing the use of violence in the pursuit of political objectives. "Israel's principal concern in the peace process has been security. This issue is of overriding importance . . . [S]ecurity is not something on which Israel will bargain or compromise. The failure of the Palestinian side to comply with both the letter and spirit of the security provisions in the various agreements has long been a source of disturbance in Israel."

According to the GOI, the Palestinian failure takes several forms: institutionalized anti-Israel, anti-Jewish incitement; the release from detention of terrorists; the failure to control illegal weapons; and the actual conduct of violent operations, ranging from the insertion of riflemen into demonstrations to terrorist attacks on Israeli civilians. The GOI maintains that the PLO has explicitly violated its renunciation of terrorism and other acts of violence, thereby significantly eroding trust between the parties. The GOI perceives "a thread, implied but nonetheless clear, that runs throughout the Palestinian submissions. It is that Palestinian violence against Israel and Israelis is somehow explicable, understandable, legitimate."

## END THE VIOLENCE

For Israelis and Palestinians alike the experience of the past several months has been intensely personal. Through relationships of kinship, friendship, religion, community and profession, virtually everyone in both societies has a link to someone who has been killed or seriously injured in the recent violence. We were touched by their stories. During our last visit to the region, we met with the families of Palestinian and Israeli victims. These individual accounts of grief were heart-rending and indescribably sad. Israeli and Palestinian families used virtually the same words to describe their grief.

When the widow of a murdered Israeli physician—a man of peace whose practice included the treatment of Arab patients—tells us that it seems that Palestinians are interested in killing Jews for the sake of killing Jews, Palestinians should take notice. When the parents of a Palestinian child killed while in his bed by an errant .50 caliber bullet draw similar conclusions about the respect accorded by Israelis to Palestinian lives, Israelis need to listen. When we see the shattered bodies of children we know it is time for adults to stop the violence.

With widespread violence, both sides have resorted to portrayals of the other in hostile stereotypes. This cycle cannot be easily broken. Without considerable determination and readiness to compromise, the rebuilding of trust will be impossible.

Cessation of Violence: Since 1991, the parties have consistently committed themselves, in all their agreements, to the path of nonviolence. They did so most recently in the two Sharm el-Sheikh summits of September 1999 and October 2000. To stop the violence now, the PA and GOI need not "reinvent the wheel." Rather, they should take immediate steps to end the violence, reaffirm their mutual commitments, and resume negotiations.

Resumption of Security Cooperation: Palestinian security officials told us that it would take some time—perhaps several weeks—for the PA to reassert full control over armed elements nominally under its command and to exert decisive influence over other armed elements operating in Palestinian areas. Israeli security officials have not disputed these assertions. What is important is that the PA make an all-out effort to enforce a complete cessation of violence and that it be clearly seen by the GOI as doing so. The GOI must likewise exercise a 100 percent effort to ensure that potential friction points, where Palestinians come into contact with armed Israelis, do not become stages for renewed hostilities.

The collapse of security cooperation in early October reflected the belief by each party that the other had committed itself to a violent course of action. If the parties wish to attain the standard of 100 percent effort to prevent violence, the immediate resumption of security cooperation is mandatory.

We acknowledge the reluctance of the PA to be seen as facilitating the work of Israeli security services absent an explicit political context (i.e., meaningful negotiations) and under the threat of Israeli settlement expansion. Indeed, security cooperation cannot be sustained without such negotiations and with ongoing actions seen as prejudicing the outcome of negotiations. However, violence is much more likely to continue without security cooperation. Moreover, without effective security cooperation, the parties will continue to regard all acts of violence as officially sanctioned.

In order to overcome the current deadlock, the parties should consider how best to revitalize security cooperation. We commend current efforts to that end. Effective cooperation depends on recreating and sustaining an atmosphere of confidence and good personal relations. It is for the parties themselves to undertake the main burden of day-to-day cooperation, but they should remain open to engaging the assistance of others in facilitating that work. Such outside assistance should be by mutual consent, should not threaten good bilateral working arrangements, and should not act as a tribunal or interpose between the parties. There was good security cooperation until last year that benefited from the good offices of the U.S. (acknowledged by both sides as useful), and was also supported indirectly by security projects and assistance from the European Union. The role of outside assistance should be that of creating the appropriate framework, sustaining goodwill on both sides, and removing friction where possible. That framework must be seen to be contributing to the safety and welfare of both communities if there is to be acceptance by those communities of these efforts.

## REBUILD CONFIDENCE

The historic handshake between Chairman Arafat and the late Prime Minister Rabin at the White House in September 1993 symbolized the expectation of both parties that the door to the peaceful resolution of differences had been opened. Despite the current violence and mutual loss of trust, both communities have repeatedly expressed a desire for peace. Channeling this desire into substantive progress has proved difficult. The restoration of trust is essential, and the parties should take affirmative steps to this end. Given the high level of hostility and mistrust, the timing and sequence of these steps are obviously crucial. This can be decided only by the parties. We urge them to begin the process of decision immediately.

Terrorism: In the September 1999 Sharm el-Sheikh Memorandum, the parties pledged to take action against "any threat or act of terrorism, violence or incitement." Although all three categories of hostilities are reprehensible, it was no accident that "terrorism" was placed at the top of the list.

Terrorism involves the deliberate killing and injuring of randomly selected noncombatants for political ends. It seeks to promote a political outcome by spreading terror and demoralization throughout a population. It is immoral and ultimately self-defeating. We condemn it and we urge that the parties coordinate their security efforts to eliminate it.

In its official submissions and briefings, the GOI has accused the PA of supporting terrorism by releasing incarcerated terrorists, by allowing PA security personnel to abet, and in some cases to conduct terrorist operations, and by terminating security cooperation with the GOI The PA vigorously denies the accusations. But Israelis hold the view that the PA's leadership has made no real effort over the past seven months to prevent anti-Israeli terrorism. The belief is, in and of itself, a major obstacle to the rebuilding of confidence.

We believe that the PA has a responsibility to help rebuild confidence by making clear to both communities that terrorism is reprehensible and unacceptable, and by taking all measures to prevent terrorist operations and to punish perpetrators. This effort should include immediate steps to apprehend and incarcerate terrorists operating within the PA's jurisdiction.

Settlements: The GOI also has a responsibility to help rebuild confidence. A cessation of Palestinian-Israeli violence will be particularly hard to sustain unless the GOI freezes all settlement construction activity. The GOI should also give careful consideration to whether settlements that are focal points for substantial friction are valuable bargaining chips for future negotiations or provocations likely to preclude the onset of productive talks.

The issue is, of course, controversial. Many Israelis will regard our recommendation as a statement of the obvious, and will support it. Many will oppose it. But settlement activities must not be allowed to undermine the restoration of calm and the resumption of negotiations.

During the half-century of its existence, Israel has had the strong support of the United States. In international forums, the U.S. has at times cast the only vote on Israel's behalf. Yet, even in such a close relationship there are some differences. Prominent among those differences is the U.S. Government's long-standing opposition to the GOI's policies and practices regarding settlements. As the then-Secretary of State, James A. Baker, III, commented on May 22, 1991:

Every time I have gone to Israel in connection with the peace process, on each of my four trips, I have been met with the announcement of new settlement activity. This does violate United States policy. It's the first thing that Arabs—Arab Governments, the first thing that the Palestinians in the territories—whose situation is really quite desperate—the first thing they raise when we talk to them. I don't think there is any bigger obstacle to peace than the settlement activity that continues not only unabated but at an enhanced pace.

The policy described by Secretary Baker, on behalf of the Administration of President George H. W. Bush, has been, in essence, the policy of every American administration over the past quarter century.

Most other countries, including Turkey, Norway, and those of the European Union, have also been critical of Israeli settlement activity, in accordance with their views that such settlements are illegal under international law and not in compliance with previous agreements.

On each of our two visits to the region there were Israeli announcements regarding expansion of settlements, and it was almost always the first issue raised by Palestinians with whom we met. During our last visit, we observed the impact of 6,400 settlers on 140,000 Palestinians in Hebron and 6,500 settlers on over 1,100,000 Palestinians in the Gaza Strip. The GOI describes its policy as prohibiting new settlements but permitting expansion of exiting settlements to accommodate "natural growth." Palestinians contend that there is no distinction between "new" and "expanded" settlements; and that, except for a brief freeze during the tenure of Prime Minister Yitzak Rabin, there has been a continuing, aggressive effort by Israel to increase the number and size of settlements.

The subject has been widely discussed within Israel. The Ha'aretz English Language Edition editorial of April 10, 2001 stated:

A government which seeks to argue that its goal is to reach a solution to the conflict with the Palestinians through peaceful means, and is trying at this stage to bring an end to the violence and terrorism, must announce an end to construction in the settlements.

The circumstances in the region are much changed from those which existed nearly 20 years ago. Yet, President Reagan's words remain relevant: "The immediate adoption of a settlements freeze by Israel, more than any other action, could create the confidence needed . . ."

Beyond the obvious confidence-building qualities of a settlement freeze, we note that many of the confrontations during this conflict have occurred at points where Palestinians, settlers, and security forces protecting the settlers, meet. Keeping both the peace and these friction points will be very difficult.

Reducing Tension: We were told by both Palestinians and Israelis that emotions generated by the many recent deaths and funerals have fueled additional confrontations, and, in effect, maintained the cycle of violence. We cannot urge one side or the other to refrain from demonstrations. But both sides must make clear that violent demonstrations will not be tolerated. We can and do urge that both sides exhibit a greater respect for human life when demonstrators confront security personnel. In addition, a renewed effort to stop the violence might feature, for a limited time, a "cooling off" period during which public demonstrations at or near friction points will be discouraged in order to break the cycle of violence. To the extent that demonstrations continue, we urge that demonstrators and security personnel keep their distance from one another to reduce the potential for lethal confrontation.

Actions and Responses: Members of the Committee staff witnessed an incident involving stone throwing in Ramallah from the perspectives, on the ground, of both sides. The people confronting one another were mostly young men. The absence of senior leadership on the IDF side was striking. Likewise, the absence of responsible security and other officials counseling restraint on the Palestinian side was obvious.

Concerning such confrontations, the GOI takes the position that "Israel is engaged in an armed conflict short of war. This is not a civilian disturbance or a demonstration or a riot. It is characterized by live-fire attacks on a significant scale [emphasis added] . . . [T]he attacks are carried out by a well-armed and organized militia . . ." Yet, the GOI acknowledges that of some 9,000 "attacks" by Palestinians against Israelis, "some 2,700 [about 30 percent] involved the use of automatic weapons, rifles, hand guns, grenades, [and] explosives of other kinds."

Thus, for the first three months of the current uprising, most incidents did not involve Palestinian use of firearms and explosives. B'Tselem reported that, "according to IDF figures, 73 percent of the incidents [from September 29 to December 2, 2000] did not include Palestinian gunfire. Despite this, it was in these incidents that most of the Palestinians [were] killed and wounded. . ." Altogether, nearly 500 people were killed and over 10,000 injured over the past seven months; the overwhelming majority in both categories were Palestinian. Many of these deaths were avoidable, as were many Israeli deaths.

Israel's characterization of the conflict, as noted above, is overly broad, for it does not adequately describe the variety of incidents reported since late September 2000. Moreover, by thus defining the conflict, the IDF has suspended its policy of mandating investigations by the Department of Military Police Investigations whenever a Palestinian in the territories dies at the hands of an IDF soldier in an incident not involving terrorism. In the words of the GOI, "Where Israel considers that there is reason to investigate particular incidents, it does so, although, given the circumstances of armed conflict, it does not do so routinely." We believe, however, that by abandoning the blanket "armed conflict short of war" characterization and by re-instituting mandatory military police investigations, the GOI could help mitigate deadly violence and help rebuild mutual confidence. Notwithstanding the danger posed by stone-throwers, an effort should be made to differentiate between terrorism and protests.

Controversy has arisen between the parties over what Israel calls the "targeting of individual enemy combatants." The PLO describes these actions as "extra-judicial executions," and claims that Israel has engaged in an "assassination policy" that is "in clear violation of Article 32 of the Fourth Geneva Convention. . . ." The GOI states that, "whatever action Israel has taken has been taken firmly within the bounds of the relevant and accepted principles relating to the conduct of hostilities."

With respect to demonstrations, the GOI has acknowledged "that individual instances of excessive response may have occurred. To a soldier or a unit coming under Palestinian attack, the equation is not that of the Israeli army versus some stone throwing Palestinian protesters. It is a personal equation."

We understand this concern, particularly since rocks can maim or even kill. It is no easy matter for a few young soldiers, confronted by large numbers of hostile demonstrators, to make fine legal distinctions on the spot. Still, this "personal equation" must fit within an organizational ethic; in this case, The Ethical Code of the Israel Defense Forces, which states, in part:

The sanctity of human life in the eyes of the IDF servicemen will find statement in all of their actions, in deliberate and meticulous planning, in safe and intelligent training and in proper execution of their mission. In evaluating the risk to self and others, they will use the appropriate standards and will exercise constant care to limit injury to life to the extent required to accomplish the mission.

Those required to respect the IDF ethical code are largely draftees, as the IDF is a conscript force. Active duty enlisted personnel, noncommissioned officers and junior officers—the categories most likely to be present at friction points—are young, often teenagers. Unless more senior career personnel or reservists are stationed at friction points, no IDF personnel present in these sensitive areas have experience to draw upon from previous violent Israeli-Palestinian confrontations. We think it is essential, especially in the context of restoring confidence by minimizing deadly confrontations, that the IDF deploy more senior, experienced soldiers to these sensitive points.

There were incidents where IDF soldiers have used lethal force, including live ammunition and modified metal-cored rubber rounds, against unarmed demonstrators throwing stones. The IDF should adopt crowd-control tactics that minimize the potential for deaths and casualties, withdrawing metal-cored rubber rounds from general use and using instead rubber baton rounds without metal cores.

We are deeply concerned about the public safety implications of exchanges of fire between populated areas, in particular between Israeli settlements and neighboring Palestinian villages. Palestinian gunmen have directed small arms fire at Israeli settlements and at nearby IDF positions from within or adjacent to civilian dwellings in Palestinian areas, thus endangering innocent, Israeli and Palestinian civilians alike. We condemn the positioning of gunmen within or near civilian dwellings. The IDF often responds to such gunfire with heavy caliber weapons, sometimes resulting in deaths and injuries to innocent Palestinians. An IDF officer told us at the Ministry of Defense on March 23, 2001 that, "When shooting comes from a building we respond, and sometimes there are innocent people in the building." Obviously, innocent people are injured and killed during exchanges of this nature. We urge that such provocations cease and that the IDF exercise maximum restraint in its responses if they do occur. Inappropriate or excessive uses of force often lead to escalation.

We are aware of IDF sensitivities about these subjects. More than once we were asked: "What about Palestinian rules of engagement? What about a Palestinian code of ethics for their military personnel?" These are valid questions.

On the Palestinian side there are disturbing ambiguities in the basic areas of responsibility and accountability. The lack of control exercised by the PA over its own security personnel and armed elements affiliated with the PA leadership is very troubling. We urge the PA to take all necessary steps to establish a clear and unchallenged chain of command for armed personnel operating under its authority. We recommend that the PA institute and enforce effective standards of conduct and accountability, both within the uniformed ranks and between the police and the civilian political leadership to which it reports.

Incitement: In their submissions and briefings to the Committee, both sides expressed concerns about hateful language and images emanating from the other, citing numerous examples of hostile sectarian and ethnic rhetoric in the Palestinian and Israeli media, in school curricula and in statements by religious leaders, politicians and others.

We call on the parties to renew their formal commitments to foster mutual understanding and tolerance and to abstain from incitement and hostile propaganda. We condemn hate language and incitement in all its forms. We suggest that the parties be particularly cautious about using words in a manner that suggests collective responsibility.

Economic and Social Impact of Violence: Further restrictions on the movement of people and goods have been imposed by Israel on the West

Bank and the Gaza Strip. These closures take three forms: those which restrict movement between the Palestinian areas and Israel; those (including curfews) which restrict movement within the Palestinian areas; and those which restrict movement from the Palestinian areas to foreign countries. These measures have disrupted the lives of hundreds of thousands of Palestinians; they have increased Palestinian unemployment to an estimated 40 percent, in part by preventing some 140,000 Palestinians from working in Israel; and have stripped away about one-third of the Palestinian gross domestic product. Moreover, the transfer of tax and customs duty revenues owed to the PA by Israel has been suspended, leading to a serious fiscal crisis in the PA.

Of particular concern to the PA has been the destruction by Israeli security forces and settlers of tens of thousands of olive and fruit trees and other agricultural property. The closures have had other adverse effects, such as preventing civilians from access to urgent medical treatment and preventing students from attending school.

The GOI maintains that these measures were taken in order to protect Israeli citizens from terrorism. Palestinians characterize these measures as "collective punishment." The GOI denies the allegation:

Israel has not taken measures that have had an economic impact simply for the sake of taking such measures or for reasons of harming the Palestinian economy. The measures have been taken for reasons of security. Thus, for example, the closure of the Palestinian territories was taken in order to prevent, or at least minimize the risks of, terrorist attacks. . . . The Palestinian leadership has made no attempt to control this activity and bring it to an end.

Moreover, the GOI points out that violence in the last quarter of 2000 cost the Israeli economy $1.2 billion (USD), and that the loss continues at a rate of approximately $150 million (USD) per month.

We acknowledge Israel's security concerns. We believe, however, that the GOI should lift closures, transfer to the PA all revenues owed, and permit Palestinians who have been employed in Israel to return to their jobs. Closure policies play into the hands of extremists seeking to expand their constituencies and thereby contribute to escalation. The PA should resume cooperation with Israeli security agencies to ensure that Palestinian workers employed within Israel are fully vetted and free of connections to terrorists and terrorist organizations.

International development assistance has from the start been an integral part of the peace process, with an aim to strengthen the socio-economic foundations for peace. This assistance today is more important than ever. We urge the international community to sustain the development agenda of the peace process.

Holy Places: It is particularly regrettable that places such as the Temple Mount/Haram al-Sharif in Jerusalem, Joseph's Tomb in Nablus, and Rachel's Tomb in Bethlehem have been the scenes of violence, death and injury. These are places of peace, prayer and reflection which must be accessible to all believers.

Places deemed holy by Muslims, Jews, and Christians merit respect, protection and preservation. Agreements previously reached by the parties regarding holy places must be upheld. The GOI and the PA should create a joint initiative to defuse the sectarian aspect of their political dispute by preserving and protecting such places. Efforts to develop interfaith dialogue should be encouraged.

International Force: One of the most controversial subjects raised during our inquiry was the issue of deploying an international force to the Palestinian areas. The PA is strongly in favor of having such a force to protect Palestinian civilians and their property from the IDF and from settlers. The GOI is just as adamantly opposed to an "international protection force," believing that it would prove unresponsive to Israeli security concerns and interfere with bilateral negotiations to settle the conflict.

We believe that to be effective such a force would need the support of both parties. We note that international forces deployed in this region have been or are in a position to fulfill their mandates and make a positive contribution only when they were deployed with the consent of all of the parties involved.

During our visit to Hebron, we were briefed by personnel of the Temporary International Presence in Hebron (TIPH), a presence to which both parties have agreed. The TIPH is charged with observing an explosive situation and writing reports on their observations. If the parties agree, as a confidence-building measure, to draw upon TIPH personnel to help them manage other friction points, we hope that TIPH contributors could accommodate such a request.

Cross-Community Initiatives: Many described to us the near absolute loss of trust. It was all the more inspiring, therefore, to find groups (such as the Parent's Circle and the Economic Cooperation Foundation) dedicated to cross-community understanding in spite of all that has happened. We commend them and their important work.

Regrettably, most of the work of this nature has stopped during the current conflict. To help rebuild confidence, the GOI and PA should jointly endorse and support the work of Israeli and Palestinian non-governmental organizations (NGOs) already involved in confidence-building through initiatives linking both sides. It is important that the PA and GOI support cross-community organizations and initiatives, including the provision of humanitarian assistance to Palestinian villages by Israeli NGOs. Providing travel permits for participants is essential. Cooperation between the humanitarian organizations and the military/security services of the parties should be encouraged and institutionalized.

Such programs can help build, albeit slowly, constituencies for peace among Palestinians and Israelis and can provide safety nets during times of turbulence. Organizations involved in this work are vital for translating good intentions into positive actions.

## RESUME NEGOTIATIONS

Israeli leaders do not wish to be perceived as "rewarding violence." Palestinian leaders do not wish to be perceived as "rewarding occupation." We appreciate the political constraints on leaders of both sides. Nevertheless, if the cycle of violence is to be broken and the search for peace resumed, there needs to be a new bilateral relationship incorporating both security cooperation and negotiations.

We cannot prescribe to the parties how best to pursue their political objectives. Yet the construction of a new bilateral relationship solidifying and transcending an agreed cessation of violence requires intelligent risk-taking. It requires, in the first instance, that each party again be willing to regard the other as a partner. Partnership, in turn, requires at this juncture something more than was agreed in the Declaration of Principles and in subsequent agreements. Instead of declaring the peace process to be "dead," the parties should determine how they will conclude their common journey along their agreed "road map," a journey which began in Madrid and continued—in spite of problems—until very recently.

To define a starting point is for the parties to decide. Both parties have stated that they remain committed to their mutual agreements and undertakings. It is time to explore further implementation. The parties should declare their intention to meet on this basis, in order to resume full and meaningful negotiations, in the spirit of their undertakings at Sharm el-Sheikh in 1999 and 2000.

Neither side will be able to achieve its principal objectives unilaterally or without political risk. We know how hard it is for leaders to act—especially if the action can be characterized by political opponents as a concession—without getting something in return. The PA must—as it has at previous critical junctures—take steps to reassure Israel on security matters. The GOI must—as it has in the past—take steps to reassure the PA on political matters. Israelis and Palestinians should avoid, in their own actions and attitudes, giving extremists, common criminals and revenge seekers the final say in defining their joint future. This will not be easy if deadly incidents occur in spite of effective cooperation. Notwithstanding the daunting difficulties, the very foundation of the trust required to re-establish a functioning partnership consists of each side making such strategic reassurances to the other.

## RECOMMENDATIONS

The GOI and the PA must act swiftly and decisively to halt the violence. Their immediate objectives then should be to rebuild confidence and resume negotiations. What we are asking is not easy. Palestinians and Israelis—not just their leaders, but two publics at large—have lost confidence in one another. We are asking political leaders to do, for the sake of their people, the politically difficult: to lead without knowing how many will follow.

During this mission our aim has been to fulfill the mandate agreed at Sharm el-Sheikh. We value the support given our work by the participants at the summit, and we commend the parties for their cooperation. Our principal recommendation is that they recommit themselves to the Sharm el-Sheikh spirit, and that they implement the decisions made there in 1999 and 2000. We believe that the summit participants will support bold action by the parties to achieve these objectives.

## END THE VIOLENCE

The GOI and the PA should reaffirm their commitment to existing agreements and undertakings and should immediately implement an unconditional cessation of violence.

Anything less than a complete effort by both parties to end the violence will render the effort itself ineffective, and will likely be interpreted by the other side as evidence of hostile intent.

The GOI and PA should immediately resume security cooperation.

Effective bilateral cooperation aimed at preventing violence will encourage the resumption of negotiations. We are particularly concerned that, absent effective, transparent security cooperation, terrorism and other acts of violence will continue and may be seen as officially sanctioned whether they are or not. The parties should consider widening the scope of security cooperation to reflect the priorities of both communities and to seek acceptance for these efforts from those communities.

We acknowledge the PA's position that security cooperation presents a political difficulty absent a suitable political context, i.e., the relaxation of stringent Israeli security measures combined with ongoing, fruitful negotiations. We also acknowledge the PA's fear that, with security cooperation in hand, the GOI may not be disposed to deal forthrightly with Palestinian political concerns. We believe that security cooperation cannot long be sustained if meaningful negotiations are unreasonably deferred, if security measures "on the ground" are seen as hostile, or if steps are taken that are perceived as provocative or as prejudicing the outcome of negotiations.

## REBUILD CONFIDENCE

The PA and GOI should work together to establish a meaningful "cooling off period" and implement additional confidence building measures, some of which were proposed in the October 2000 Sharm el-Sheikh Statement and some of which were offered by the U.S. on January 7, 2001 in Cairo.

The PA and GOI should resume their efforts to identify, condemn and discourage incitement in all its forms.

The PA should make clear through concrete action to Palestinians and Israelis alike that terrorism is reprehensible and unacceptable, and that the PA will make a 100 percent effort to prevent terrorist operations and to punish perpetrators. This effort should include immediate steps to apprehend and incarcerate terrorists operating within the PA's jurisdiction.

The GOI should freeze all settlement activity, including the "natural growth" of existing settlements.

The kind of security cooperation desired by the GOI cannot for long co-exist with settlement activity described very recently by the European Union as causing "great concern" and by the U.S. as "provocative."

The GOI should give careful consideration to whether settlements which are focal points for substantial friction are valuable bargaining chips for future negotiations or provocations likely to preclude the onset of productive talks.

The GOI may wish to make it clear to the PA that a future peace would pose no threat to the territorial contiguity of a Palestinian State to be established in the West Bank and the Gaza Strip.

The IDF should consider withdrawing to positions held before September 28, 2000 which will reduce the number of friction points and the potential for violent confrontations.

The GOI should ensure that the IDF adopt and enforce policies and procedures encouraging non-lethal responses to unarmed demonstrators, with a view to minimizing casualties and friction between the two communities. The IDF should:

Re-institute, as a matter of course, military police investigations into Palestinian deaths resulting from IDF actions in the Palestinian territories in incidents not involving terrorism. The IDF should abandon the blanket characterization of the current uprising as "an armed conflict short of war," which fails to discriminate between terrorism and protest.

Adopt tactics of crowd-control that minimize the potential for deaths and casualties, including the withdrawal of metal-cored rubber rounds from general use.

Ensure that experienced, seasoned personnel are present for duty at all times at known friction points.

Ensure that the stated values and standard operating procedures of the IDF effectively instill the duty of caring for Palestinians in the West Bank and Gaza Strip as well as Israelis living there, consistent with The Ethical Code of the IDF.

The GOI should lift closures, transfer to the PA all tax revenues owed, and permit Palestinians who had been employed in Israel to return to their jobs; and should ensure that security forces and settlers refrain from the destruction of homes and roads, as well as trees and other agricultural property in Palestinian areas. We acknowledge the GOI's position that actions of this nature have been taken for security reasons. Nevertheless, their economic effects will persist for years.

The PA should renew cooperation with Israeli security agencies to ensure, to the maximum extent possible, that Palestinian workers employed within Israel are fully vetted and free of connections to organizations and individuals engaged in terrorism.

The PA should prevent gunmen from using Palestinian populated areas to fire upon Israeli populated areas and IDF positions. This tactic places civilians on both sides at unnecessary risk.

The GOI and IDF should adopt and enforce policies and procedures designed to ensure that the response to any gunfire emanating from Palestinian populated areas minimizes the danger to the lives and property of Palestinian civilians, bearing in mind that it is probably the objective of gunmen to elicit an excessive IDF response.

The GOI should take all necessary steps to prevent acts of violence by settlers.

The parties should abide by the provisions of the Wye River Agreement prohibiting illegal weapons.

The PA should take all necessary steps to establish a clear and unchallenged chain of command for armed personnel operating under its authority.

The PA should institute and enforce effective standards of conduct and accountability, both within the uniformed ranks and between the police and the civilian political leadership to which it reports.

The PA and GOI should consider a joint undertaking to preserve and protect holy places sacred to the traditions of Muslims, Jews, and Christians. An initiative of this nature might help to reverse a disturbing trend: the increasing use of religious themes to encourage and justify violence.

The GOI and PA should jointly endorse and support the work of Palestinian and Israeli non-governmental organizations (NGOs) involved in cross-community initiatives linking the two peoples. It is important that these activities, including the provision of humanitarian aid to Palestinian villages by Israeli NGOs, receive the full backing of both parties.

## RESUME NEGOTIATIONS

We reiterate our belief that a 100 percent effort to stop the violence, an immediate resumption of security cooperation and an exchange of confidence building measures are all important for the resumption of negotiations. Yet none of these steps will long be sustained absent a return to serious negotiations.

It is not within our mandate to prescribe the venue, the basis or the agenda of negotiations. However, in order to provide an effective political context for practical cooperation between the parties, negotiations must not be unreasonably deferred and they must, in our view, manifest a spirit of compromise, reconciliation and partnership, notwithstanding the events of the past seven months.

In the spirit of the Sharm el-Sheikh agreements and understandings of 1999 and 2000, we recommend that the parties meet to reaffirm their commitment to signed agreements and mutual understandings, and take corresponding action. This should be the basis for resuming full and meaningful negotiations.

The parties are at a crossroads. If they do not return to the negotiating table, they face the prospect of fighting it out for years on end, with many of their citizens leaving for distant shores to live their lives and raise their children. We pray they make the right choice. That means stopping the violence now. Israelis and Palestinians have to live, work, and prosper together. History and geography have destined them to be neighbors. That cannot be changed. Only when their actions are guided by this awareness will they be able to develop the vision and reality of peace and shared prosperity.

Suleyman Demirel
9th President of the Republic of Turkey

Thorbjoern Jagland
Minister of Foreign Affairs of Norway

George J. Mitchell, Chairman
Former Member and Majority Leader of the United States Senate

Warren B. Rudman
Former Member of the United States Senate

Javier Solana
High Representative for the Common Foreign and Security Policy, European Union

Source:
http://www.yale.edu/lawweb/avalon/mideast/mitchell_plan.htm

Palestinian-Israeli Security Implementation Work Plan
(Tenet cease-fire plan)
(as published in Ha'aretz, June 14, 2001)

The security organizations of the Government of Israel (GOI) and of the Palestinian Authority (PA) reaffirm their commitment to the security agreements forged at Sharm al-Sheikh in October 2000 embedded in the Mitchell Report of April 2001.

The operational premise of the workplan is that the two sides are committed to a mutual, comprehensive cease-fire, applying to all violent activities, in accordance with the public declaration of both leaders. In addition, the joint security committee referenced in this workplan will resolve issues that may arise during the implementation of this workplan.

The security organizations of the GOI and PA agree to initiate the following specific, concrete, and realistic security steps immediately to reestablish security cooperation and the situation on the ground as they existed prior to 28 September.

1. The GOI and the PA will immediately resume security cooperation.
   - A senior-level meeting of Israeli, Palestinian, and US security officials will be held immediately and will reconvene at least once a week, with mandatory participation by designated senior officials.
   - Israeli-Palestinian DCOs will be reinvigorated. They will carry out their daily activities, to the maximum extent possible, according to the standards established prior to 28 September 2000. As soon as the security situation permits, barriers to effective cooperation—which include the erection of walls between the Israeli and Palestinian sides—will be eliminated and joint Israeli-Palestinian patrols will be reinitiated.
   - US-supplied video conferencing systems will be provided to senior-level Israeli and Palestinian officials to facilitate frequent dialogue and security cooperation.
2. Both sides will take immediate measures to enforce strict adherence to the declared cease-fire and to stabilize the security environment.
   - Specific procedures will be developed by the senior-level security committee to ensure the secure movement of GOI and PA security personnel traveling in areas outside their respective control, in accordance with existing agreements.
   - Israel will not conduct attacks of any kind against the Palestinian Authority Ra'is facilities: the headquarters of Palestinian security, intelligence, and police organization; or prisons in the West Bank and Gaza.
   - The PA will move immediately to apprehend, question, and incarcerate terrorists in the West Bank and Gaza and will pro-

vide the security committee the names of those arrested as soon as they are apprehended, as well as a readout of actions taken.

- Israel will release all Palestinians arrested in security sweeps who have no association with terrorist activities.
- In keeping with its unilateral cease-fire declaration, the PA will stop any Palestinian security officials from inciting, aiding, abetting, or conducting attacks against Israeli targets, including settlers.
- In keeping with Israel's unilateral cease-fire declaration, Israeli forces will not conduct "proactive" security operations in areas under the control of the PA or attack against innocent civilian targets.
- The GOI will re-institute military police investigations into Palestinian deaths resulting from IDF actions in the West Bank and Gaza in incidents not involving terrorism.

3. Palestinian and Israeli security officials will use the security committee to provide each other, as well as designated US officials, terrorist threat information, including information on known or suspected terrorist operation in—or moving to—areas under the other's control.

- Legitimate terrorist and threat information will be acted upon immediately, with follow-up actions and results reported to the security committee.
- The PA will undertake preemptive operations against terrorists, terrorist safehouses, arms depots, and mortar factories. The PA will provide regular progress reports of these actions to the security committee.
- Israeli authorities will take action against Israeli citizens inciting, carrying out, or planning to carry out violence against Palestinians, with progress reports on these activities provided to the security committee.

4. The PA and GOI will move aggressively to prevent individuals and groups from using areas under their respective control to carry out acts of violence. In addition, both sides will take steps to ensure that areas under their control will not be used to launch attacks against the other side nor be used as refuge after attacks are staged.

- The security committee will identify key flash points, and each side will inform the other of the names of senior security personnel responsible for each flash point.
- Joint Standard Operating Procedures (SOP's) will be developed for each flash point. These SOP's will address how the two sides handle and respond to security incidents; the mechanisms

for emergency contact; and the procedures to deescalate security crises.

- Palestinian and Israeli security officials will identify and agree to the practical measures needed to enforce "no demonstration zones" and "buffer zones" around flash points to reduce opportunities for confrontation. Both sides will adopt all necessary measures to prevent riots and to control demonstration, particularly in flash point areas.

- Palestinian and Israeli security officials will make a concerted effort to locate and confiscate illegal weapons, including mortars, rockets, and explosives, in areas under their respective control In addition, intensive efforts will be made to prevent smuggling and illegal production of weapons. Each side will inform the security committee of the status and success of these efforts.

- The Israeli Defense Forces (IDF) will adopt additional non-lethal measures to deal with Palestinian crowds and demonstrators, and more generally, seek to minimize the danger to lives and property of Palestinian civilians in responding to violence.

5. The GOI and the PA, through the auspices of the senior-level security committee, will forge—within one week of the commencement of security committee meetings and resumption of security cooperation—an agreed-upon schedule to implement the complete redeployment of IDF forces to positions held before 28 September 2000.

- Demonstrable on-the-ground redeployment will be initiated within the first 48 hours of this one-week period and will continue while the schedule is being forged.

6. Within one week of the commencement of security committee meetings and resumption of security cooperation, a specific timeline will be developed for the lifting of interal closures as well as for the reopening of internal roads, the Allenby Bridge, Gaza Airport, Port of Gaza, and border crossings. Security checkpoints will be minimized according to legitimate security requirements and following consultation between the two sides.

- Demonstrable on-the-ground actions on the lifting of the closures will be initiated within the first 48 hours of this one-week period and will continue while the timeline is being developed. The parties pledge that even if untoward events occur, security cooperation will continue through the joint security committee.

Source: http://www.israel.org/mfa/go.asp?MFAH0khz0

The Saudi Peace Plan March 28, 2002

"The Council of Arab States at the summit level at its 14th ordinary session, reaffirming the resolution taken in June 1996 at the extraordinary Arab summit that a just and comprehensive peace in the Middle East is the strategic option of the Arab countries, to be achieved in accordance with international legality, and which would require a comparable commitment on the part of the Israeli government;

"Having listened to the statement made by his royal highness Prince Abdullah bin Abdul Aziz, Crown prince of the Kingdom of Saudi Arabia, in which his highness presented his initiative calling for full Israeli withdrawal from Arab territories occupied since June 1967, in implementation of Security Council resolutions 242 and 338, reaffirmed by the Madrid conference of the 1991 and the land-for-peace principle, and Israel's acceptance of an independent Palestinian state with East Jerusalem as its capital, in return for the establishment of normal relations in the context of comprehensive peace with Israel, emanating from the conviction of the Arab countries that a military solution to the conflict will not achieve peace or provide security for the parties, the council:

1. Requests Israel to request its policies and declare that a just peace is its strategic option as well
2. Further calls upon Israel to affirm: Full Israeli withdrawal from all territories occupied since 1967, including the Syrian Golan Heights to the June 4, 1967 lines as well as the remaining occupied Lebanese territories in the south of Lebanon; II Achievement of a just solution to the Palestinian refugee problem to be agreed upon in accordance with U.N. General Assembly Resolution 194; III The acceptance of the establishment of sovereign independent Palestinian state on the Palestinian territories occupied since June 4, 1967 in the West Bank and Gaza Strip, with East Jerusalem as its capital.
3. Consequently, the Arab countries affirm the following: Consider the Arab-Israeli conflict ended, and enter into a peace agreement with Israel, and provide security for all the states of the region; Establish normal relations with Israel in the context of this comprehensive peace.
4. Assures the rejection of all forms of Palestinian patriation which conflict with special circumstances of the Arab host countries.
5. Calls upon the government of Israel and Israel's to accept this initiative in order to safeguard the prospects for peace and stop the further shedding of blood, enabling the Arab countries and Israel to live in peace and good neighbour lines and provide future generations with security, stability and prosperity.

6. Invites the International community and all countries and organizations to support this initiative.

7. Requests the chairman of the summit to form a special committee composed of some of its concerned member states and the secretary general of the League of Arab States to pursue the necessary contacts to gain support for this initiative at all levels, particularly from the United Nations, the Security Council, the United States of America, the Russian Federation, the Moslem states and the European Union."

Source:http://www.mideastweb.org/SaudiPeace.htm

## Text of President George W. Bush's Address on the Middle East June 25, 2002

*Following is a transcript of President Bush's speech from June 25, 2002 on the Middle East.*

"For too long, the citizens of the Middle East have lived in the midst of death and fear. The hatred of a few holds the hopes of many hostage. The forces of extremism and terror are attempting to kill progress and peace by killing the innocent. And this casts a dark shadow over an entire region.

For the sake of all humanity, things must change in the Middle East.

It is untenable for Israeli citizens to live in terror. It is untenable for Palestinians to live in squalor and occupation. And the current situation offers no prospect that life will improve. Israeli citizens will continue to be victimized by terrorists, and so Israel will continue to defend herself, and the situation of the Palestinian people will grow more and more miserable.

My vision is two states, living side by side, in peace and security. There is simply no way to achieve that peace until all parties fight terror.

Yet at this critical moment, if all parties will break with the past and set out on a new path, we can overcome the darkness with the light of hope.

Peace requires a new and different Palestinian leadership, so that a Palestinian state can be born.

I call on the Palestinian people to elect new leaders, leaders not compromised by terror. I call upon them to build a practicing democracy based on tolerance and liberty.

If the Palestinian people actively pursue these goals, America and the world will actively support their efforts. If the Palestinian people meet these goals, they will be able to reach agreement with Israel and Egypt and Jordan on security and other arrangements for independence.

And when the Palestinian people have new leaders, new institutions and new security arrangements with their neighbors, the United States of America will support the creation of a Palestinian state, whose borders and certain aspects of its sovereignty will be provisional until resolved as part of a final settlement in the Middle East.

In the work ahead, we all have responsibilities. The Palestinian people are gifted and capable and I'm confident they can achieve a new birth for their nation.

A Palestinian state will never be created by terror. It will be built through reform. And reform must be more than cosmetic change or a veiled attempt to preserve the status quo. True reform will require entirely new political and economic institutions based on democracy, market economics and action against terrorism.

Today, the elected Palestinian legislature has no authority, and power is concentrated in the hands of an unaccountable few. A Palestinian state can only serve its citizens with a new constitution which separates the powers of government.

The Palestinian parliament should have the full authority of a legislative body. Local officials and government ministers need authority of their own and the independence to govern effectively.

The United States, along with the European Union [EU] and Arab states, will work with Palestinian leaders to create a new constitutional framework and a working democracy for the Palestinian people. And the United States, along with others in the international community, will help the Palestinians organize and monitor fair, multiparty local elections by the end of the year, with national elections to follow.

Today, the Palestinian people live in economic stagnation, made worse by official corruption. A Palestinian state will require a vibrant economy, where honest enterprise is encouraged by honest government.

The United States, the international donor community and the World Bank stand ready to work with Palestinians on a major project of economic reform and development. The United States, the EU, the World Bank and the International Monetary Fund are willing to oversee reforms in Palestinian finances, encouraging transparency and independent auditing. And the United States, along with our partners in the developed world, will increase our humanitarian assistance to relieve Palestinian suffering.

Today, the Palestinian people lack effective courts of law and have no means to defend and vindicate their rights. A Palestinian state will require a system of reliable justice to punish those who prey on the innocent. The United States and members of the international community stand ready to work with Palestinian leaders to establish, finance and monitor a truly independent judiciary.

Today, Palestinian authorities are encouraging, not opposing terrorism.

This is unacceptable. And the United States will not support the establishment of a Palestinian state until its leaders engage in a sustained fight against the terrorists and dismantle their infrastructure.

This will require an externally supervised effort to rebuild and reform the Palestinian security services. The security system must have clear lines of authority and accountability, and a unified chain of command.

America's pursuing this reform along with key regional states. The world is prepared to help, yet ultimately these steps toward statehood depend on the Palestinian people and their leaders. If they energetically take the path of reform, the rewards can come quickly. If Palestinians embrace democracy, confront corruption and firmly reject terror, they can count on American support for the creation of a provisional state of Palestine.

With a dedicated effort, this state could rise rapidly, as it comes to terms with Israel, Egypt and Jordan on practical issues such as security. The final borders, the capital and other aspects of this state's sovereignty will be negotiated between the parties as part of a final settlement.

Arab states have offered their help in this process, and their help is needed.

I've said in the past that nations are either with us or against us in the war on terror. To be counted on the side of peace, nations must act. Every leader actually committed to peace will end incitement to violence in official media and publicly denounce homicide bombings. Every nation actually committed to peace will stop the flow of money, equipment and recruits to terrorist groups seeking the destruction of Israel, including Hamas, Islamic Jihad and Hezbollah.

Every nation actually committed to peace must block the shipment of Iranian supplies to these groups and oppose regimes that promote terror, like Iraq.

And Syria must choose the right side in the war on terror by closing terrorist camps and expelling terrorist organizations.

Leaders who want to be included in the peace process must show by their deeds an undivided support for peace.

And as we move toward a peaceful solution, Arab states will be expected to build closer ties of diplomacy and commerce with Israel, leading to full normalization of relations between Israel and the entire Arab world.

Israel also has a large stake in the success of a democratic Palestine. Permanent occupation threatens Israel's identity and democracy. A stable, peaceful Palestinian state is necessary to achieve the security that Israel longs for.

So I challenge Israel to take concrete steps to support the emergence of a viable, credible Palestinian state.

As we make progress toward security, Israel forces need to withdraw fully to positions they held prior to September 28, 2000. And consistent with the recommendations of the Mitchell committee, Israeli settlement activity in the occupied territories must stop.

The Palestinian economy must be allowed to develop. As violence subsides, freedom of movement should be restored, permitting innocent Palestinians to resume work and normal life. Palestinian legislators and officials, humanitarian and international workers, must be allowed to go about the business of building a better future. And Israel should release frozen Palestinian revenues into honest, accountable hands.

I've asked Secretary [of State Colin L.] Powell to work intensively with Middle Eastern and international leaders to realize the vision of a Palestinian state, focusing them on a comprehensive plan to support Palestinian reform and institution building.

Ultimately, Israelis and Palestinians must address the core issues that divide them if there is to be a real peace, resolving all claims and ending the conflict between them.

This means that the Israeli occupation that began in 1967 will be ended through a settlement negotiated between the parties, based on U.N. Resolutions 242 and 338, with Israeli withdrawal to secure and recognized borders.

We must also resolve questions concerning Jerusalem, the plight and future of Palestinian refugees, and a final peace between Israel and Lebanon and [between] Israel and a Syria that supports peace and fights terror.

All who are familiar with the history of the Middle East realize that there may be setbacks in this process. Trained and determined killers, as we have seen, want to stop it. Yet the Egyptian and Jordanian peace treaties with Israel remind us that, with determined and responsible leadership, progress can come quickly.

As new Palestinian institutions and new leaders emerge, demonstrating real performance on security and reform, I expect Israel to respond and work toward a final status agreement.

With intensive effort by all of us, agreement could be reached within three years from now. And I and my country will actively lead toward that goal.

I can understand the deep anger and anguish of the Israeli people. You've lived too long with fear and funerals, having to avoid markets and public transportation, and forced to put armed guards in kindergarten classrooms. The Palestinian Authority has rejected your offered hand and trafficked with terrorists. You have a right to a normal life. You have a right to security. And I deeply believe that you need a reformed, responsible Palestinian partner to achieve that security.

I can understand the deep anger and despair of the Palestinian people. For decades you've been treated as pawns in the Middle East conflict. Your interests have been held hostage to a comprehensive peace agreement that never seems to come, as your lives get worse year by year.

You deserve democracy and the rule of law. You deserve an open society and a thriving economy. You deserve a life of hope for your children.

An end to occupation and a peaceful democratic Palestinian state may seem distant, but America and our partners throughout the world stand ready to help, help you make that possible as soon as possible.

If liberty can blossom in the rocky soil of the West Bank and Gaza, it will inspire millions of men and women around the globe, who are equally weary of poverty and oppression, equally entitled to the benefits of democratic government.

I have a hope for the people of Muslim countries. Your commitments to morality and learning and tolerance led to great historical achievements, and those values are alive in the Islamic world today. You have a rich culture, and you share the aspirations of men and women in every culture. Prosperity and freedom and dignity are not just American hopes or Western hopes, they are universal human hopes. And even in the violence and turmoil of the Middle East, America believes those hopes have the power to transform lives and nations.

This moment is both an opportunity and a test for all parties in the Middle East: an opportunity to lay the foundations for future peace; a test to show who is serious about peace and who is not.

The choice here is stark and simple. The Bible says, "I have set before you life and death . . . therefore choose life . . . " The time has arrived for everyone in this conflict to choose peace and hope and life.

Thank you very much.

Source: http://www.whitehouse.gov/news/releases/2002/06/ 20020624-3.html

# SELECTED BIBLIOGRAPHY

## BOOKS AND MONOGRAPHS

'Abd al-Jawad, Salih, *The Israeli Assassination Policy in the Aqsa Intifada.* East Jerusalem: Jerusalem Media & Communication Center, 2001.

Abu 'Amr, Ziyad, *Islamic fundamentalism in the West Bank and Gaza: Muslim Brotherhood and Islamic Jihad.* Bloomington: Indiana University Press, 1994.

Adams, James, *The Financing of Terror: the PLO, IRA, Red Brigades and M-19, and Their Money Supply.* New York: Simon and Schuster, 1980.

Alexander, Yonah, *Middle East Terrorism: Current Threats and Future Prospects.* Aldershot: Dartmouth, 1994.

Alexander, Yonah, *Middle East Terrorism: Selected Group Profiles.* Washington: Jewish Institute for National Security Affairs, 1994.

Alexander, Yonah and Sinai, Joshua, *Terrorism: the PLO Connection.* New York: Crane Russak, 1989.

Amer, Z. Abu, *Islamic Fundamentalism in the West Bank and Gaza: Muslim Brotherhood and Islamic Jihad.* Indiana: Indiana Press University, 1994.

Appleby, R. Scott, *Spokesmen for the Despised: Fundamentalist Leaders of the Middle East.* Chicago: University of Chicago Press, 1997.

Aronson, Geoffrey, *Israel, Palestinians, and the Intifada: Creating Facts on the West Bank.* New York: Routledge, Chapman and Hall, 1990.

Aruri, Naseer Hasan, *Palestinian Refugees: the Right of Return.* London; Sterling VA: Pluto Press, 2001.

Asia, Ilan, *The Quest for Arab Territorial Continuity as a Focus of the Middle East Conflict.* Ariel, Israel: Ariel Center for Policy Research, 1998.

Asmar, Marwan, *Intifada II: Media and Politics.* Amman: Ad-Dustour Commercial Presses, 2001.

Ashrawi, Hanan and Lederman, Jim, *The Coming of Age: an Anatomy of the Palestinian Intifada.* Tunis: Palestinian Liberation Organization, Unified Information, 1988.

Ateek, Naim Stifan and Prior, Michael, *Holy Land, Hollow Jubilee: God, Justice, and the Palestinians.* London: Melisende, 1999.

Bard, Mitchell Geoffrey, *Myths and Facts: a Guide to the Arab-Israeli Conflict.* Chevy Chase, MD: America Israeli Cooperative Enterprise, 2001.

Barghouti, Mustafa, *The Post-Oslo Impasse.* Washington DC: The Center for Policy Analysis on Palestine, 1998.

Bar-Siman-Tov, Yaacov, *Israel and the Intifada: Adaptation and Learning.*

Jerusalem: The Leonard Davis Institute for International Relations, The Hebrew University of Jerusalem, 2000.

Bawley, Dan and Salpeter, Elihu, *Fire in Beirut: Israel's War in Lebanon with the PLO*, Briarcliff Manor NY: Stein and Day, 1984.

Becker, Jillian, *The PLO: the Rise and Fall of the Palestinian Liberation Organization*. New York: St. Martin's Press, 1984.

Beilin, Yossi, *Touching Peace: from the Oslo Accords to a Final Agreement*. London: Weidenfeld & Nicolson, 1999.

Benvenisti, Meron, *Intimate Enemies Jews and Arabs in a Shared Land*. Berkeley: University of California Press, 1995.

Ben-Yehuda, Hemda and Sandler, Shmuel, *The Arab-Israeli Conflict Transformed: Fifty Years of Interstate and Ethnic Crises*. Albany, NY: State University of New York Press, 2002.

Beres, Louis Rene, *Israel's Survival Imperatives: the Oslo Agreements in International Law and National Strategy*. Ariel, Israel: Ariel Center for Policy Research, 1998.

Binder, Leonard, *Ethnic Conflict and International Politics in the Middle East*. Gainsville, FL: University Press of Florida, 1999.

Bishara, Marwan, *Palestine/Israel: Peace or Apartheid: Prospects for Resolving the Conflict*. Halifax, N.S.: Fernwood Pub., 2001.

Bix, Herbert P., *The Occupied Territories Under Israeli Rule: on the Origins of the Intifada*. Sheffield: Dept. of Politics, University of Sheffield, 1991.

Bleving, Leonard C., *The PLO: A Victory in Terrorism?* Fort Leavenworth, Kan.: US Army Command and General Staff College, 1991.

Bornstein, Avram, *Crossing the Green Line Between the West Bank and Israel*. Philadelphia, PA: University of Pennsylvania Press, 2001.

Bregman, Ahron, *Israel's War: From the 1947 Palestine War to the Al-Aqsa Intifada*. London: Routledge, 2002.

Bregman, Ahron and El-Tahri, Jihad, *The Fifty Years' War: Israel and the Arabs*. New York: TV Books, 1999.

Bryren, Rex, *Echoes of the Intifada: Regional Repercussions of the Palestinian-Israeli Conflict*. Boulder: Westview Press, 1991.

Bryren, Rex, *Sanctuary and Survival: the PLO in Lebanon*. Boulder; London: Westview Press, Pinter Publishers, 1990.

Buchanan, Andrew S., *Peace with Justice: a History of the Israeli-Palestinian Declaration of Principles on Interim Self-Government Arrangements*. Houndmills, Basingstoke, Hampshire: Macmillan Press, 2000.

Buckley, Richard and King, John, *Middle East Stalemate: What Hopes for Progress Now?* Cheltenham: Understanding Global Issues, 1999.

Carey, Roane, *The New Intifada: Resisting Israel's Apartheid*. London: Verso, 2001.

Cattan, Henry, *The Palestine Question*. London: Saqi, 2000.

Cohen, Stuart, Kanovsky, Eliyahu and Inbar, Efraim, *Military, Economic and*

*Strategic Aspects of the Middle East Peace Process*. Ramat Gan, Israel: Bar-Ilan University, 1995.

Cordesman, Anthony H., *Peace and War: the Arab-Israeli Military Balance Enters the 21st Century*. Westport, Conn.: Praeger, 2002.

Cubert, Harold M., *The PFLP's Changing Role in the Middle East*. London: F.Cass, 1997.

Dajani, Souad R., *Eyes Without Country: Searching for a Palestinian Strategy of Liberation*. Philadelphia: Temple University Press, 1995.

Ditchek, Janice, *The Palestine National Council and the PLO*. New York: Anti-Defamation League of B'nai B'rith, 1985.

Djerejian, Edward P., *Strategic Equation of Peace: the Negotiations Between Israel, Syria and Lebanon*. Tel Aviv, Israel: Tel Aviv University, 1999.

Dolan, David, *Israel in Crisis: What Lies Ahead?* Grand Rapids, MI: Fleming H. Revell, 2001.

Downing, David, *Yasser Arafat*. Oxford: Heinemann Library, 2002.

Elon, Amos, *A Blood-Dimmed Tide: Dispatches From the Middle East*. London: Penguin, 2001.

Esposito, John L., *Political Islam: Revolution, Radicalism, or Reform?* Boulder: Lynne Rienner Publishers, 1997.

Finkelstein, Norman G., *The Rise and Fall of Palestine: A Personal Account of the Intifada Years*. Minneapolis: University of Minnesota Press, 1996.

Finkelstein, Norman G., *Image and Reality of the Israel-Palestine Conflict*. London: Verso, 2001.

Frangi, Abdallah, *The PLO and Palestine*. London: Zed, 2001.

Frankel, Glenn, *Beyond the Promised Land: Jews and Arabs on the Hard Road to a New Israel*. New York: Simon & Schuster, 1996.

Freedman, Robert Owen, *The Intifada: Its Impact on Israel, the Arab World and the Superpowers*. Miami: Florida International University Press, 1991.

Freedman, Robert Owen, *The Middle East and the Peace Process: the Impact of the Oslo Accords*. Gainsville: University Press of Florida, 1998.

Freund, Wolfgang, *Palestinian Perspectives*. Frankfurt: Peter Lang 1999.

Friedman, Thomas L., *From Beirut to Jerusalem*. New York: Anchor Books, 1995.

Gabriel, Richard A., *Operation Peace for Galilee: the Israeli-PLO War in Lebanon*. New York: Hill and Wang, 1984.

Gazit, Mordechai, *Israeli Diplomacy and the Quest for Peace*. London: Franck Cass, 2002.

Gefen, Aba, *Israel at a Crossroads*. Jerusalem: Gefen Pub. 2001.

Giacaman, George and Lønning, Dag Jørund, *After Oslo: New Realities, Old Problem*. London: Pluto Press, 1998.

Gilbert, Martin, *The Arab-Israeli Conflict—Its History in Maps*. London: Weidenfeld and Nicolson, 1979.

Gilboa, Amos, *The Threat of PLO Terrorism*. Jerusalem: Ministry of Foreign Affairs, 1985.

Ginat, J and Perkins, Edward J., *The Palestinian Refugees: Old Problems—New Solutions*. Norman, OK: University of Oklahoma Press, 2001.

Gordon, Neve and Lopez, George A., *Terrorism in the Arab-Israeli Conflict*, Notre Dame: University of Notre Dame, 1999.

Gowers, Andrew and Walker Tony, *Behind the Myth: Yasser Arafat and the Palestinian Revolution*. London: Corgi, 1991.

Gresh, Alain, *The PLO: the Struggle Within: Towards an Independent Palestinian State*. London: Zed Books, 1988.

Gruen, George E., *The PLO and the Palestinian Uprising: Their Tactics and Declared Objectives*. New York: American Jewish Committee, 1988.

Hamid, Rashid, *What is the PLO?* London: PLO, 1981.

Hilewitz, Yehuda, *PLO and Palestinian-Inspired Terrorism, 1982–1985: the Continuing Record of Violence*. New York: Anti-Defamation League of B'nei B'rith, 1985.

Hiro, Dilip, *Sharing the Promised Land: a Tale of the Israelis and Palestinians*. New York: Olive Branch Press, 1999.

Holliday, Laurel, *Why do They Hate Me: Young Lives Caught in War and Conflict*. New York: Pocket Books, 1999.

Hunter, Robert F., *The Palestinian Uprising: a War by Other Means*. Berkeley: University of California Press, 1993.

Hunter, Shireen, *The PLO After Tripoli*. Washington, D.C.: Center for Strategic and International Studies, Georgetown University, 1984.

Inbari, Pinhas, *The Palestinians Between Terrorism and Statehood*. Brighton: Sussex Academic Press, 1996.

Jamal, Amal Ahmad, *Mobilization Under Control: the PLO and the Palestinians in the West Bank and the Gaza Strip*. Yarka, Israel: A.A. Jamal, 1996.

Kaleh, Hala and Calderini, Simonetta, *The Intifada: the Palestinian Uprising in the West Bank and Gaza Strip: A Bibliography of Books and Articles, 1987–1992*. Oxford: Middle East Libraries Committee, 1993.

Kaminer, Reuven, *The Politics of Protest: the Israeli Peace Movement and the Palestinian Intifada*. Brighton, UK: Sussex Academic Press, 1996.

Kanovsky, Eliyahu, *Arab-Israel Peace Agreements Since Camp David: a Look Backward and a Look Ahead*. Ariel, Israel: Ariel Center for Policy Research, 1997.

Karsh, Efraim, *Between War and Peace: Dilemmas of Israeli Security*. Portland: F. Cass, 1996.

Katz, Samuel M., *Israel Versus Jibril: the Thirty-Year War Against a Master Terrorist*. New York: Paragon House, 1993.

Khamenei, Ali, *We Support the Intifada*. London: Center for Islamic Political Studies, 2001.

Khatchadourian, Haig, *The Quest for Peace Between Israel and the Palestinians*. New York: Peter Land Publishing, 2000.

Kirisci, Kemal, *The PLO and World Politics: a Study of Mobilization of Support for the Palestinian Cause*. New York: St. Martin's Press, 1986.

Klein, Morton A., *Six years of Palestinian Arab Violations of the Oslo Accords—an Assessment of Palestinian Arab Compliance Since the Signing of the Israel-PLO Accords*, September 13, 1993–September 13, 1999. New York: Zionist Organization of America, 1999.

Klein, Yitzhak, *Israel's War With the Palestinians: Sources, Political Objectives, and Operational Means*. Shaarei Tikva, Israel: The Ariel Center for Policy Research, 2001.

Laffin, John, *The PLO Connections*. London: Corgi Books, 1983.

La Guardia, Anton, *Holy Land, Unholy War: Israelis and Palestinians*. London: John Murray, 2001.

Laqueuer, Walter and Rubin, Barry M., *The Israeli-Arab Reader: a Documentary History of the Middle East Conflict*. New York: Penguin Books, 2001.

Lesch, Ann Mosely and Tessler, Mark A., *Israel, Egypt and the Palestinians: From Camp David to Intifada*. Bloomington: Indiana University Press, 1989.

Levitt, Wendy, *Intifada: The Palestinian's Popular Uprising*. London: Kegan Paul, 1990.

Livingstone, Neil C. and Halevy, David, *Inside the PLO: Covert Units, Secret Funds, and the War Against Israel and the United States*. Washington: Morrow, 1990.

Lewis Bernard, *The Palestinians and the PLO: a Historical Approach*. New York: American Jewish Committee, 1975.

Lustick, Ian, *The Conflict With Israel in Arab Politics and Society*. New York: Garland, 1994.

Lustick, Ian, *From Wars Toward Peace in the Arab-Israeli Conflict,* New York: Garland Publishers, 1994.

Makovsky, David, *Making Peace with the PLO: the Rabin Government's Road to the Oslo Accords*. Boulder: Westview Press, 1999.

Masadeh, Mohamad Taisir, *The Search for Security in the Middle East Between Israel and Neighboring Countries*. Carlisle Barracks, PA: US Army War College, 2000.

McDowall, David, *The Palestinians: the Road to Nationhood*. London: Minority Rights Publications, 1995.

Merari, Ariel, *PLO: Core of World Terror*. Jerusalem: Carta, 1983.

Miller, Aaron David, *The PLO and the Politics of Survival*. New York: Praeger, 1983.

Mishal, Shaul, *The PLO Under Arafat: Between Gun and Olive Branch*, New Haven: Yale University Press, 1986.

Mishal, Shaul and Aharoni, Re'uven, *Speaking Stones: Communiqués From the Intifada Underground*. Syracuse, NY: Syracuse University Press, 1994.

Mollen, Bjorn, *Three Futures for Israel and Palestine*. Copenhagen: Copenhagen Peace Research Institute, 1999.

Moses-Hrushovski, Rena and Moses, Rafael, *Grief and Grievance: The*

*Assassination of Yitzhak Rabin.* London: Minerva Press, 2000.

Mussalam, Sami, *The Palestinian Liberation Organization—Its Function and Structure.* Brattleboro, VT: Amana Books, 1990.

Naaz, Farah, *The Road to Peace: the Israeli-Palestinian Conflict.* New Delhi, India: Institute for Defense Studies and Analyses, 2000.

Nacer, Zabout, *A Child of the Intifada.* London: Minerva, 2001.

Nassar, Jamal R. and Heacock, Roger, *Intifada: Palestine at the Crossroads.* New York: Praeger, 1990.

Norton, Augustus R. and Greenberg, Martin Harry, *The International Relations of the Palestinian Liberation Organization.* Carbondale: Southern Illinois University Press, 1989.

Nusaybah, Sirri, *Palestine: a State is Born.* The Hague: Palestine Information Office, 1990.

O'Ballance, Edgar, *The Palestinian Intifada.* New York: St. Martin's Press, 1998.

Oren, Michael, *PLO, Nexus for International Terror.* Jerusalem: Jerusalem Center for Public Affairs, Jerusalem Institute for Federal Studies, Center for Jewish Community Studies, 1983.

Ovendale, Ritchie, *The Origins of the Arab-Israeli Wars.* London: Longman, 1999.

Peretz, Don, *Intifada: The Palestinian Uprising.* Boulder: Westview Press, 1990.

Rabinovich, Itamar, *Waging Peace: Israel and the Arabs at the End of the Century.* New York: Farar, Straus and Giroux, 1999.

Randal, Jonathan C., *The Tragedy of Lebanon: Christian Warlords, Israeli Adventurers and the PLO.* New York: Viking Press, 1983.

Rapoport, David C., *Inside Terrorist Organizations.* London: Frank Cass Co., 2001.

Reich, Bernard, *Arab-Israeli Conflict and Conciliation: A Documentary History.* Westport, CT: Greenwood Press, 1995.

Robinson, Glenn E., *Building a Palestinian State: the Incomplete Revolution.* Bloomington: Indiana University Press, 1997.

Rubin, Barry M., *Inside the PLO: Officials, Notables, and Revolutionaries.* Washington DC: Washington Institute for Near East Policy, 1989.

Rubin, Barry M., *Israel, the Palestinian Authority, and the Arab States,* Ramat Gan, Israel: Bar Ilan University 1998.

Rubin, Barry M., *The PLO: a Declaration of Independence?* Washington, DC: Washington Institute for Near East Policy, 1988.

Rubin, Barry M., *Revolution Until Victory? The Politics and History of the PLO.* Cambridge: Harvard University Press, 1994.

Ruebner, Joshua, *Israel National Unity Government and Implications for the Peace Process.* Washington, DC: Congressional Research Service, Library of Congress, 2001.

Sacco, Joe, *Palestine.* Seattle: Fantagraphic Books, 2001.

Said, Edward W., *The End of the Peace Process: Oslo and After.* New York: Vintage Books, 2001.

Savir, Uri, *The Process: 1,100 Days That Changed the Middle East.* New York: Vintage Books, 1998.

Schiff, Z., and Ya'ari, Ehud, *Intifada, the Palestinian Uprising, Israel's Third Front.* New York: Simon & Schuster, 1989.

Schoenberg, Harris O., *A Mandate for Terror: the United Nations and the PLO.* New York: Shapolsky Publishers, 1989.

Scott, Ivan, *Jew vs. Arab: Sibling Rivalry of the Ages.* Fort Bragg, CA: Lost Coast Press, 2001.

Sela, Avraham and Ma'oz, Moshe, *The PLO and Israel: From Armed Conflict to Political Solution, 1964–1994.* New York: St. Martin's Press, 1997.

Shalev, Aryeh, *The Intifada: Causes and Effects.* Boulder: Westview Press, 1991.

Shemesh, Moshe, *The Palestinian Entity, 1959–1974: Arab Politics and the PLO.* London: Frank Cass, 1996.

Shipler, David K., *Arab and Jew: Wounded Spirits in a Promised Land.* New York: Penguin Books, 2002.

Shlaim, Avi, *The Iron Wall: Israel and the Arab World.* New York: W.W. Norton, 2001.

Shlaim, Avi and Rogan, Eugene L., *Rewriting the Palestine War: 1948 and the History of the Arab-Israeli Conflict.* Cambridge: Cambridge University Press, 2001.

Schou, Arild, *The Emergence of a Public Political Elite in the West Bank During the Palestinian Uprising (1987–1991).* Oslo: NIBR, 1996.

Smith Charles P., *Palestine and the Arab-Israeli Conflict.* Boston: St. Martin's Press, 2001.

Spedding, David, *The Leadership of the Intifada.* Oxford: St. Antony's College, 1999.

Stav Arie, *Israel and a Palestinian State: Zero Sum Game?* Tel Aviv: Zmora-Bitan, 2001.

Stav, Arie, *Palestine Will Rise Upon the Ruins of the State of Israel.* Shaare Tikva, Israel: 2000.

Stein, Janice Gross, *The Widening Gyre of Negotiation: From Management to Resolution in the Arab-Israeli Conflict.* Jerusalem: The Hebrew University, 1999.

Susser, Asher, *Double Jeopardy: PLO Strategy Toward Israel and Jordan.* Washington, DC: Washington Institute for Near East Policy, 1987.

Susser, Asher, *The PLO and the Palestinian Entity.* London: Anglo-Israel Association, 1989.

Towell, Larry, Darwish, Mahmud and Backmann, René, *Then Palestine.* New York: Aperture, 1998.

Tsiddon-Chatto, Yoash, *Israel-Arabia: Eye to Eye with the Future.* Israel: Ariel Center for Policy Research, 2001.

Wagner, Heather Lehr, *Israel and the Arab World.* Philadelphia: Chelsea House, 2002.

Wallach, Janet and Wallach John, *Arafat: in the Eyes of the Beholder.* Secacy, NJ: Carol Publishers Group, 1990.

Watson, Geoffrey R., *The Oslo Accords International Law and the Israeli-Palestinian Peace Agreements.* Oxford: Oxford University Press, 2000.

Yaari, Ehud, *Strike Terror: the Story of Fatah.* New York: Sabra Books, 1970.

## ARTICLES

Ackerman, Seth, "Al-Aqsa Intifada and the US Media," *Journal of Palestine Studies,* 30, no.2, 2001.

AbuKhalil, As`ad, "Review Essay—George Habash and the Movement of Arab Nationalists: Neither Unity nor Liberation," *Journal of Palestine Studies,* 28, no,4, 1999.

Al-Jarbawi, Ali, "The Position of Palestinian Islamists on the Palestine-Israel Accord," *The Muslim World,* 83, nos. 1–2, January–April 1994.

Bligh, Alexander, "The Intifada and the New Political Role of the Israeli-Arab Leadership," *Middle Eastern Studies,* 35, no.1, Jan.1999.

Budeiri, Musa, "The Nationalist Dimension of Islamic Movements in Palestinian Politics," *Journal of Palestine Studies,* 24, no.3, spring 1995.

Cook, Mary C., "Arafat-Rabin Agreement Comes at Depths of PLO Financial Crisis." *Washington Report on Middle East Affairs Special Report,* November/December 1993.

Cubert, Harold M., "The PFLP's Changing Role in the Middle East," *Peace Research Abstracts,* 37, no.5, 2000.

Esposito, John L. and Piscatori, James P., "Democratization and Islam," *Middle East Journal,* 45, no.3, summer 1991.

Falah, Ghazi, "Intifadat Al-Aqsa and the Bloody Road to Palestinian Independence," *Political Geography,* February 2001.

Falk, Richard, "International Law and the al-Aqsa Intifada," *Middle East Report,* 30, no.4, 2000.

Fricsh, Hillel, "The Evolution of Palestinian Nationalist Islamic Doctrine: Territorializing a Universal Religion," *Canadian Review in Nationalism,* 21, nos. 1–2, 1994.

Garfinkle, Adam, "Israel and Palestine: a Precarious Partnership," *Washington Quarterly,* 20, summer1997.

Gee, John R., "Unequal Conflict: the Palestinians and Israel," *Peace Research Abstracts,* 38, no.1, 2001.

Glass, Charles, " The Scene is Set for Another Lebanon," *New Statesman,* 130, 2001.

Halkin, Hillel, "Intifada II—Israel's Nightmare," *Commentary,* 110, no.5, 2000.

Heller, Mark A., "Towards a Palestinian State," *Survival,* 39, summer 1997.

Honig, Parnass Tikva, "The Al-Aqsa Intifada: Taking Off the Masks," *New Politics,* 2001, winter, VIII.

Ionnides, Chistos P., "The PLO and the Iranian Revolution," *American-Arab Affairs*, 10, fall 1990.

Keller, Adam, "The Middle East: Hope is a Scarce Commodity," *New Politics*, summer 2001, VIII.

Lewis, Bernard, "Rethinking the Middle East," *Foreign Affairs*, 71, no.4, Fall 1992.

Litvak, Meir, "The Islamization of the Palestinian-Israeli Conflict: the Case of Hamas," *Middle East Studies*, 34, no.1, 1998.

Luft, Gal, "Who is Winning the Intifada?," *Commentary*, 112, no.1, July/Aug. 2001.

Mayer, Tomas, "Pro-Iranian Fundamentalism in Gaza," *Religious Radicalism and Politics in the Middle East*, edited by E. Sivan and M. Friedman. Albany: State University of New York Press, 1990.

Monshipouri, Mahmood, "The PLO Versus Hamas: Peace, Democratization and Islamic Radicalism," *Middle East Policy*, 4, no.3, 1996.

Muslin, Muhammad, "Palestinian Civil Society," *The Middle East Journal*, v.47, spring 1993.

Newman, David, " From Peace to War: Relighting the Flames of the Israel-Palestine Conflict," *Boundary and Security Bulletin*, fall 2001.

Nirenstein, Fiamma, "How suicide bombers are made," *Commentary*, 112. no.2, Sept. 2001.

Norton, Augustus Richard, Telhami, Shibley, Robinson, Glenn E., Peretz, Don, Alterman, Jon B., Xavuz, M. Hahan, and Gunter Michael M., "The Middle East: is the peace process dead?," *Current History*, January 2001.

Paz, Reuven, "Hizballah and Fatah: A New Alliance Against Israel." *ICT*, October 22, 2000.

Peck, Mike, "Tanzim: Arafat's Secret Army?" *Soldier of Fortune*, 26, no.1, January 1, 2001.

Peled, Alisa Rubin, "Towards Autonomy? The Islamic Movement's Quest for Control of Islamic Institutions in Israel," *The Middle East Journal*, 55, no.3, summer 2001.

Perlmutter, Amos, "The Israel—PLO Accord is Dead," *Foreign Affairs*, 74, May/June 1995.

Podhoretz, Norman, "Intifada II—Death of an Illusion?," *Commentary*, 110, no.5, 2000.

Pundak, Ron, "From Oslo to Taba: What Went Wrong?," *Survival*, autumn, 2001.

Robinson, Glenn E., "Palestine after Arafat," *Washington Quarterly*, 23, no.4, autumn 2000.

Satloff, Robert, "Islam in the Palestinian Uprising," *Orbis*, 33, no3, summer 1989.

Satloff, Robert, "The Karine-A Affair and the War on Terrorism," *The National Interest*, 67, 2002.

Sayigh, Yezid, "Arafat and the Anatomy of a Revolt," *Survival*, 43, no.3, autumn 2001.

Sayigh, Yezid, "Palestine's Prospects," *Survival*, 42, no.4, winter 2000/2001.

Schlze, Kirsten E., "Camp David and the Al-Aqsa Intifada: an Assessment of the State of the Israeli-Palestinian Peace Process, July–December 2000," *Studies in Conflict and Terrorism*, 24, no.3, May/June 2001.

Shaked, Roni, "The Tanzim: Fatah's Fighters on the Ground," *Yediot Achronot*, October 3, 2000.

Shikaki, Khalil, "Long War in the Making—Palestinians Divided," *Foreign Affairs*, 81, no.1, 2002.

Singer, Joel, "Mayday for Oslo," *National Interest*, 55, spring 1999.

Steinberg, Matti, "The PLO and Palestinian Islamic Fundamentalism," *Jerusalem Quarterly*, 52, 1989.

Steinberg, Matti, "The Worldview of Habash's 'Popular Front,'" *Jerusalem Quarterly*, 47, summer 1998.

Tutunji, Jenab; Khaldi Kamal, "A Binational State in Palestine: the National Choice for Palestinians and the Moral Choice for Israelis," *International Affairs*, 73, Jan. 1997.

Usher, Graham, "Fatah's Tanzim: Origins and Politics, *Middle East Report MERIP*, 30, no.217, part 4, 2000.

Usher, Graham, "Letter from Jerusalem: Impact of Islamic Suicide Bombings on Relations Between Israel and the Occupied Territories," *New Statesman and Society*, 9, 1996.

Viorst, Milton, "Middle East Peace Mirage on the Horizon?," *Washington Quarterly*, 23, no.1, winter 2000.

*Patterns of Global Terrorism*, 2001, United States Department of State, May 2001.

"Arafat's choice," *The Economist*, 361, 2001.

"Arafat's Latest Climb-Down Reflects a Weakening Domestic Position. Watch Out for Hamas Resurgence," *Middle East International*, no.621, 2000.

"Hamas and Arafat's Men," *The Economist*, 350, no.8101, 1999.

"Hamas and the PLO," *The Economist*, 332, no7879, September 3, 1994.

"Hamas 1, PLO 0," *The New Republic*, 211, no.24, December 12, 1994.

"Palestinians Look to Lebanon's Example," *The Economist*, 354, no. 8163, 2000.

"Popular, Extreme and an Alternative to Arafat. Also Why the Suicide Bombers Keep Dying, and the Charity Accused of Terrorist Links," *Time*, December 17, 2001.

"Sharon's Strategy, If He Has One," *The Economist*, 361, 2001.

## PRIMARY SOURCES, PERIODICALS, AND NEWSPAPERS

al-Aseer
al-Ayyam (Jerusalem)
al-Bayadir al-Siyasi (East Jerusalem)
Biladi—Jerusalem Times (East Jerusalem)
Al-Esteqlal
Filastin (Gaza)
Filastin-al Muslima (London)
Filastin al-Thawra
Ha'aretz (Tel Aviv)
Ha-Mizrah he-Hadash (Jerusalem)
al-Hayat (London)
al-Hayat al-Jadida (Gaza)
al-Istiqlal (Gaza)
al-Jareeda
al-Karmel
Kol Ha'ir (Jerusalem)
Kol Yerushalayim (Jerusalem)
Majjallat al-Dirasat al-Filastiniyya
al-Manar (East Jerusalem)
al-Massar (Ramallah)
Ma'ariv (Tel Aviv)
al-Mujtama` (Kuwait)
al-Nahar (East Jerusalem)
The New Republic (Washington DC)
News from Within (Jerusalem)
The Observer (London)
Palestine Chronicle
Palestine Times (London)
al-Quds (East Jerusalem)
Qira`at Siyasiyya (Florida)
al-Rasid (noncirculating internal Hamas report)
al-Risala (circulating internal Hamas report)
al-Sabar (Jerusalem)
al-Sharq al-Awsat (Paris)
Sawt al-Haqq wal-Hurriyya (Umm Al-Fahm)
Shu'un Filastiniyya (Nicosia)
al-Tahlil al-Siyasi (circulating internal Hamas report)
Voice of Palestine radio
al-Wasat (London)
al-Watan (Gaza)
al-Watan al-`Arabi (Paris)
WAFA—Palestine News Agency
Yediot Aharonot (Tel Aviv)

## WEB SITES

Al-Aqsa Martyrs Brigades
http://www.terrorismanswers.com/groups/ alaqsa.html
Al-Aqsa Martyrs Brigades. See Shahar, Yael, "The al-Aqsa Martyrs
Brigades, a political tool with an edge,"
http://www.ict.org.il/articles/article_det.cfm?articleid=430
Ariel Sharon biography
http://www.danpal.dk/vidensbase/baggrund/ bg-0.33.htm
Battle of Jenin
http://www.time.com/time/2002/jenin/
BBC: History of Middle East Conflict
http://news.bbc.co.uk/hi/english/in_depth/middle_east/2000/mide
ast_peace_process/newsid_340000/340237.stn
Camp David II: Assumptions and Consequences
http://www.brookings.edu/views/articles/telhami/
Chjanuary2001.htm
Democratic Front for the Liberation of Palestine (DFLP)
http://www.ict.org.il/inter%5Fter/orgdet.cfm?orgid=11
"Rejection and Imposition." Official Fatah website editorial.
http://www.fateh.net/e_editor/01/150701.htm
Fatah and the PFLP. See Karmon, Eli, "Fatah and the Popular Front for
the Liberation of Palestine: International Terrorism Strategies
(1968–1990).
http://www.ict.org.il/articles/articledet.cfm?articleid=145
Force 17
http://www.ict.org.il/inter55Fter/orgdet.cfm?orgid=86
Hamas
http://www.ict.org.il/inter_ter/orgdet.cfm?orgid=13
History of the Arab Israeli conflict
http://www.arab2.com/biography/Arab-Israeli-Conflict.htm
Islamic Resistance Movement (Hamas)
http://www.palestine-info.com/hamas
Intifada
http://www.intifada.com
Israeli Defense Forces (IDF) counter-terrorist operation and Jenin background information
http://www.mfa.gov.il/mfa/go.asp?MFAH01920
Israeli Foreign Ministry
http://www.israel.org/mfa
Israeli-Palestinian Interim Agreement
http://www.israel.org/mfa/go.asp?MFAH00qa0
MEMRI—The Middle East Media Research Institute, source for
translated materials,
http://www.memri.org

Middle East Crisis: Camp David, the Al-Aqsa Intifada and the prospects
for the peace process
http://parliament.uk/commons/lob/resarch/rp2001/rp01-009.pdf
Middle East history and references
http://www.mideastweb.org/history.htm
Palestinian Islamic Jihad (PIJ)
http://web.nps.navy.mil/~library/tsp/pij.htm
Palestinian Liberation Organization (PLO)
http://www.palestinehistory.com
http://ict.org.il/inter_ter/orgdet.cfm?orgid=31
http://www.arab.net/palestine/history/pe%5Fplo.html
http://www.terrorism.com/terrorism/PLO.shtml
Palestinian National Authority
Palestinian Terrorism led by Yasser Arafat's Tanzim and Force 17
http://www.aipac.org/arafattanzim.pdf
Palestinian Security Services. See Luft, Gal, "The Palestinian Security
Services: Between Police and Army," June 14, 1999.
www.ict.org.il/articles/articledet.cfm?articleid=79
Palestinian Media Watch
http://www.pmw.org.il
Popular Front for the Liberation of Palestine—General Command
(PFLP-GC)
http://www.ict.org.il/inter55Fter/orgdet.cfm?orgid=32
Popular Front for the Liberation of Palestine (PFLP)
http://www.pflp-pal.org/about.html
Profile: Al-Aqsa Martyrs Brigades
http://news.bbc.co.uk/hi/english/world/middle%5Feast/
newsid%5F1760
Profile: Marwan Barghouti
http://news.bbc.co.uk/hi/english/in%5Fdepth/middle%5Feast/
2001/israel
Review essay: The Oslo Peace Process through three lenses
http://www.mepc.org/journal/9810%5Frubner.html
Tanzim
http://www.idf.il/english/news/tanzim.stm
Tanzim: Fatah's fighters on the ground
http://www.israel-mfa.gov.il.mfa/go.asp?MFAH0i0p0
Terrorism Q&A: Al Aqsa Martyrs Brigades
http://www.cnn.com/SPECIALS/2002/cfr/stories/al.aqsa.martyrs
Terrorism: Questions and Answers: Flashpoint: Israeli' Palestinian conflict
http://www.terrorismanswers.com/policy/israel.html
Palestinian-Israeli Conflict
http://www.usnewsclassroom.com/resources/activities/
act001023.html

Palestinian-Israeli Conflict. See Marcus, Itamar, "Rape, Murder, Violence and War for Allah Against the Jews: summer 2000 on Palestinian Television." *Palestinian Media Watch*, September 11, 2000, http://www.pmw.org.il/report-30.html

Palestinian-Israeli Conflict. See Radlauer, Don, "An Engineered Tragedy, Statistical Analysis of Casualties in the Palestinian-Israeli Conflict, September 2000–June 2002," *ICT*, June 2002. www.ict.org.il

Palestinian-Israeli Conflict. See Wurmser, Meyrav, "Terrorism and a Palestinian State." *MEMRI*, www.memri.org/staff/staff04.html

Who is Barghouti? http://www.jpost.com/Editions/2002/04/16/News/News.47056.html www.pna.net

Yasser Arafat http://www.aipac.org/documents/AIPACmemo031202.html

Yasser Arafat. See Kimhi, Shaul, Even, Shmuel and Post, Jerrold, "Yasir Arafat, Psychological Profile and Strategic Analysis," The International Policy Institute for Counterterrorism, http://www.ict.org.il/articles/yasir_arafat.htm

Yasser Arafat. See Naveh, Dani, "Involvement of Arafat, PA Senior Officials, and Apparatuses in Terrorism Against Israel,Corruption and Crime," www.mfa.gov.il/mfa/go.asp?MFAH0lom0

Paz, Reuven, "Qa'idat al-Jihad, A new name on the road to Palestine." *ICT*, June 2002, www.ict.org.il

## AUDIO-VIDEO

*Beyond the Green Line*, New York: Filmakers Library, 1990.

*The 50 Years War—Israel and the Arabs*, Burbank, CA: PBS DVD Video; Warner Home, 2000.

*Gaza Strip, Spring 2001*, Seattle, WA: Arab Film Distribution, 2002.

*In Search of Peace: Part One: 1948–1967*, Los Angeles: Moriah Films, 2000.

*Inside the Intifada*, New York, United Jewish appeal, Dept. of Communications/Public Relations, 1990.

*Israel vs. The PLO—the Invasion of Lebanon*, Oak Forest, Il: MPI Home Video, 1989.

*Palestine: 1890s–1990s*, Princeton, NJ: Films for the Humanities, 2000.

*PLO*, Clarksburg, NJ: Alden Films 2001.

*Search for Solid Ground—the Intifada Through Israeli Eyes*, New York: Anti-Defamation League, in association with Hadassah, 1990.

*Seeds of Hatred*, Clarksburg, NJ: Alden Films, 2001.

*The Road to Peace—Israelis and Palestinians*, New York: First Run Icarus Films, 1995.

*The Shifting Sands—a History of the Middle East,* New York: PolyGram Video, 1991.

*Voices for Peace Video—Cases of Jews and Arabs in Israel,* Denver: M.A. Watson and R. Hazan, 2000.

*Yasser Arafat—Terrorist or Peacemaker,* New York: A&E Home Video, 1996.